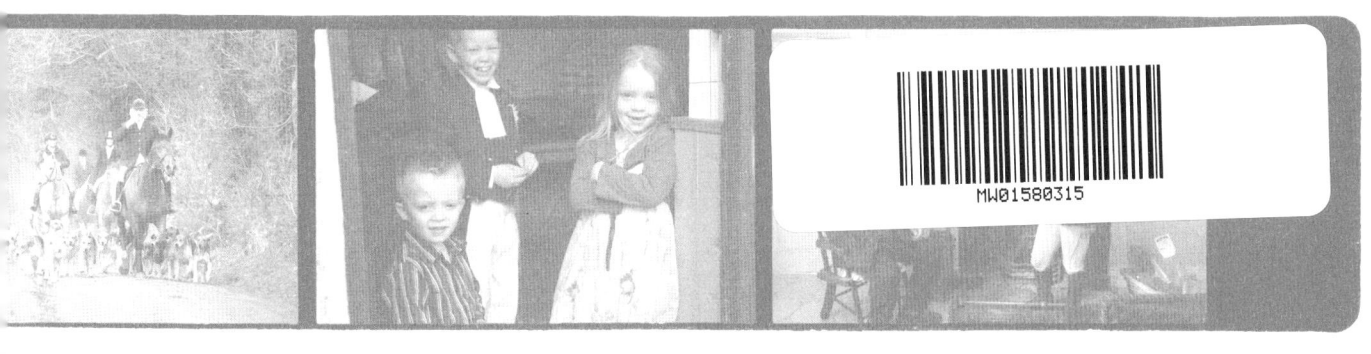
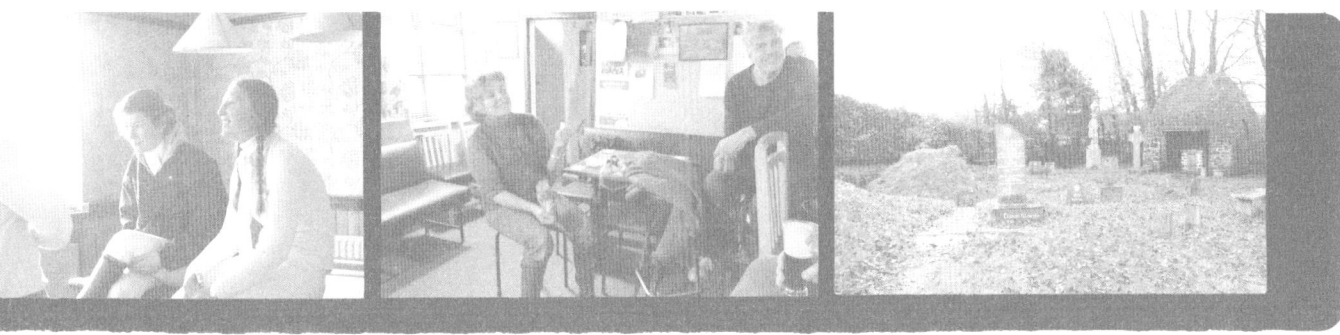
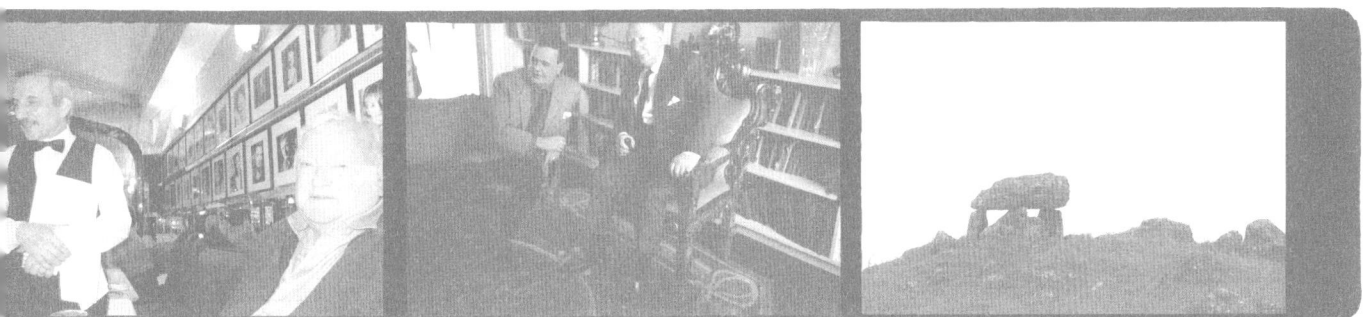
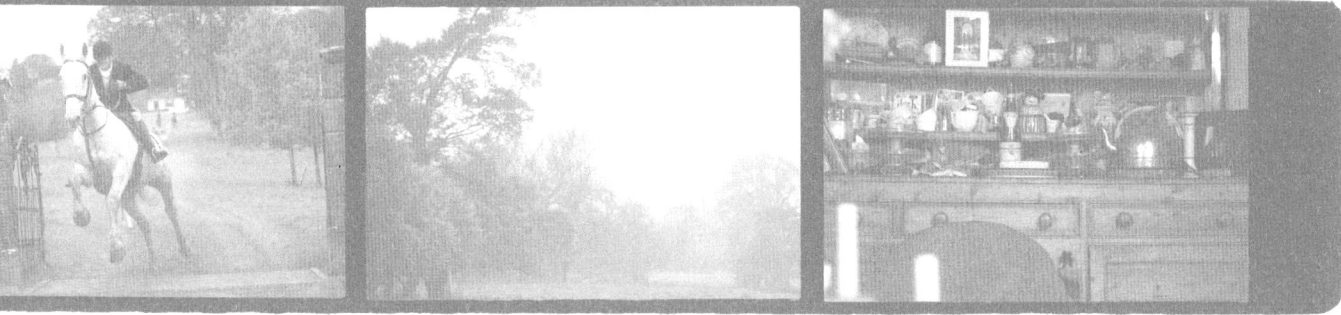
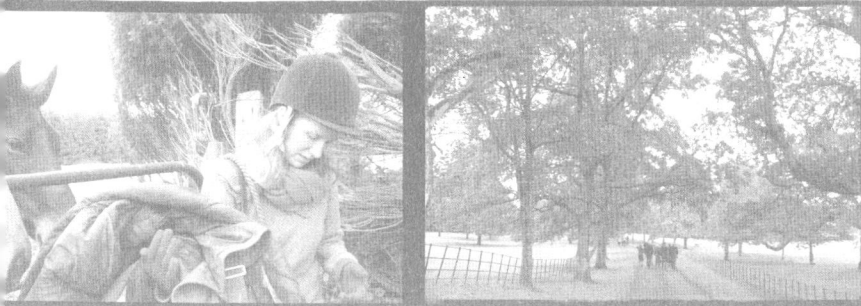

To Patrick

— who caroline tells me you are now an Irish citizen)

best wishes from another admirer of Ireland —

Susan Wood
Dec 6 2018

SUSAN WOOD
IRELAND

SUSAN WOOD
IRELAND

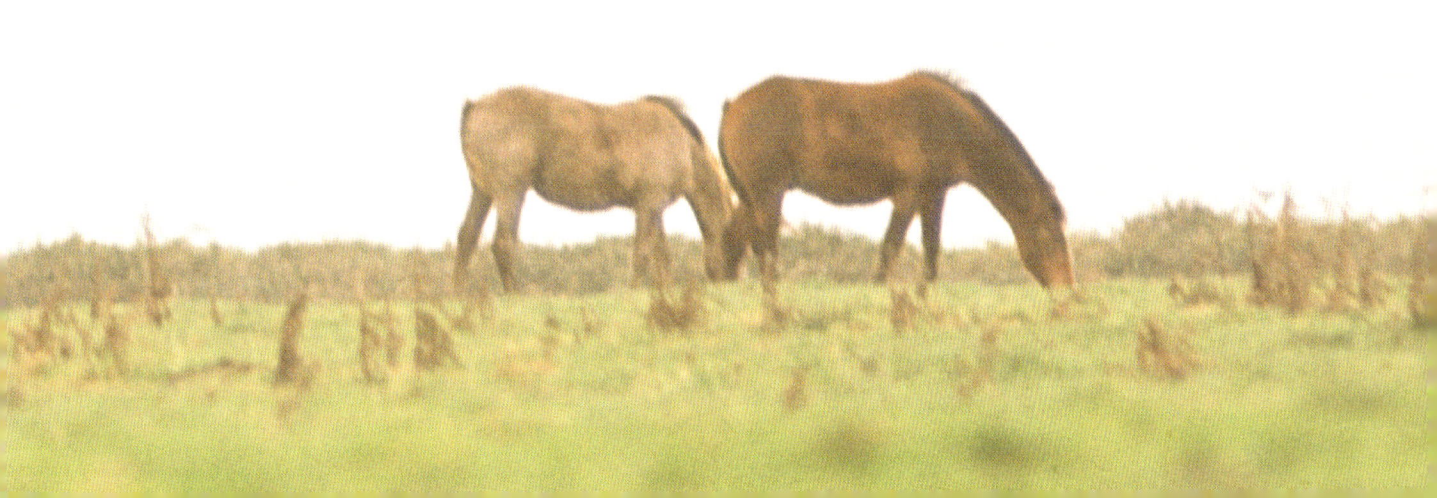

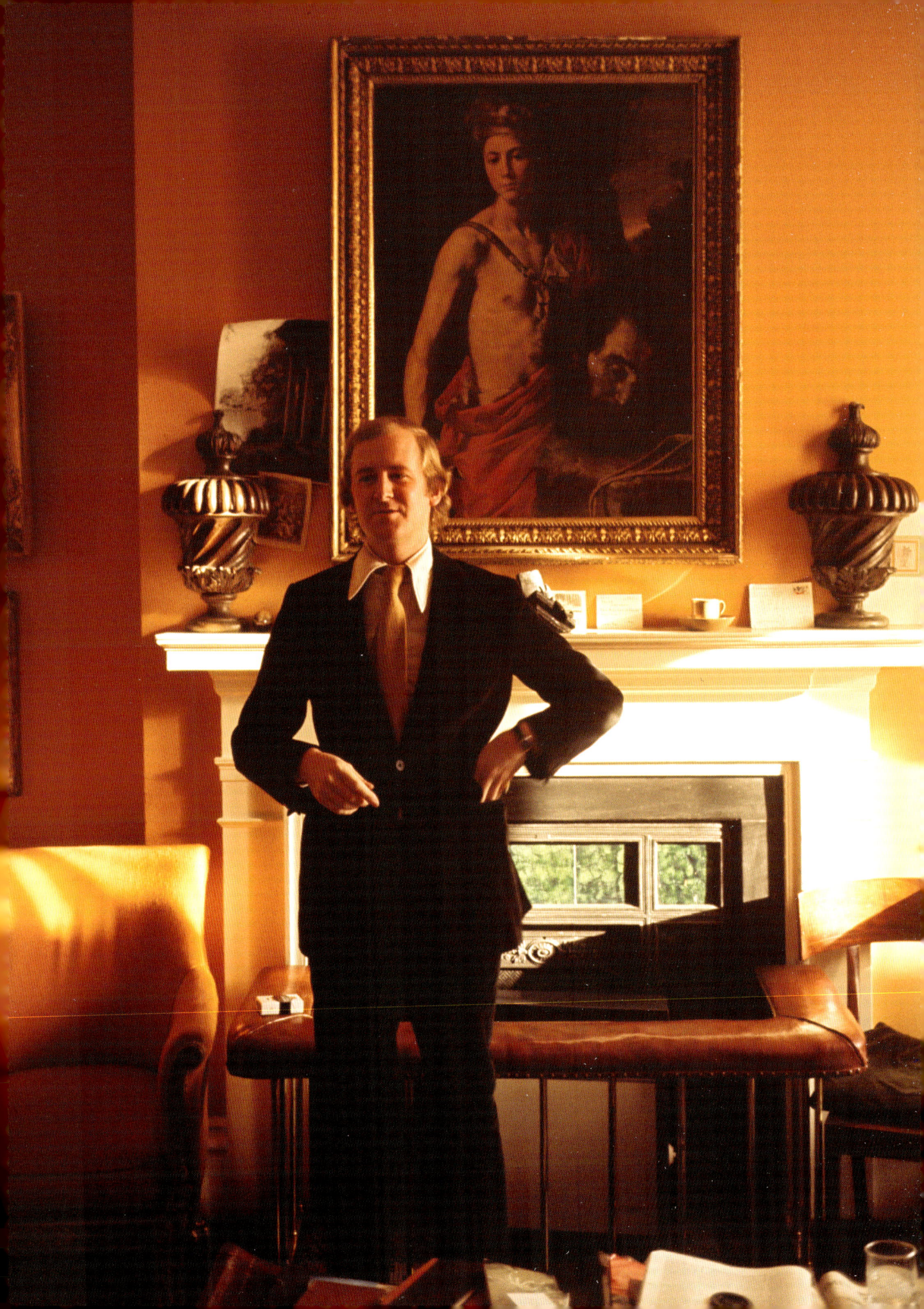

I dedicate these Ireland photographs

1968 to 2018

to

DESMOND FITZGERALD

and the good people of

THE IRISH GEORGIAN SOCIETY

who encouraged me to do this book.

First published 2018 by
THE LILLIPUT PRESS LTD
62–63 Sitric Road, Arbour Hill, Dublin 7, Ireland
www.lilliputpress.ie

Text © Susan Wood, 2018
Photographs © Susan Wood, 2018

ISBN 978 1 84351 745 0

All rights reserved. No part of this publication may be reproduced
in any form or by any means without the prior permission of the publisher.

A CIP record is available from the British Library.

1 3 5 7 9 10 8 6 4 2

Design by Niall McCormack
Printed in Poland by Drukarnia Skleniarz

Introduction	2
Garech Browne	9
A Singular Country	37
Marina Guinness, Family & Friends	67
J.P. Donleavy	87
Tim Pat Coogan	97
Hector McDonnell	103
The Hunt	113
Desmond FitzGerald	121
Coda	137
Notes on photographs	143

SUSAN WOOD
IRELAND

This is a simple book about love and friendship.

I fell in love with Ireland and its first glimmerings in the handsome, wry, verbal, self-deprecating transplanted Irish I came to know in America. I married two of them – though not of course at the same time. When I went to work in London in 1968 for British *Vogue*, its spunky editor Beatrix Miller sent me on to Ireland to photograph and to write about it. No pre-plan. Ireland found me as much as I found Ireland, and I came away with lifelong friendships.

I've been back many times since and I hope that my photographs have captured the land's beauty, the charm of its old customs, country cattle sales and fox hunts as well as the spirit and energy of those Irish men and women who let me into their homes and lives.

My first sojourn in the sixties, rambling in a car on small roads or by foot through narrow lanes, led me into the landscapes, scenes and events depicted here. In many instances, I felt I was channeling the work of nineteenth or twentieth-century artists such as Corot, Millet or Jack Yeats, figures who broke from the tradition of painting only portraits of royals or scenes from mythology and religion and instead portrayed the populace at home or at a picnic by the Seine. The true lives of people were their beat – as they were mine. And the misty light of Ireland helped me achieve a painterly style, aided by a year studying folklore and myth with Joseph Campbell at Sarah Lawrence College. That was my photographic take.

Throughout the seventies and nineties, and into the new century, up until what seems like yesterday, I kept returning, photographing many of my friends old and new. The subjects are random yet have a commonality. The connecting sinew is their patriotism as recorders and guardians of Ireland's culture, its history, ancient music, poetry, centuries-old architecture and art.

Garech Browne along with Paddy Moloney, the brilliant lead piper of the Chieftains, founded Claddagh Records in 1959 to support traditional music and the spoken word preserved in readings by Austin Clarke, Derek Mahon, John Montague and others. He owned Luggala as Luggala owned him. I stayed there many times; a restorative experience. Its preservation and upkeep has made it a prized gem of the Irish people.

Garech and I met as I journeyed through Ireland in 1968. Later, he brought Purna, his Indian princess wife, to visit in my new 25th-floor New York apartment in Olympic Tower

A selection of my work over the decades.

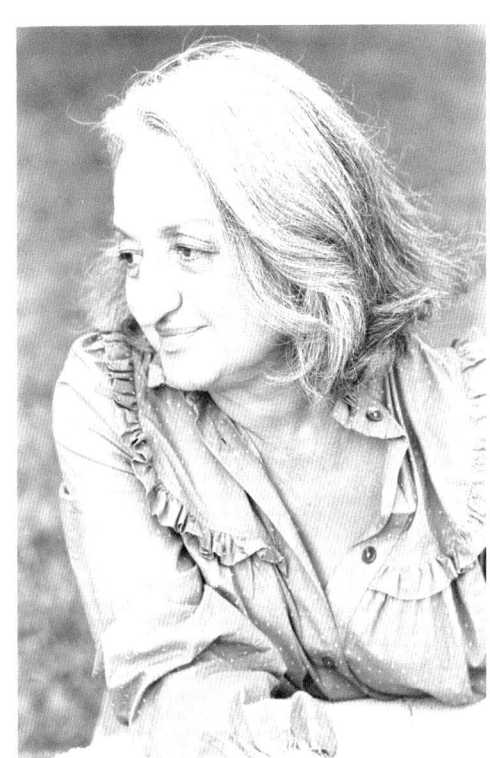

Betty Friedan, Sag Harbor, NY, 1981

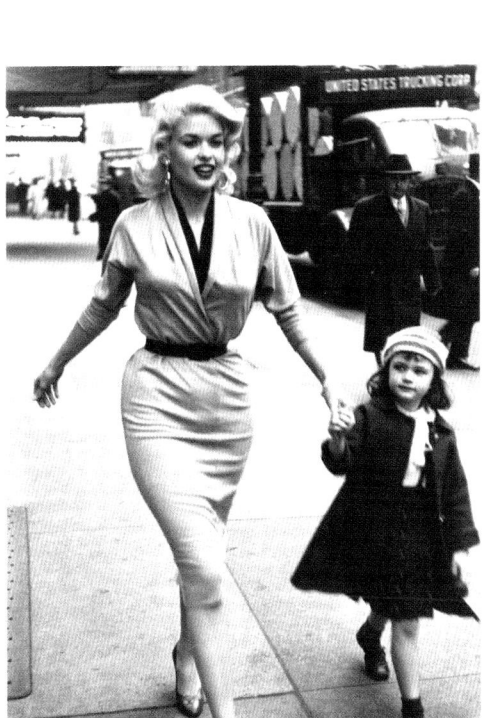

Jayne Mansfield, New York, 1955

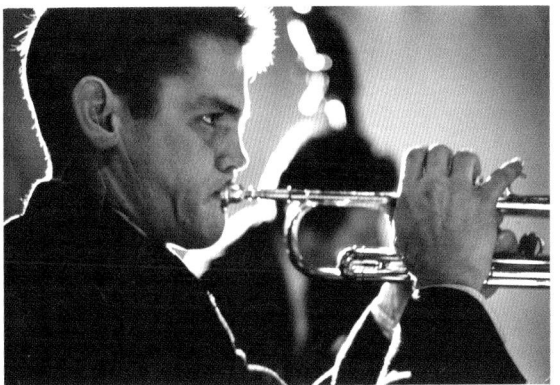

Chet Baker, New York, 1957

on that leg of their honeymoon. It had a wall of glass with a vertiginously thrilling view of the spires of St Patrick's Cathedral, whose fireproof metal embellishments came from my grandfather Louis Retman's small foundry. He was an immigrant boy aged six when he came from Odessa to North America, building his own brick-and-granite Beaux Arts house and workshop in fulfillment of the American Dream.

Marina, dear friend, muse and activist has the three 'b's – beauty, brains and breeding. She is a Guinness on her father's side, and could be called princess on her mother's, but finds the idea of 'title' ridiculous as she is a proud citizen of a republic. She offers Dracula or Vlad the Impala as her progenitor when pressed on this subject.

Her mother Mariga, descended from a long ago Lithuanian King, had co-founded the Irish Georgian Society with her husband Desmond to save Ireland's crumbling heritage from the wrecking ball when I first met her in the late sixties among the derelict houses of Mountjoy Square. We see their daughter Marina at the confirmation party of Paddy Doran, one of a traveller family she has adopted and vice versa. Encouraged by her to learn 'can-do by doing', he and his brother Liam have modelled for Violet's father, the photographer Perry Ogden. The boys' dad, Tommy Doran, is a talented concertina player and fixer of old jogging carts.

Marina has made a cosy full-scale recording studio at her home Pickering Forest where the famous and locals have recorded, from Kila to Glen Hansard. Her patriotism finds expression in personal acts of courage and spontaneity, running a blockade to Belfast with a truckload of potatoes and supporting individual poets and artists. A poster of Gerry Adams hangs over her stove and on her sideboard sits a boggle-head Trump doll, given by Rupert Murdoch who bet her five dollars that he would win the election.

I first heard of Donleavy in the seventies at a lunch where *The Ginger Man* was receiving great praise. One begrudger said, 'Donleavy's no writer; he just sat in the pub with all of us and listened to our words and ran off to the stalls to scribble them down.'

I revisited *The Ginger Man* after forty years, a terrific read with bittersweet laughs. Sebastian Dangerfield, the Ginger Man, and his band of American brothers on the GI Bill at Trinity College are short on money, morals, condoms and drink – scallywags the lot of them. Their adventures are rowdy, bawdy, happy and sad, and make for a great movie. This tale heralded the sixties in what we now label the sexual revolution. Women today would call Donleavy's Gingerman a misogynist; probably Donleavy too. But as literary misogynists go, J P.'s is small potatoes compared to the nasty men introduced to us later by Edward Albee, Phillip Roth and Norman Mailer.

Was J.P. a model for the libidinous Ginger Man, who tried to have it all on someone else's dime? His friend and muse Marina Guinness took me to his demesne on which stood a fine Georgian mansion, a hundred-acre farm and some cattle; inside, J.P. and his son Philip led a spartan life in an unheated house where J.P.'s written words and anything else about him or by his hand – drafts, scribbles, lawsuits, jottings, doodles, notes – rested in large cardboard file boxes occupying the floor space where furniture perhaps once stood.

My favourite photograph from this shoot in Westmeath catches Philip and Marina, tired caregivers having a break in the kitchen: an unadorned picture of life with famous men.

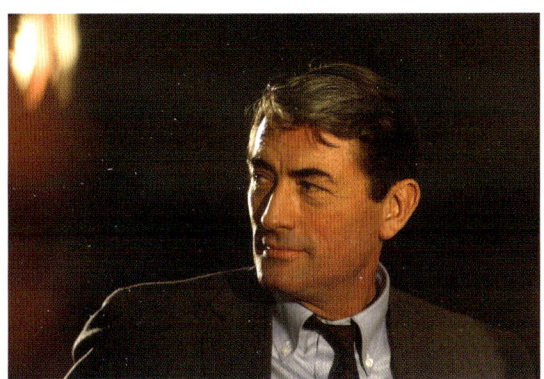
Gregory Peck on the set of *Mirage*, 1964

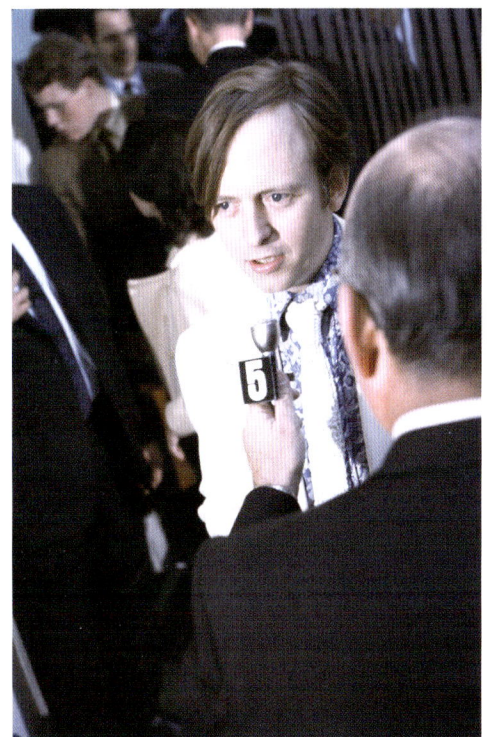
Tom Wolfe, New York, 1968

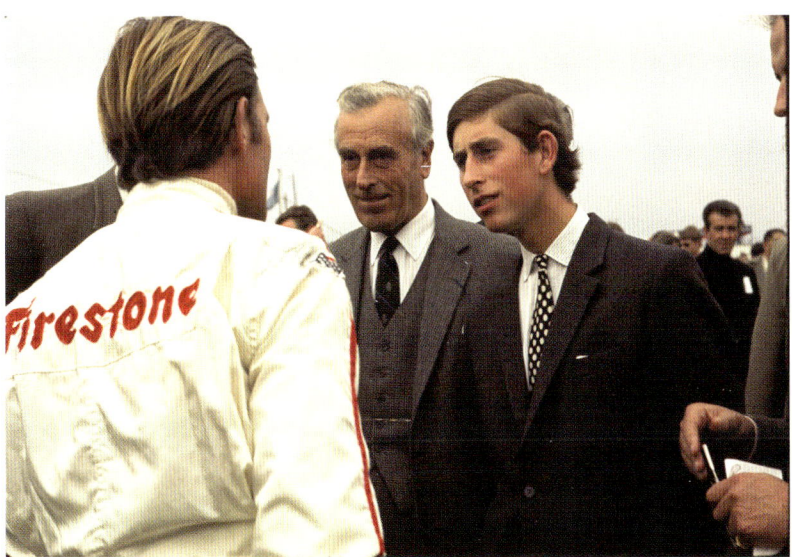
Lord Louis Mountbatten and Prince Charles speaking to Graham Hill, 1970

Tim Pat Coogan wrote the authoritative history of the Irish revolution and brought Michael Collins to the forefront of that revolution at a time when his significant role had been downplayed. My collage of him imposed on a sculpture of Michael Collins in a salesroom window in St Stephen's Green is a happy accident. Michael Collins is very much in Tim Pat's head and, because of his work, he is now in everyone else's.

Hector McDonnell is a twenty-first century Renaissance man: amusing, charming, talented, and practised in art and music. He writes wonderful books, humorous and serious, about Irish art, vernacular poetry, primordial history, and even St Patrick, illustrating them with superb line drawings.

His paintings sell in fine-art galleries across the world and perhaps the spur of fashioning a living has helped him to keep his focus on his art. His piano riffs of classical music are exceptional – his facial expressions sublime or sorrowful – attuned to the score.

I met Hector first as an impecunious artist looking for a place where he might paint in NYC. I had that for him and we became great friends, with him making use of my country house and my visiting Glenarm in County Antrim. Staying there with Hector and his wife Wendy, the two sides of Hector are revealed in his early morning attire. On one occasion I caught him on camera in his posh Turnbull & Asser surah silk robe, and on another morning as we met in the kitchen to warm ourselves by the Aga, he sported flannel PJs imprinted with Mickey Mouse.

I stumbled upon foxhounds of the Galway Blazers being walked on a narrow road on my ramble from Limerick to Dublin in 1968. Little was I to know when I married Joe Haggerty that I would acquire a wonderful stepdaughter, Leah Haggerty Clark, who rides with this pack on the weekdays, while on Sundays she is joint-master of the County Roscommon Hunt, where all are equal in the thrill of the chase. A love of horses from her time at Foxcroft and as a child in Locust Valley Long Island now results in her breeding, breaking, hunting and selling on. She has over a dozen horses under training in Ireland, yielding a joy that any athlete feels in accomplishment.

Desmond FitzGerald, The Black Knight of Glin, identified the work of 'Irish artists whose work was labelled either anonymous or European', and firmly placed them in the pantheon of Irish art. In restoring Glin Castle and presiding over the Irish Georgian Society for decades, he fulfilled a mission of preserving Ireland's architectural treasures and material culture for future generations and through his scholarship achieved world-wide recognition for Irish builders and craftsmen.

The last three subjects I had the opportunity to photograph in Ireland were in November 2017. Eliza Geoghan, a child of three, using her computer in a restaurant in Roundwood, the light giving a glow to her face, a La Tour angel lit by a candle, symbol of Ireland's future; Bono and his wife Ali Hewson, Garech Browne and John Boorman, talking over lunch; and four Belfast girls I met on the Belfast to Dublin train, who grew up Catholic and Protestant. For them the Troubles long over, harbingers of happier days. I deeply regret Garech's demise. He would have enjoyed getting to know these youngsters. It was our last lunch. I shall miss him very much.

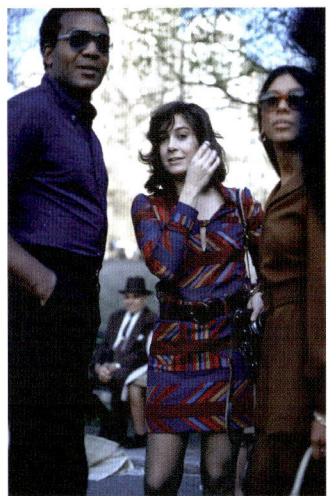
Susan Wood with Jim Brown, New York, 1968

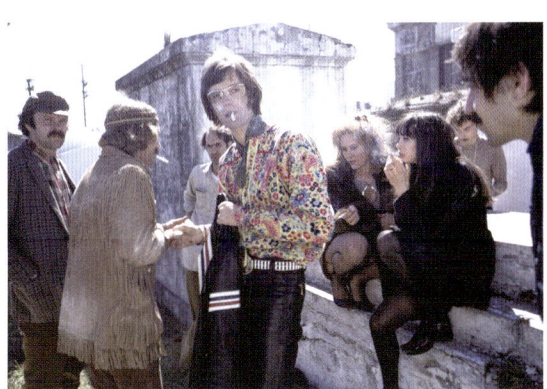
Easy Rider, New Orleans, Louisiana, 1968

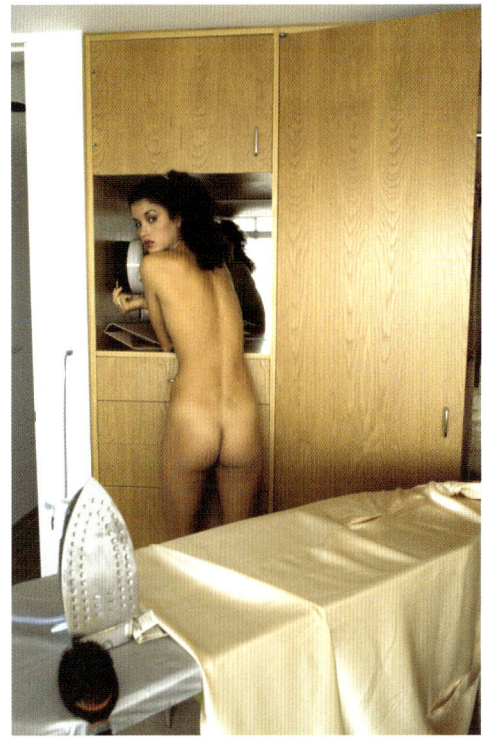
Janice Dickinson, Hamptons, New York, 1978

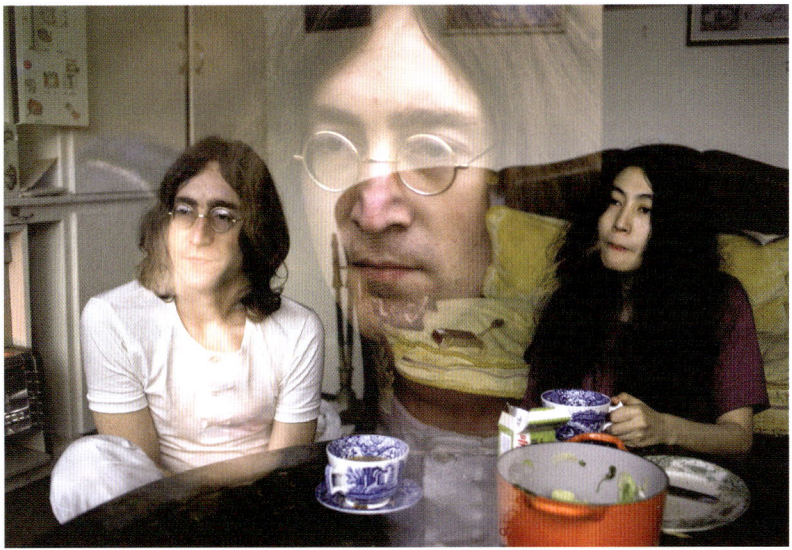
John Lennon and Yoko Ono, London, England, 1968

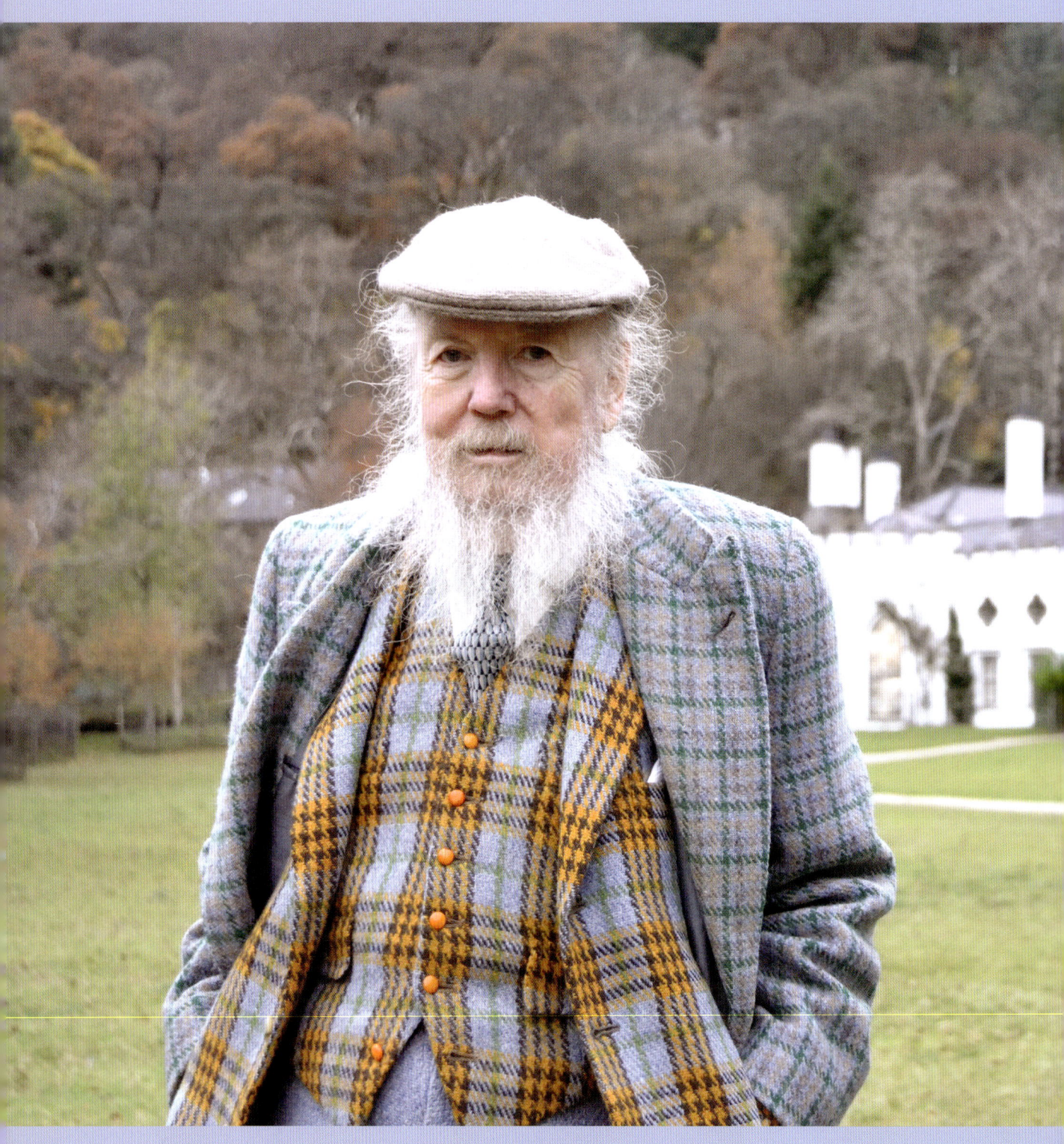

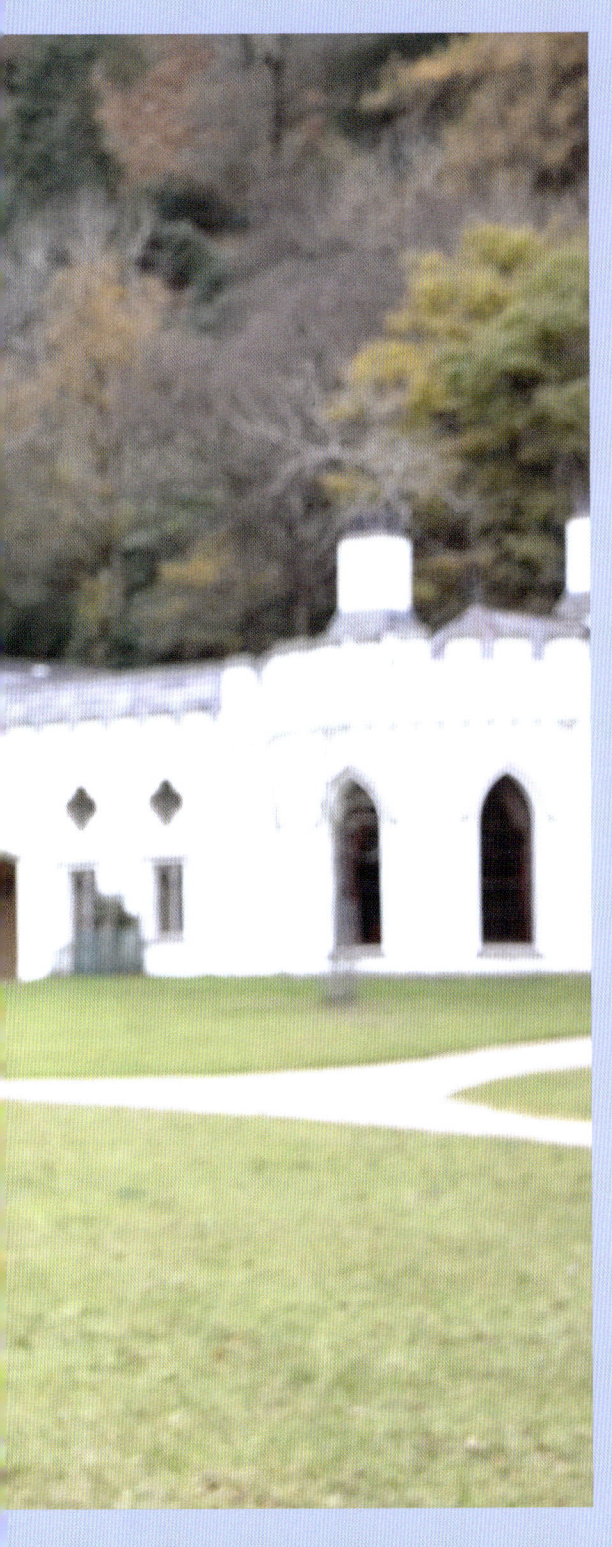

Garech Browne

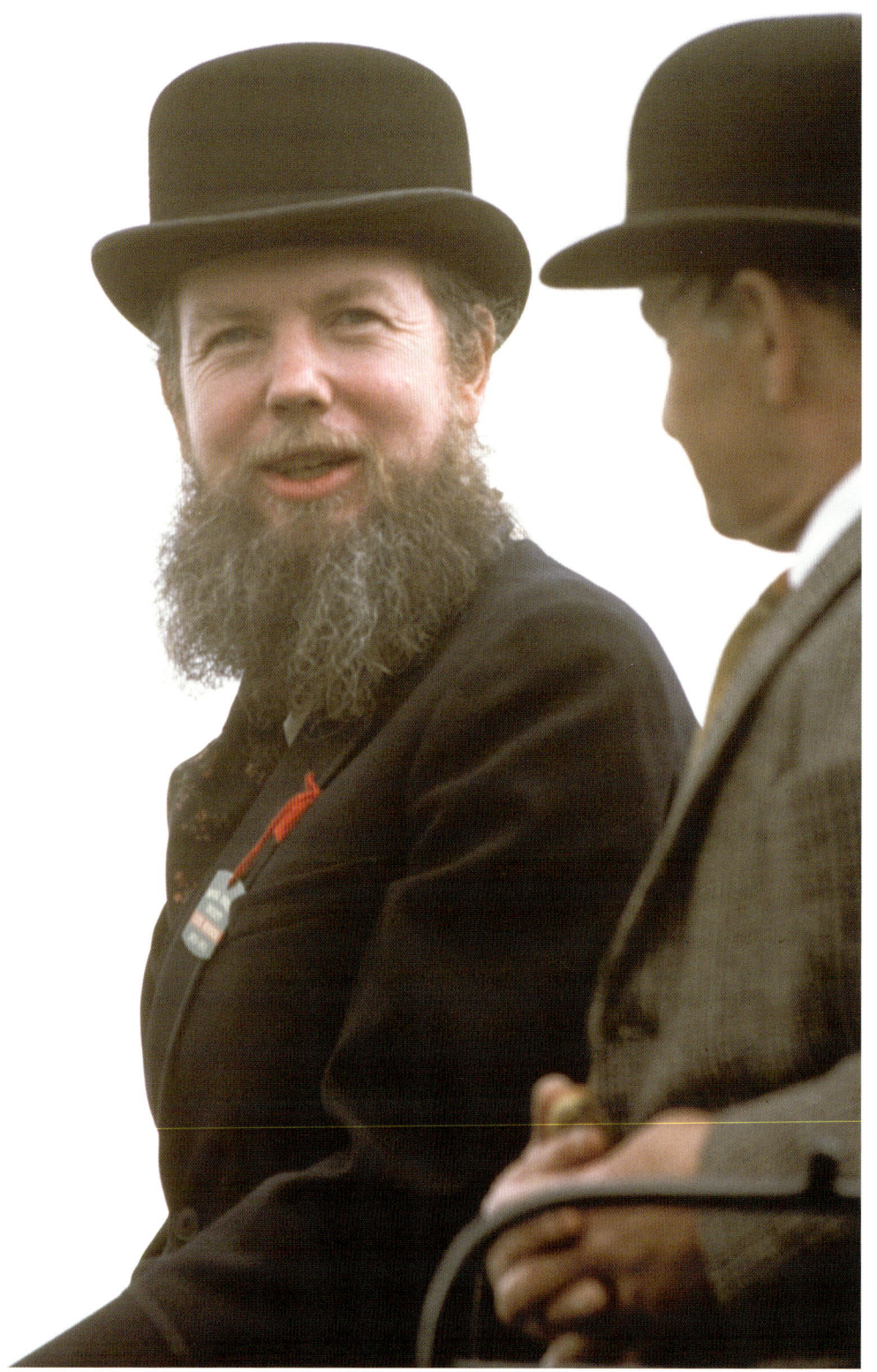

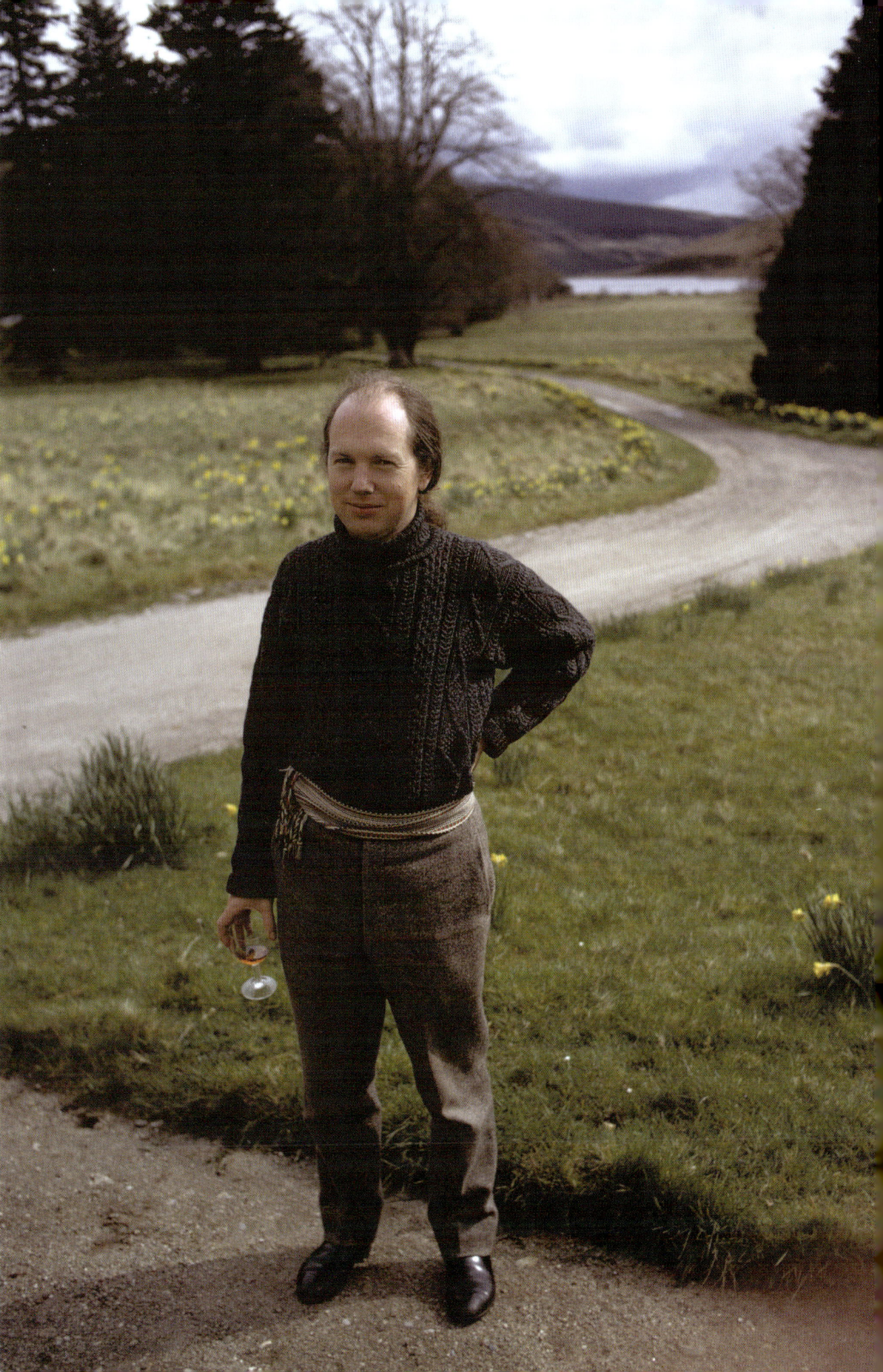

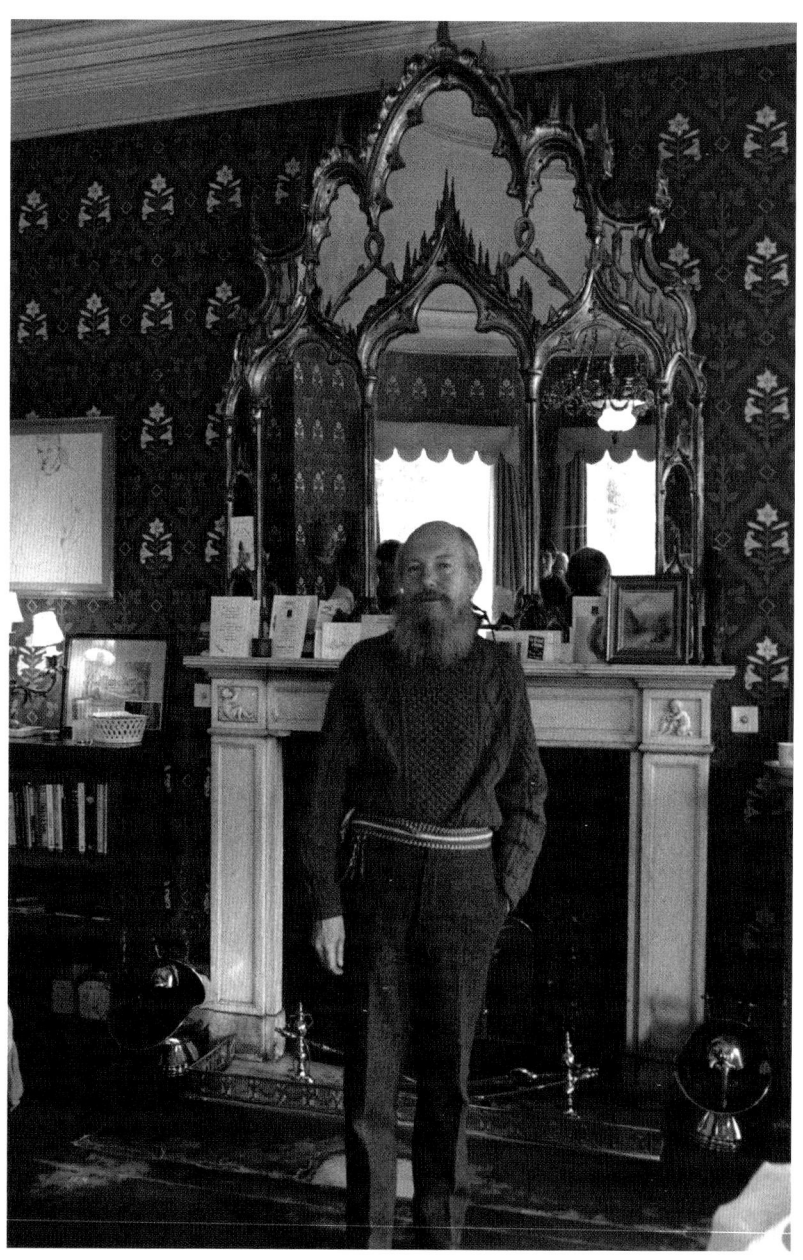

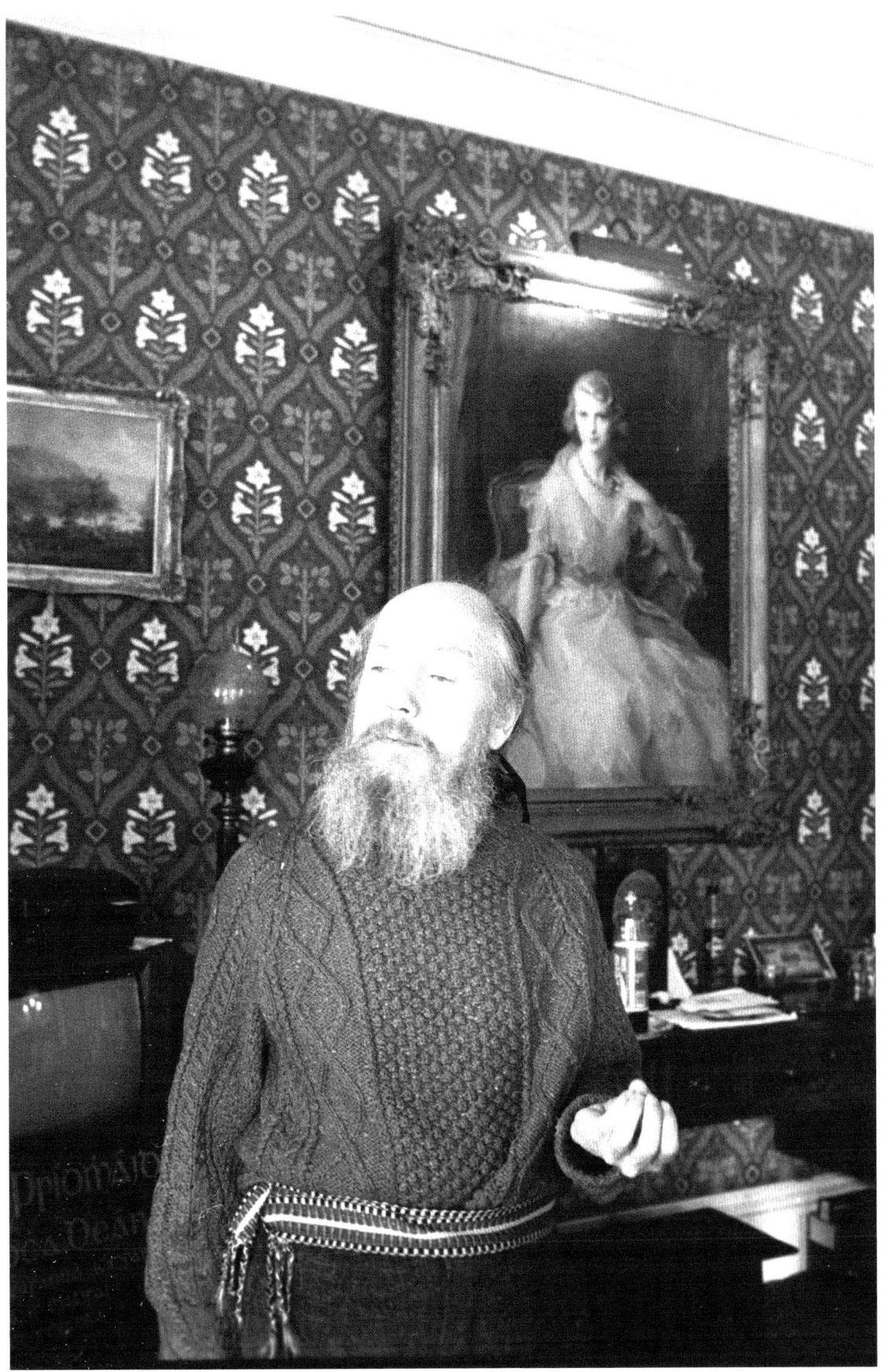

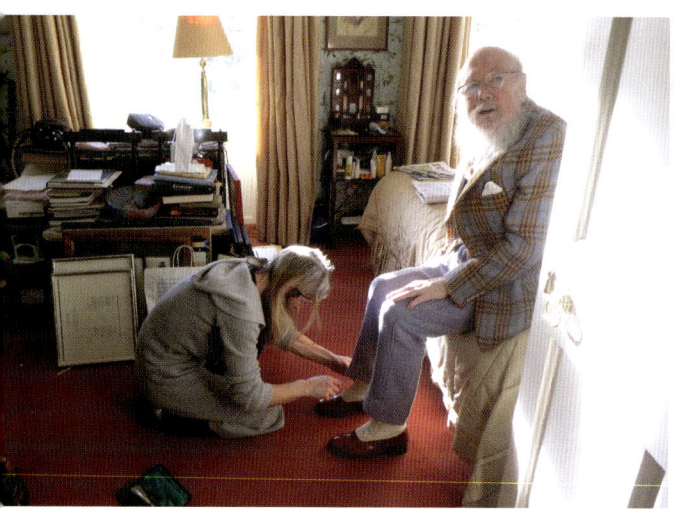
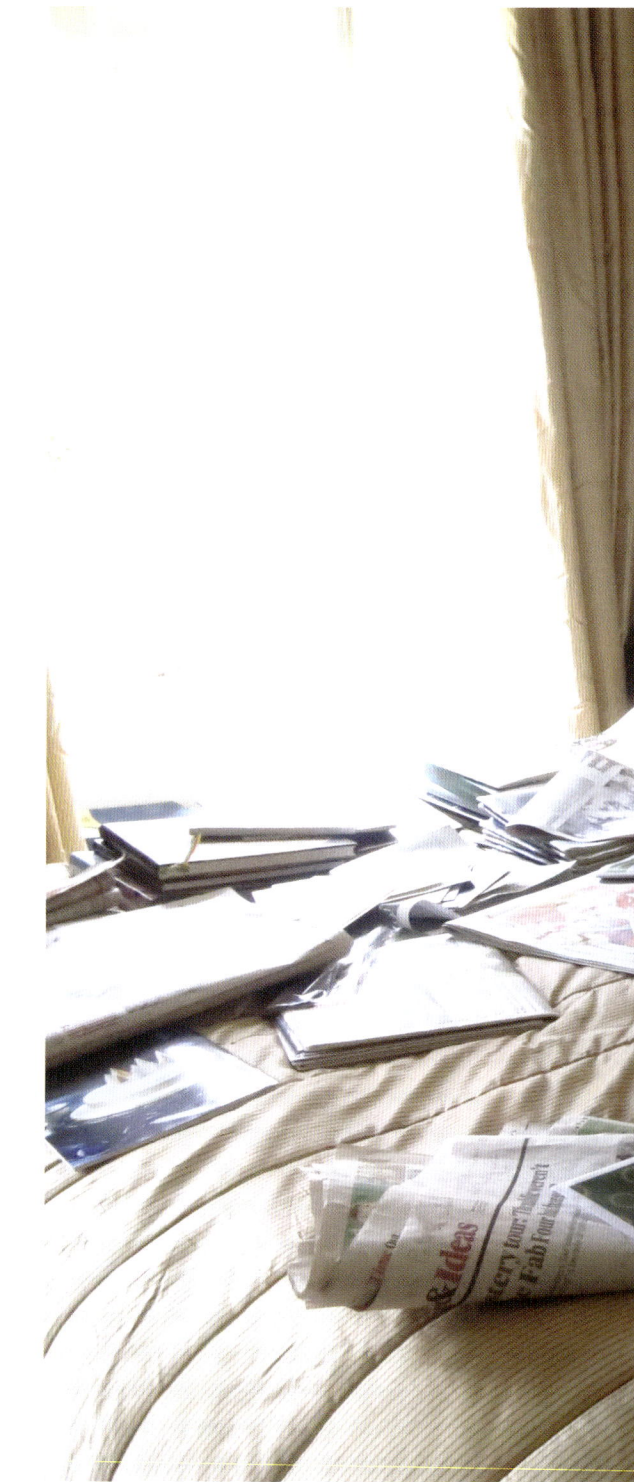

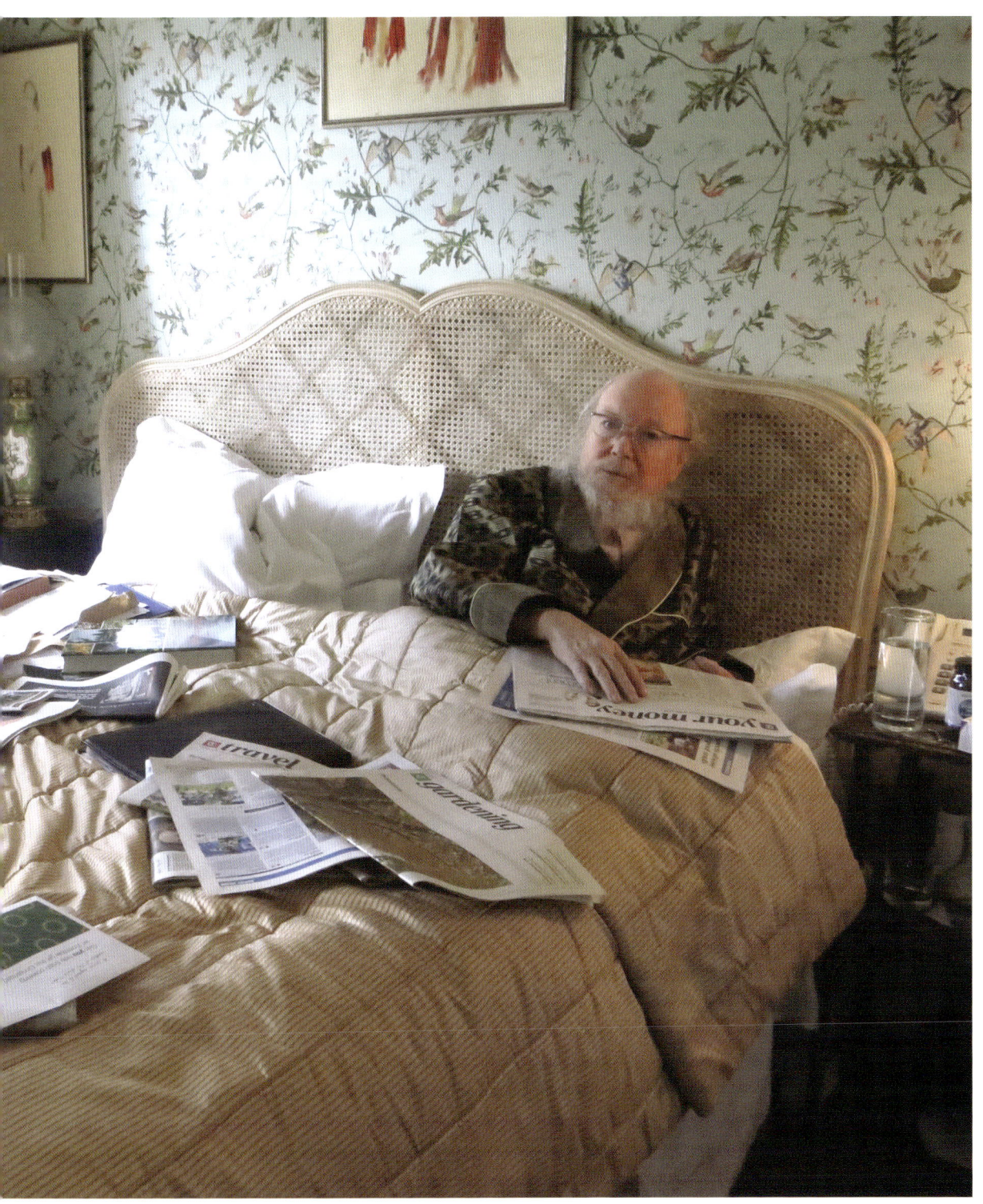

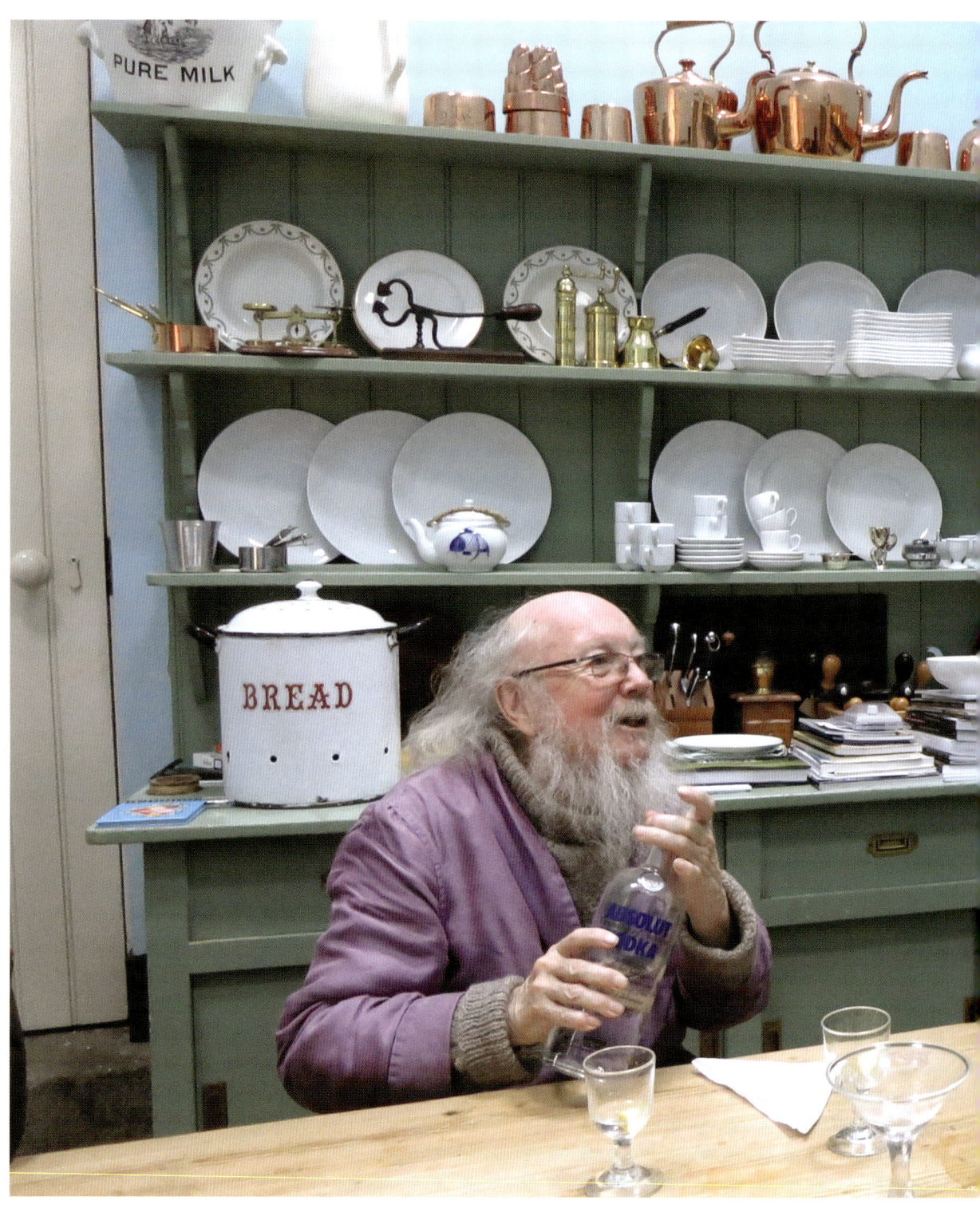

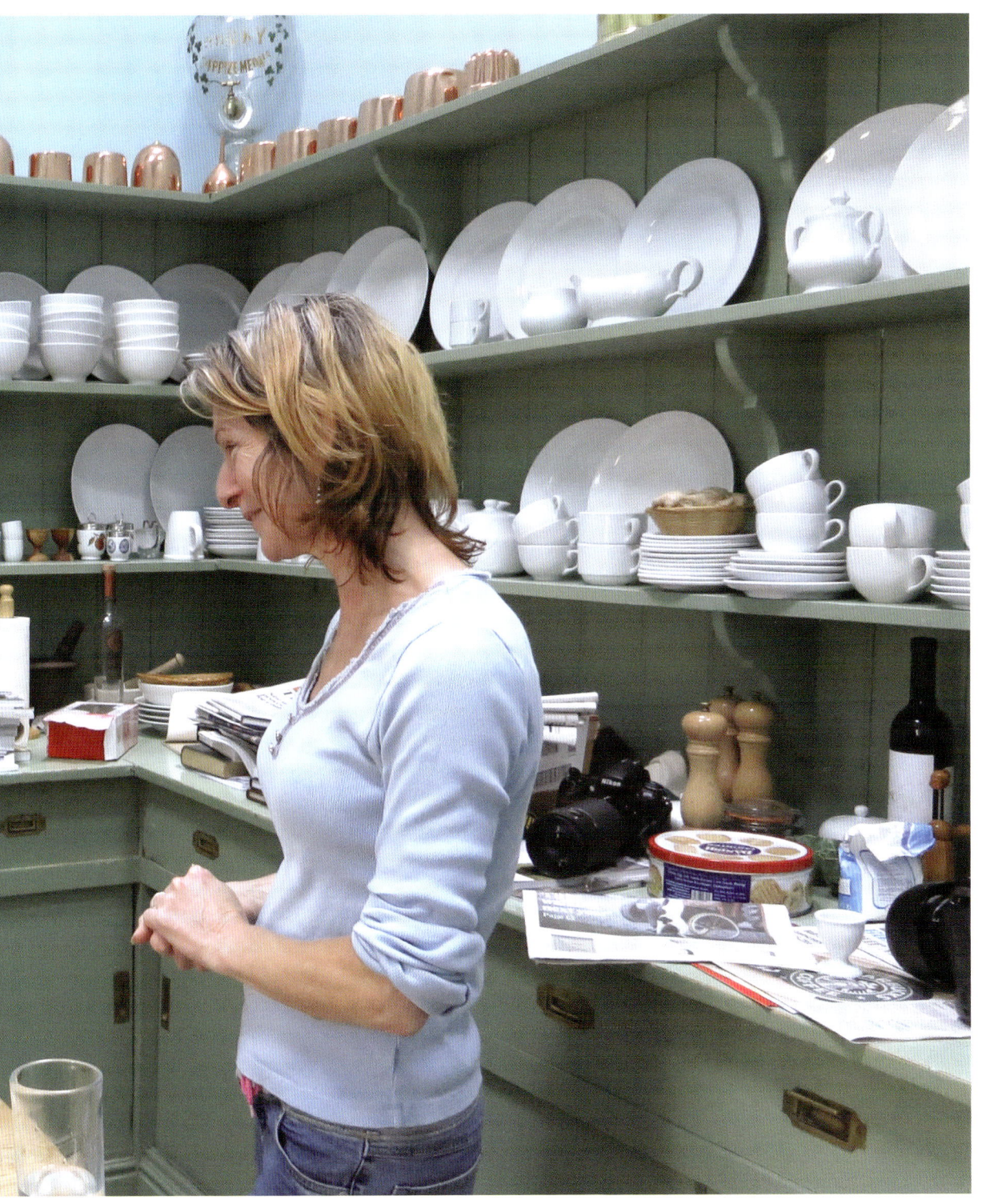

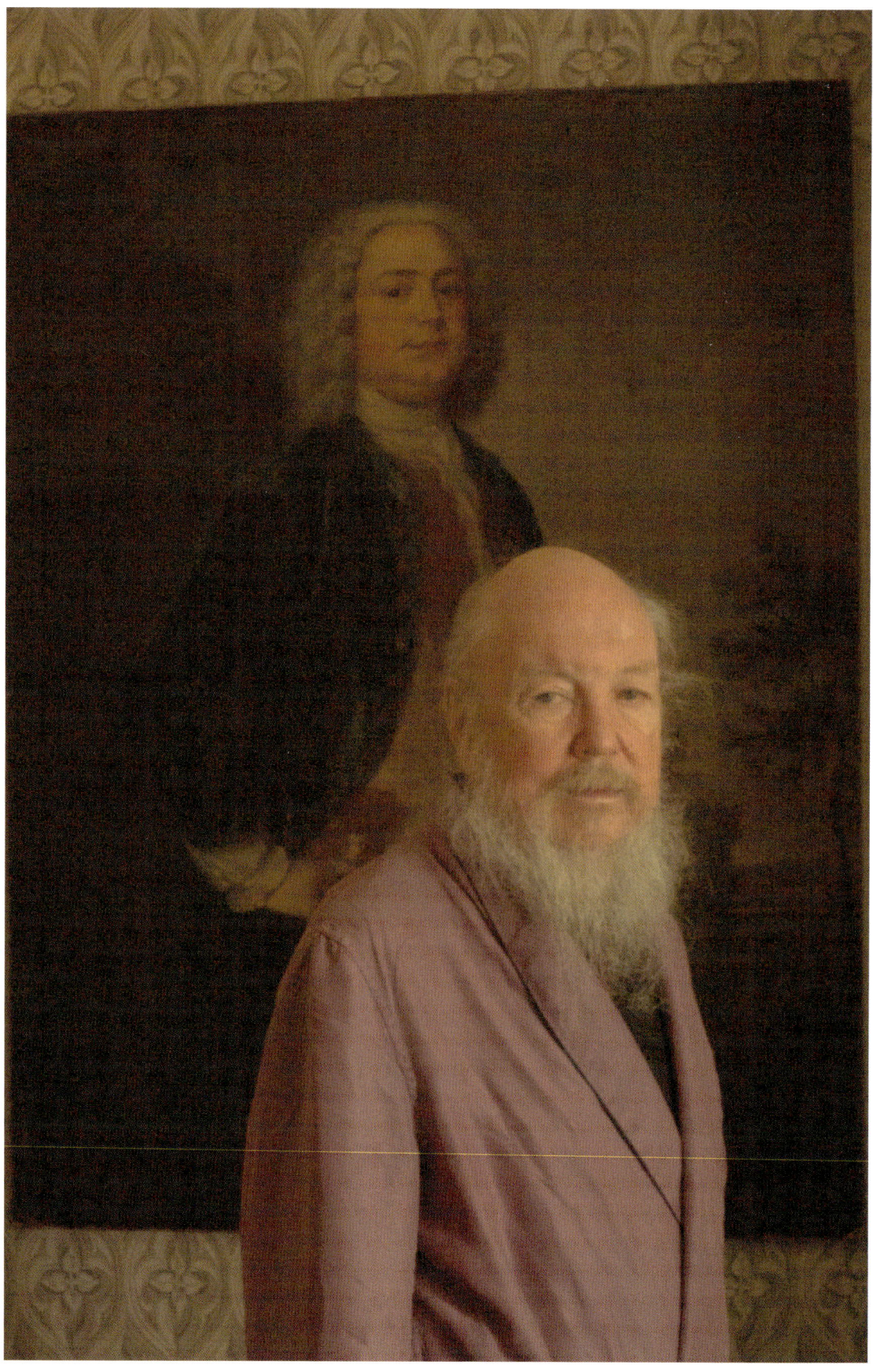

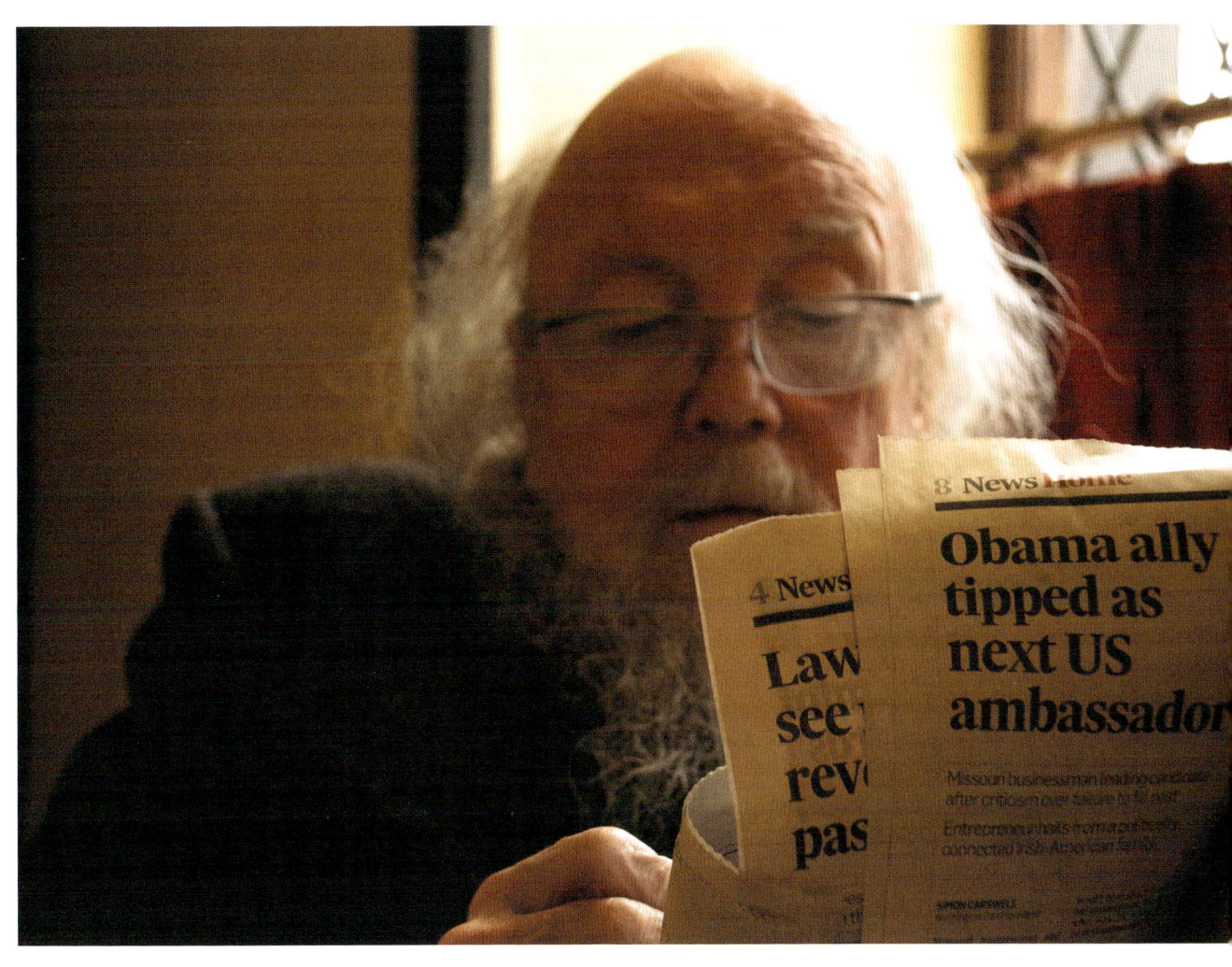

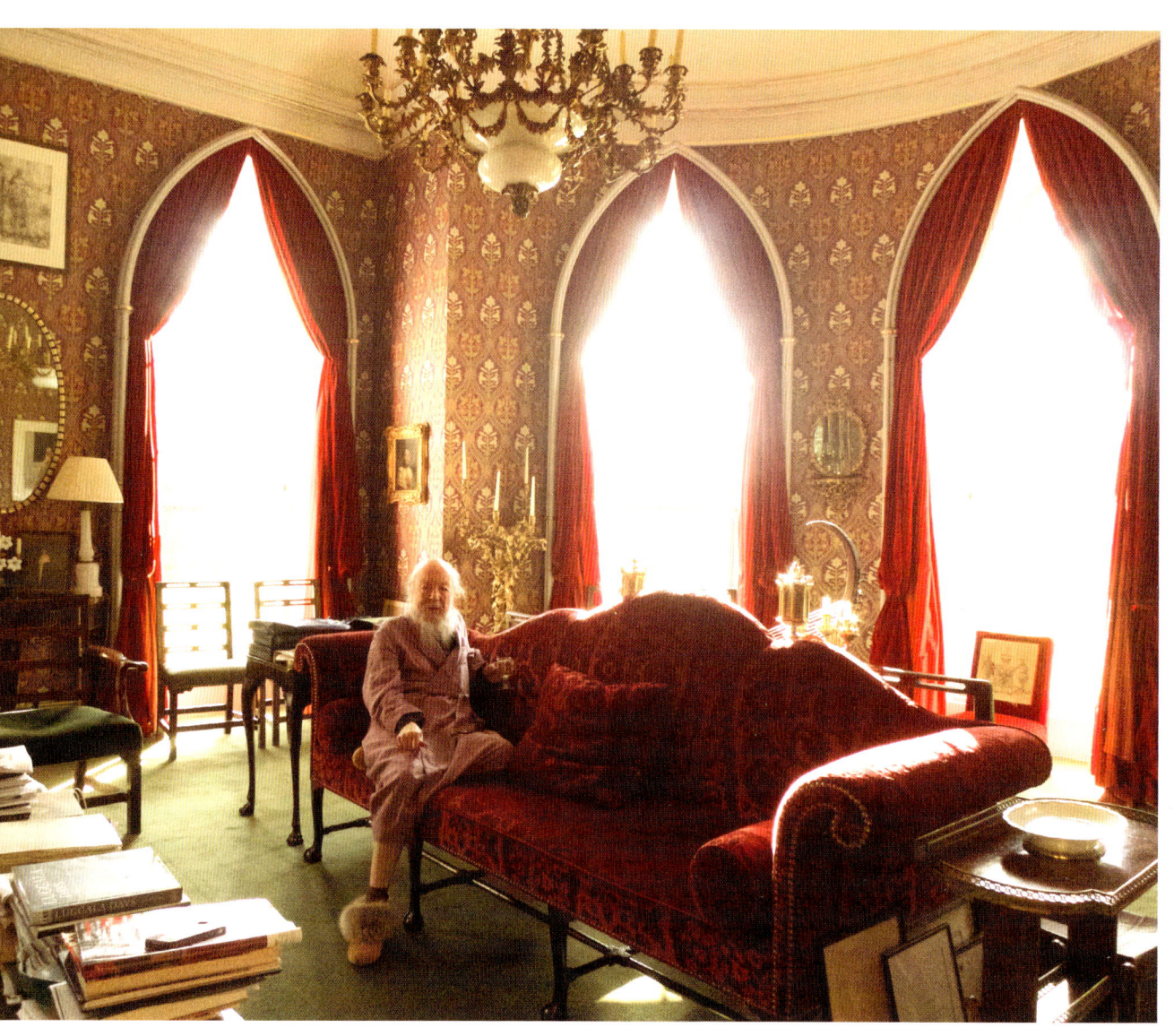

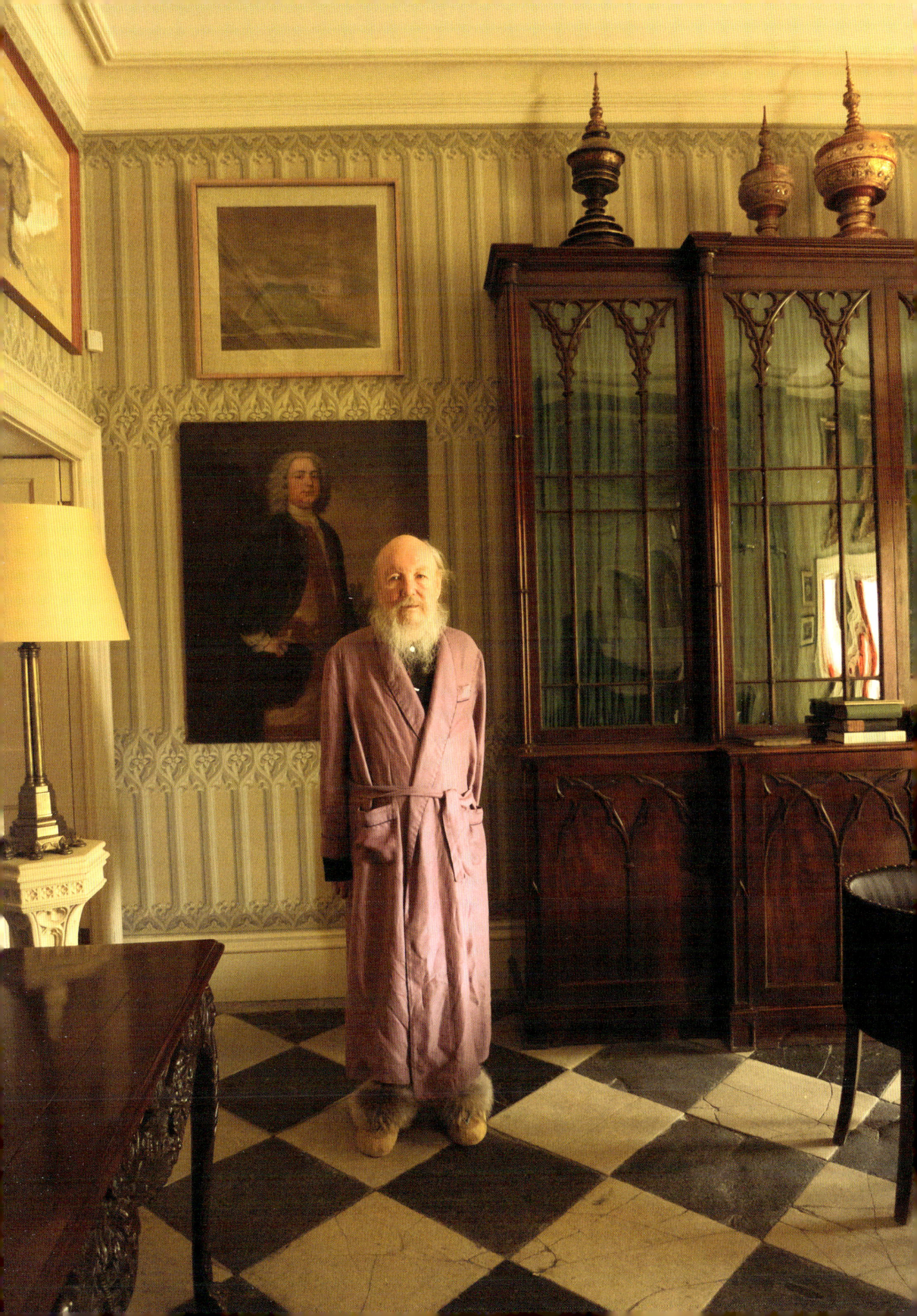

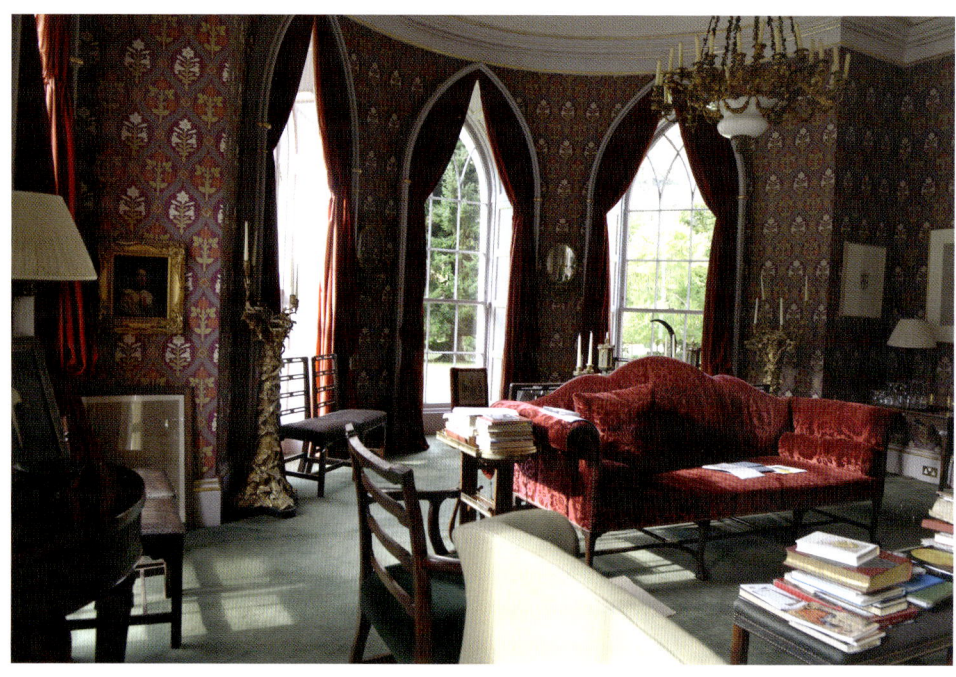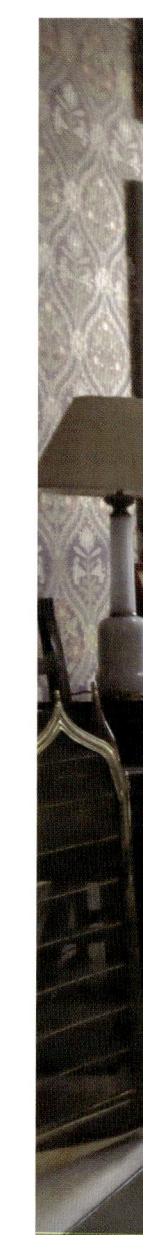

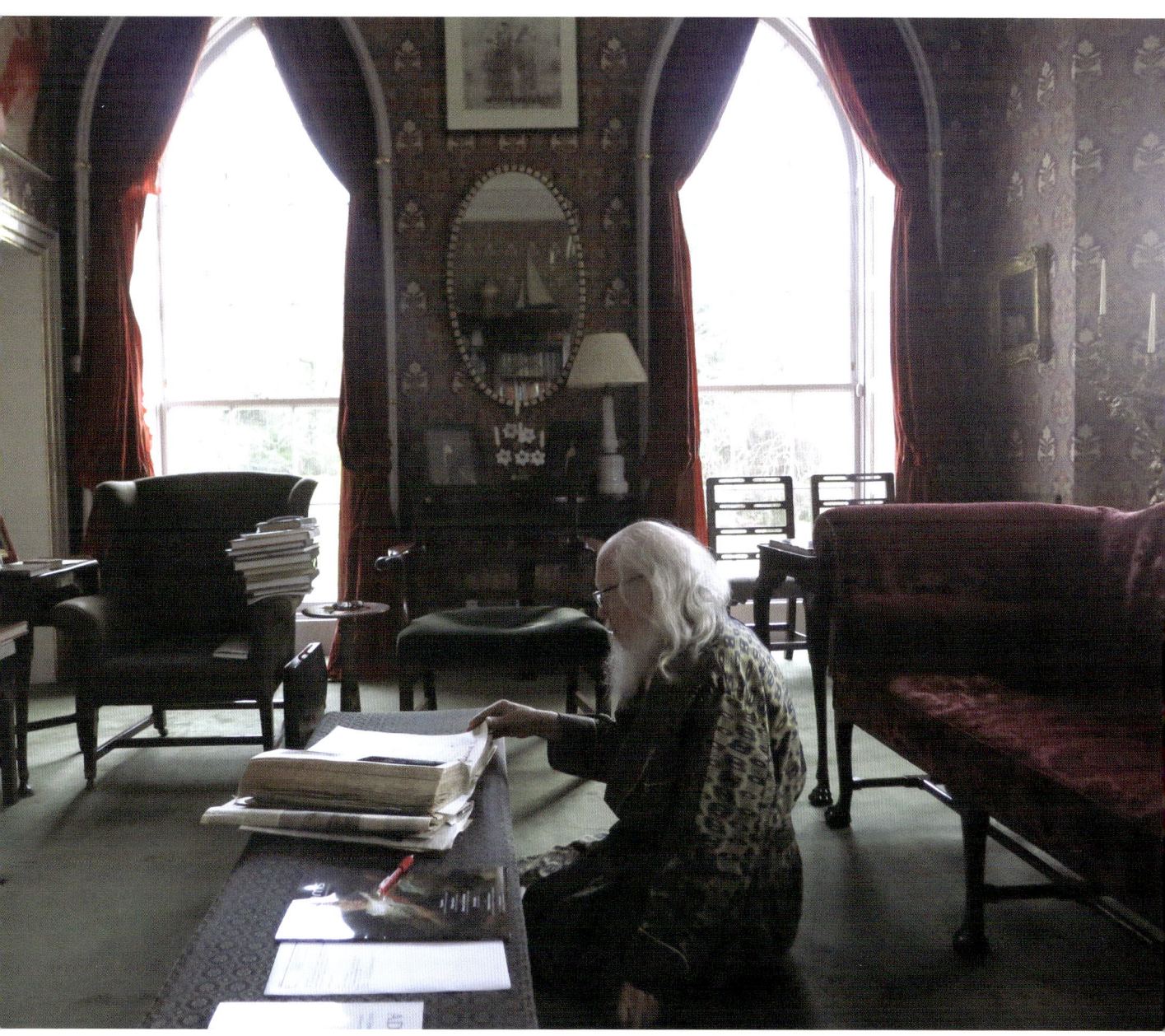

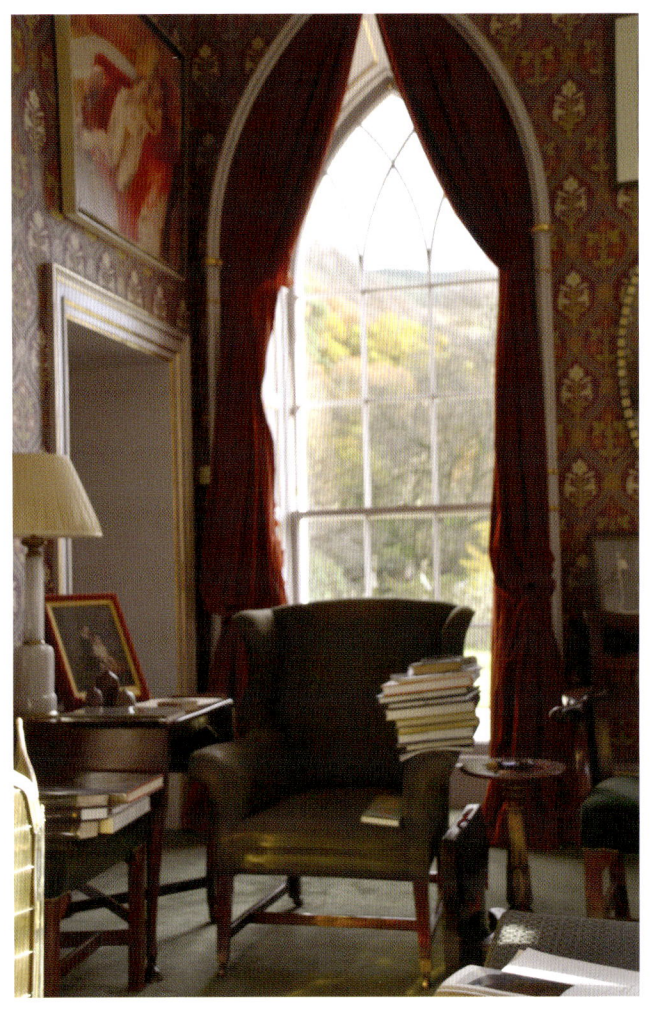
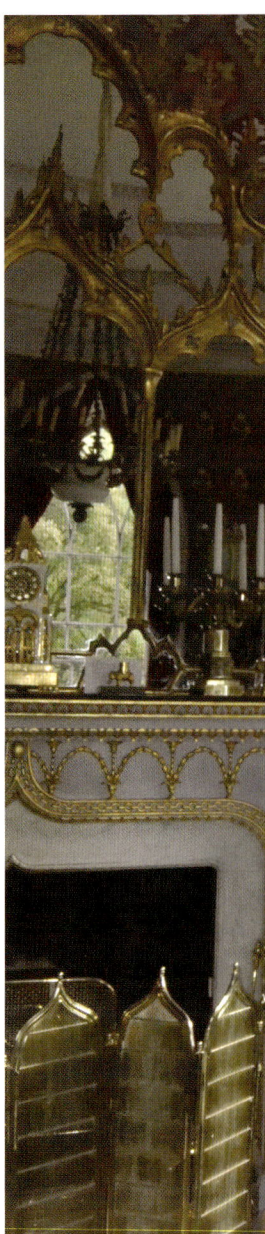
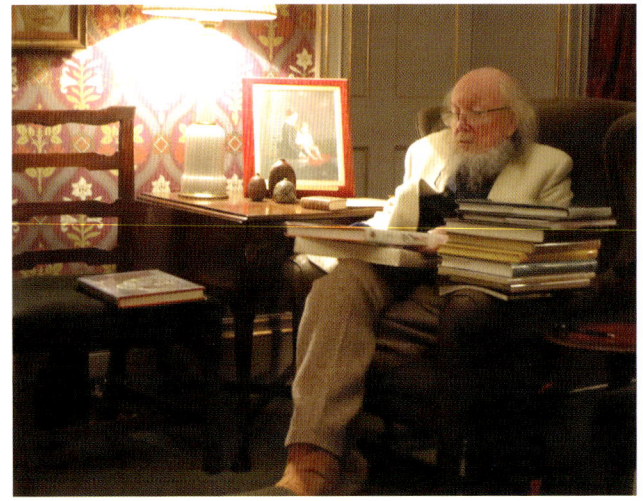

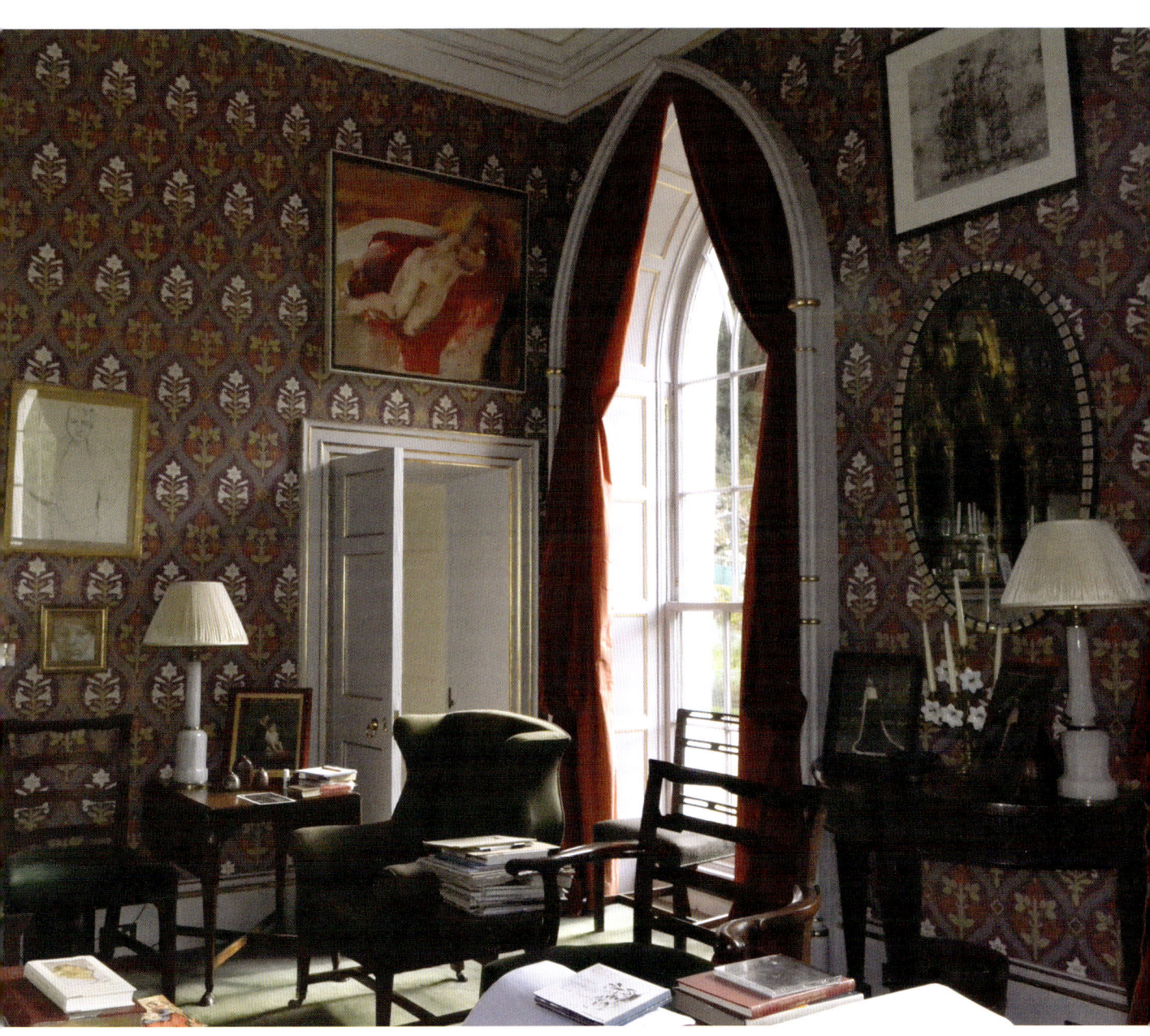

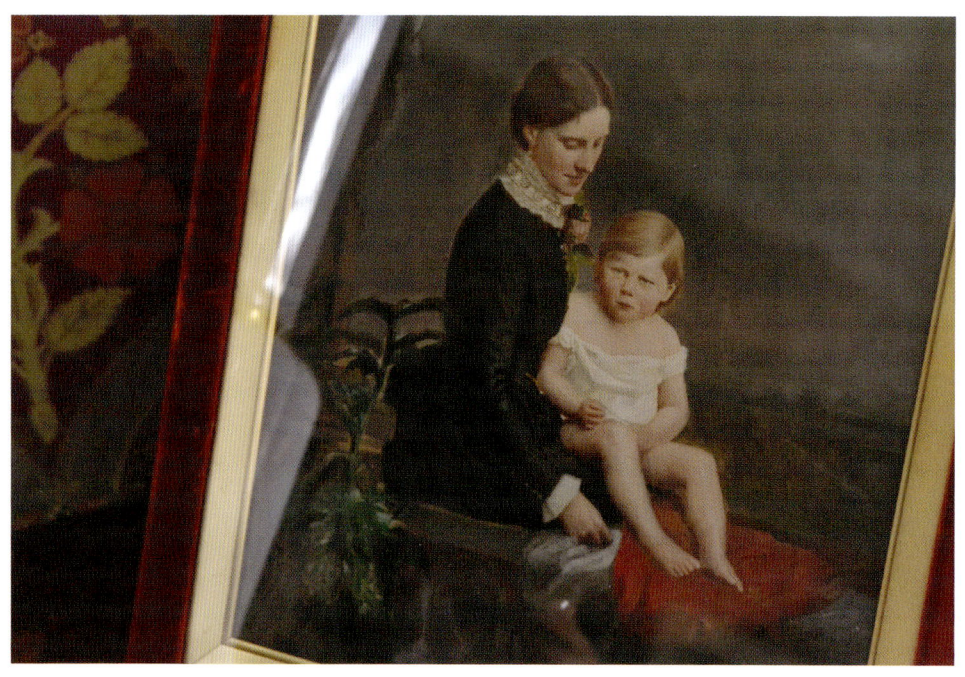

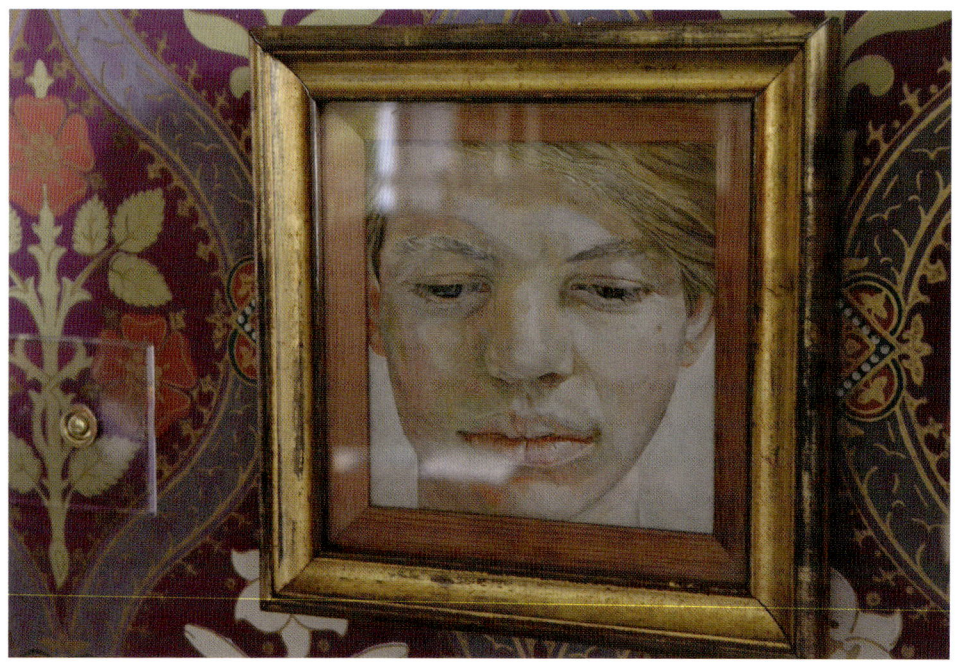

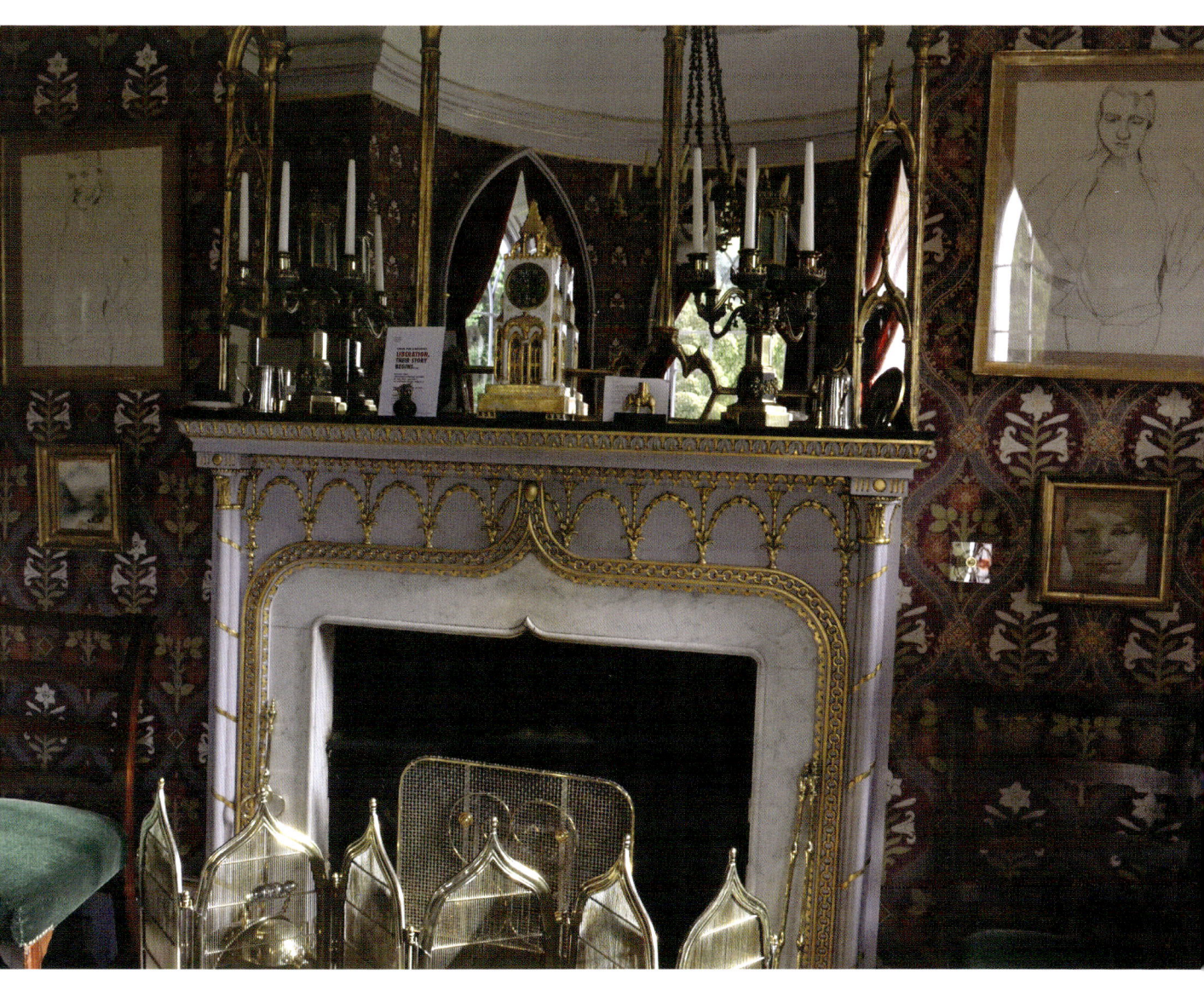

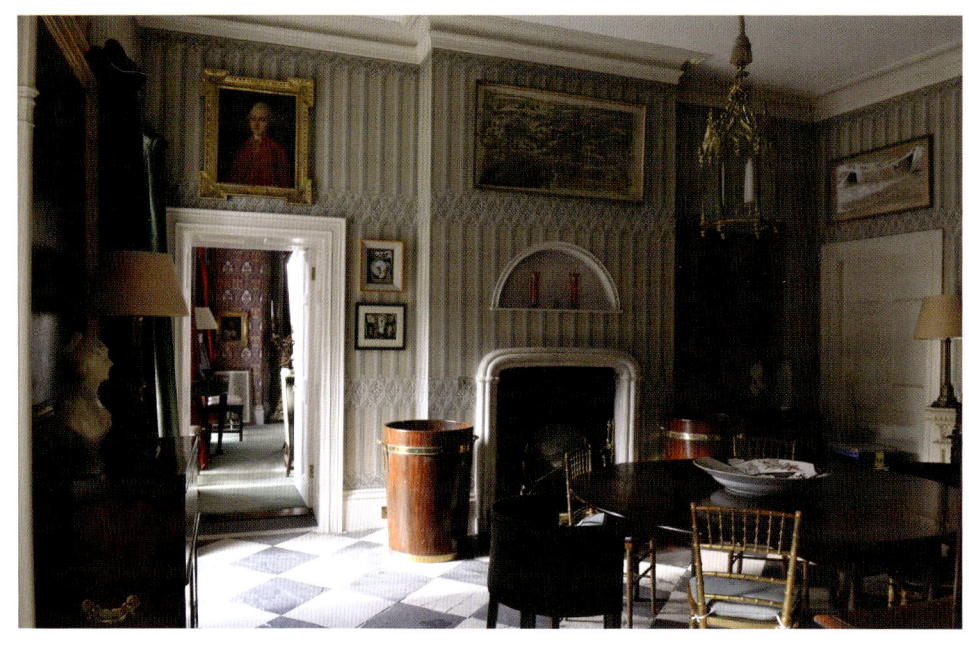

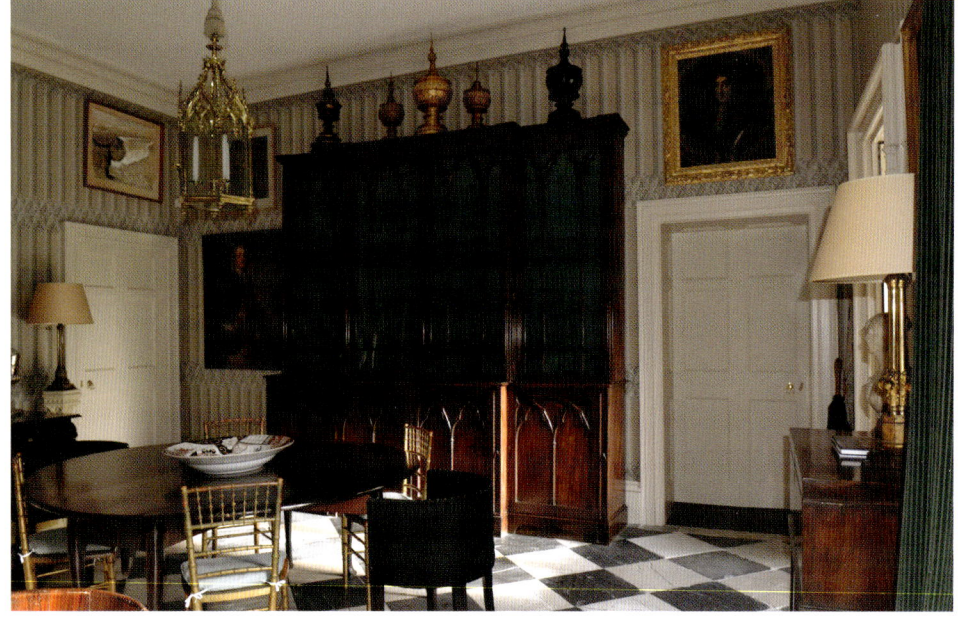

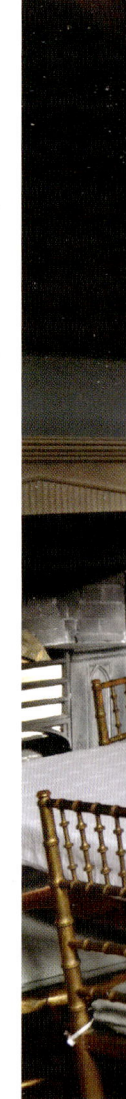

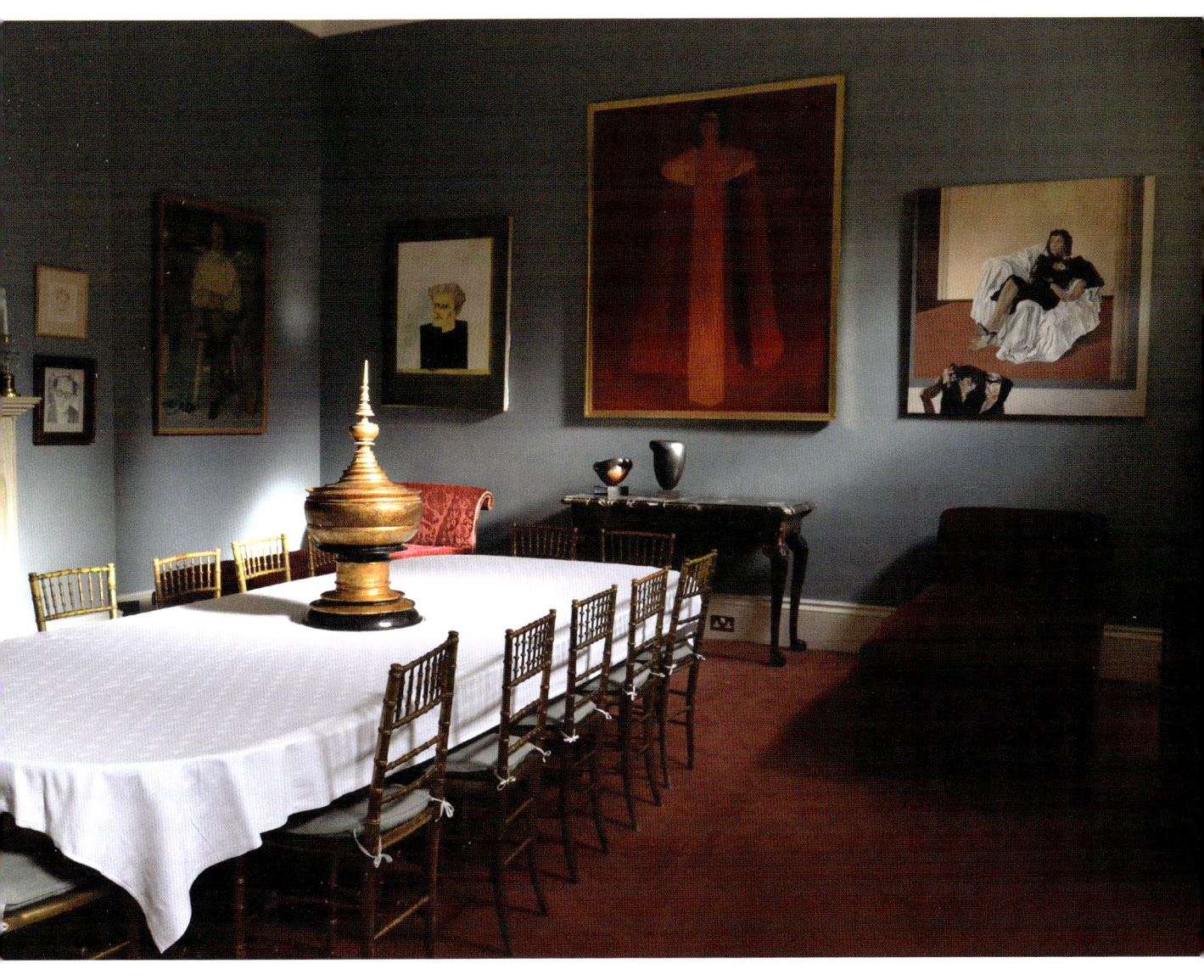

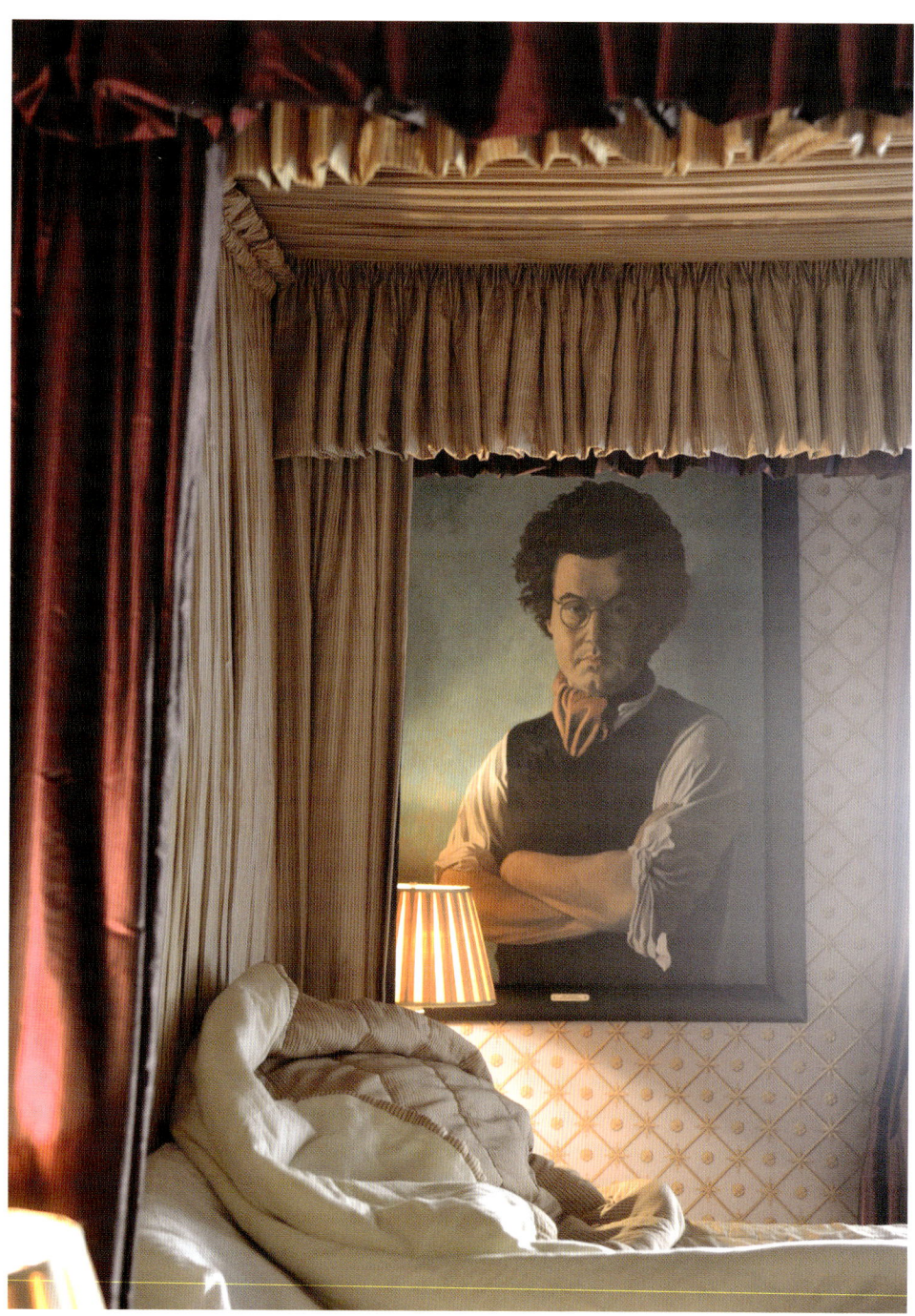

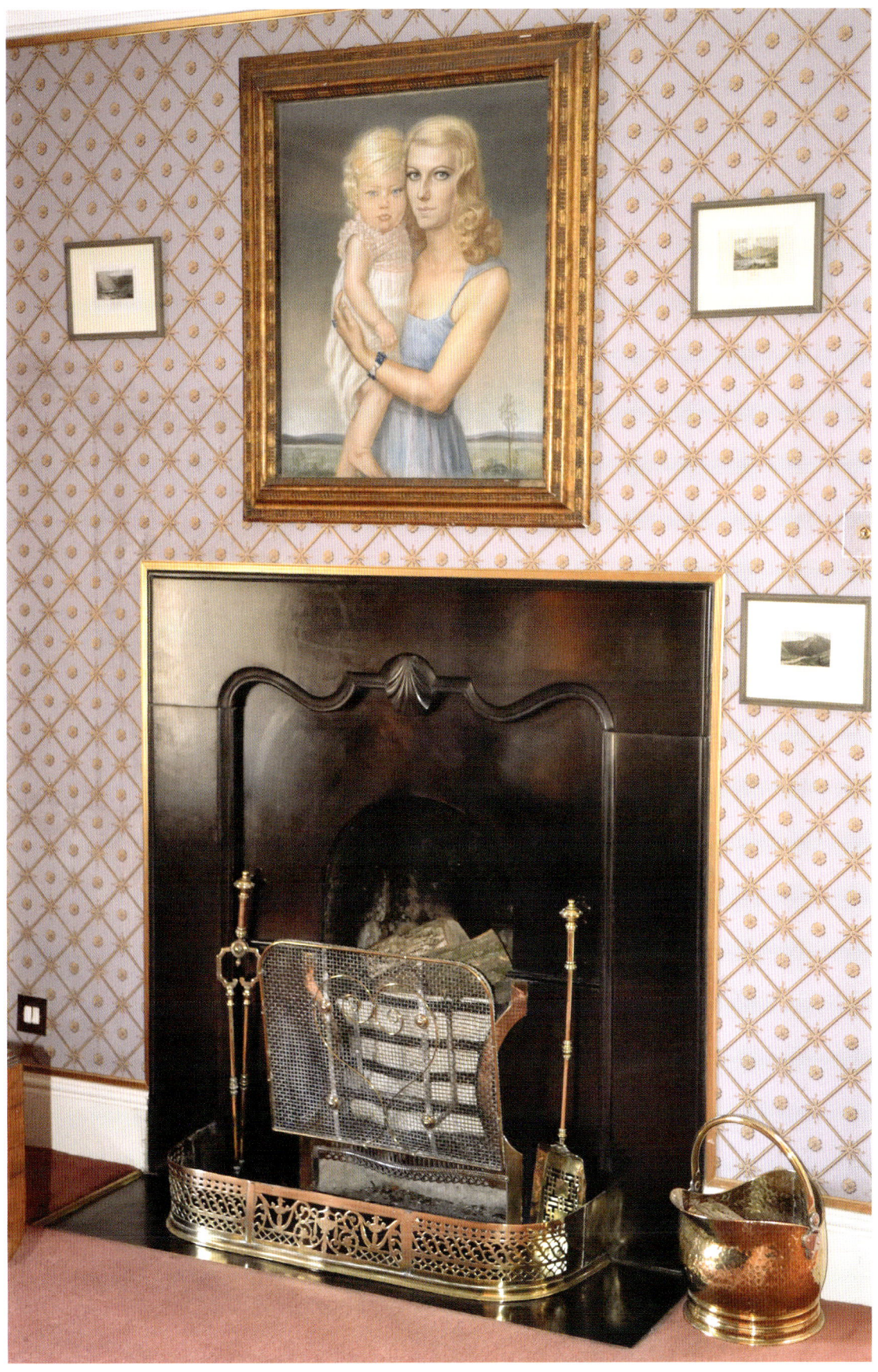

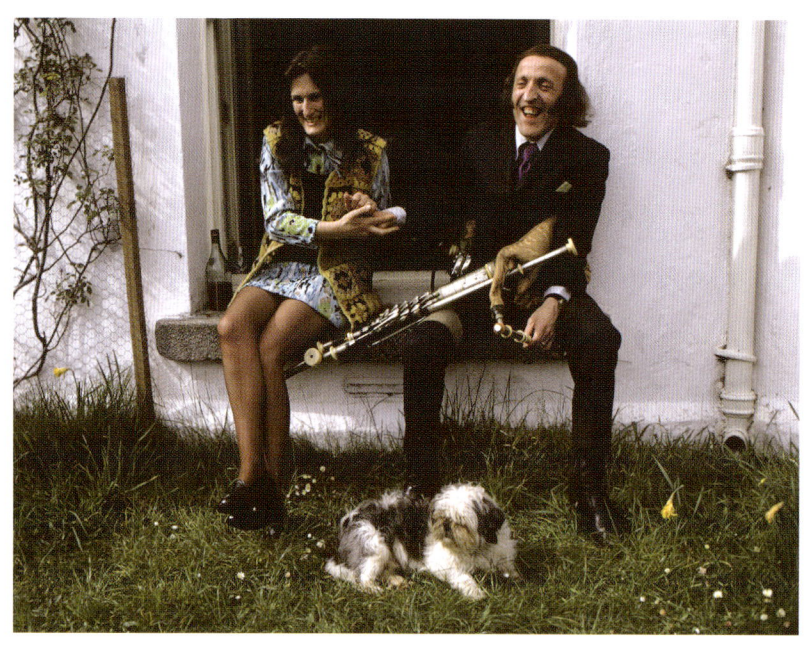
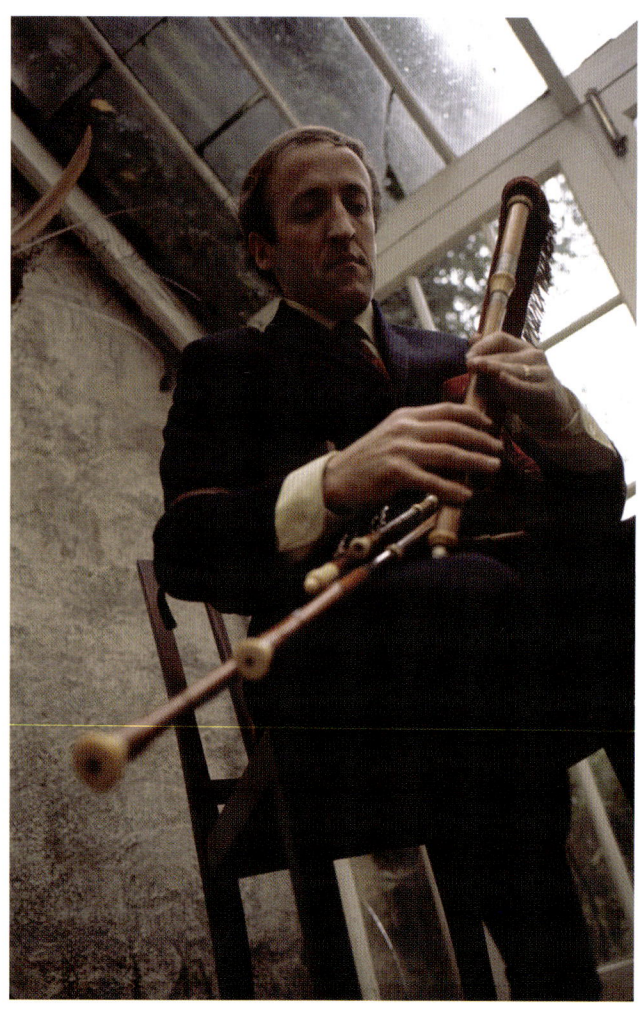

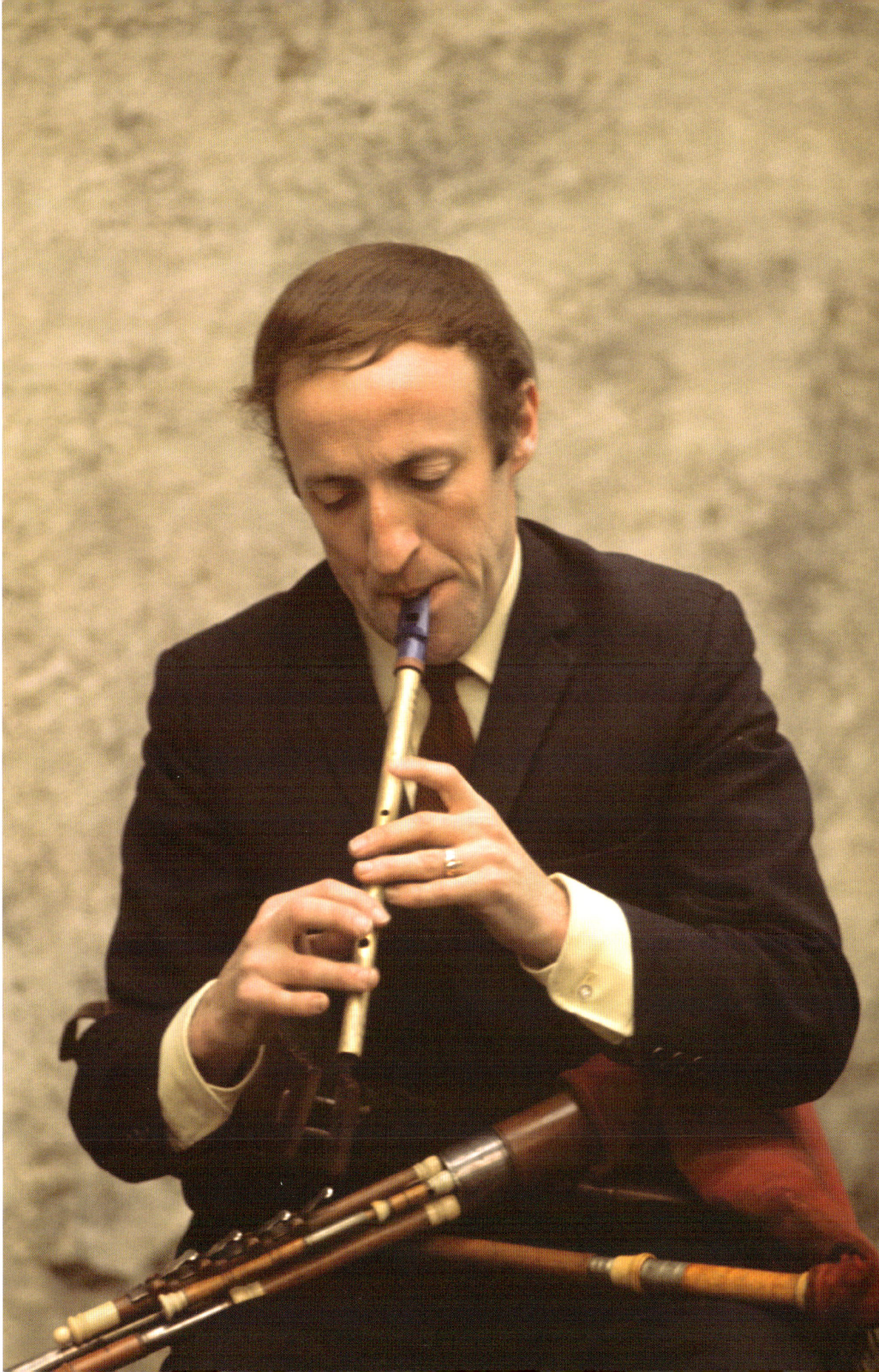

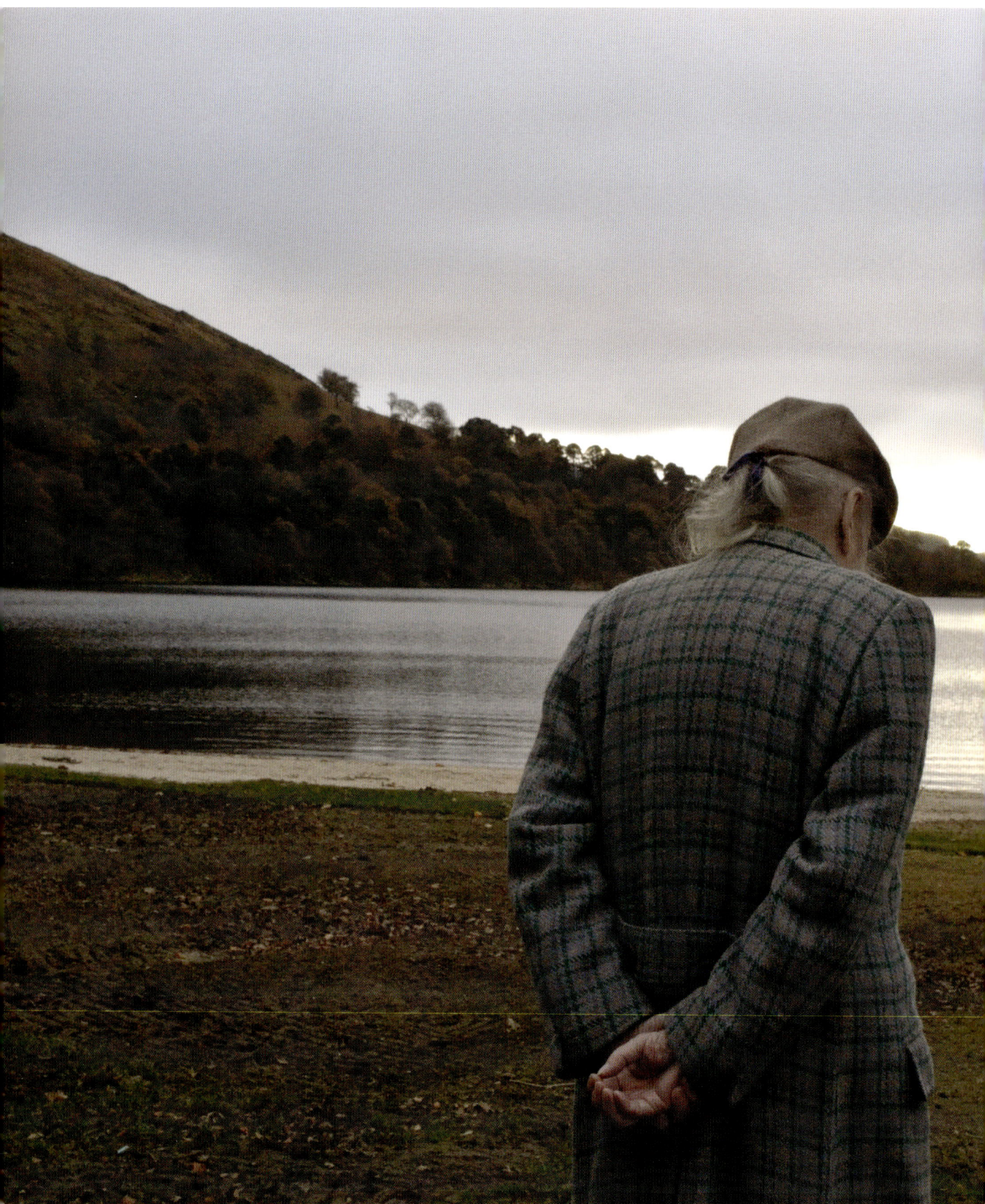

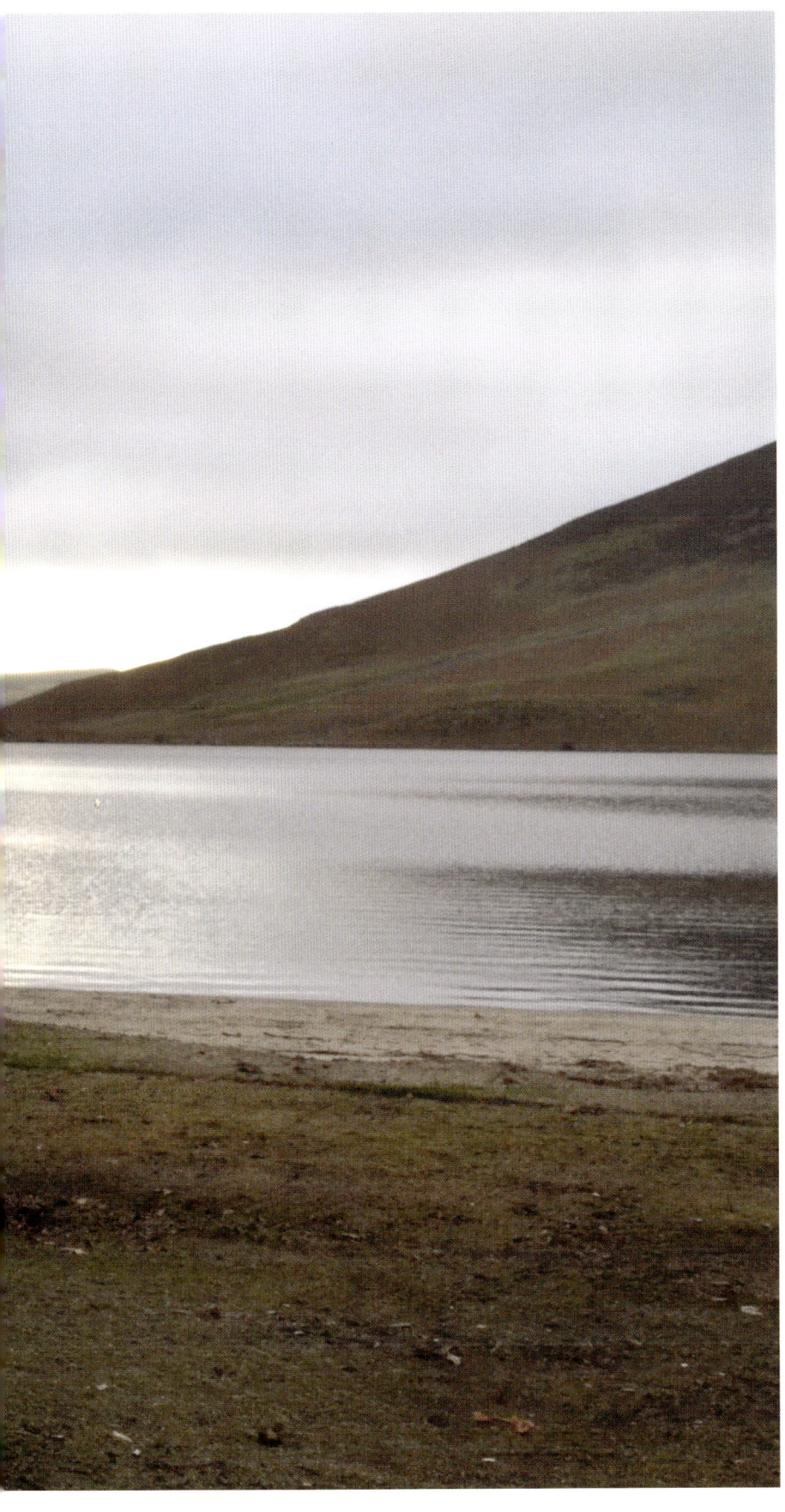

A Singular Country

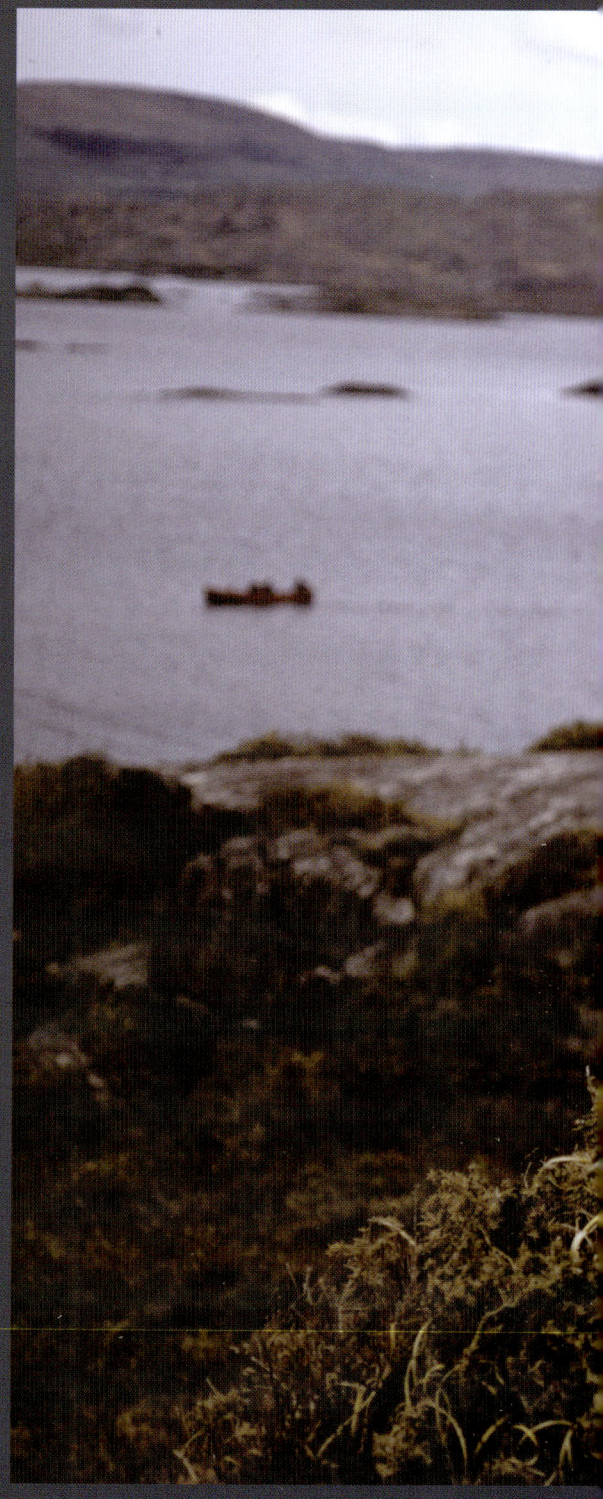

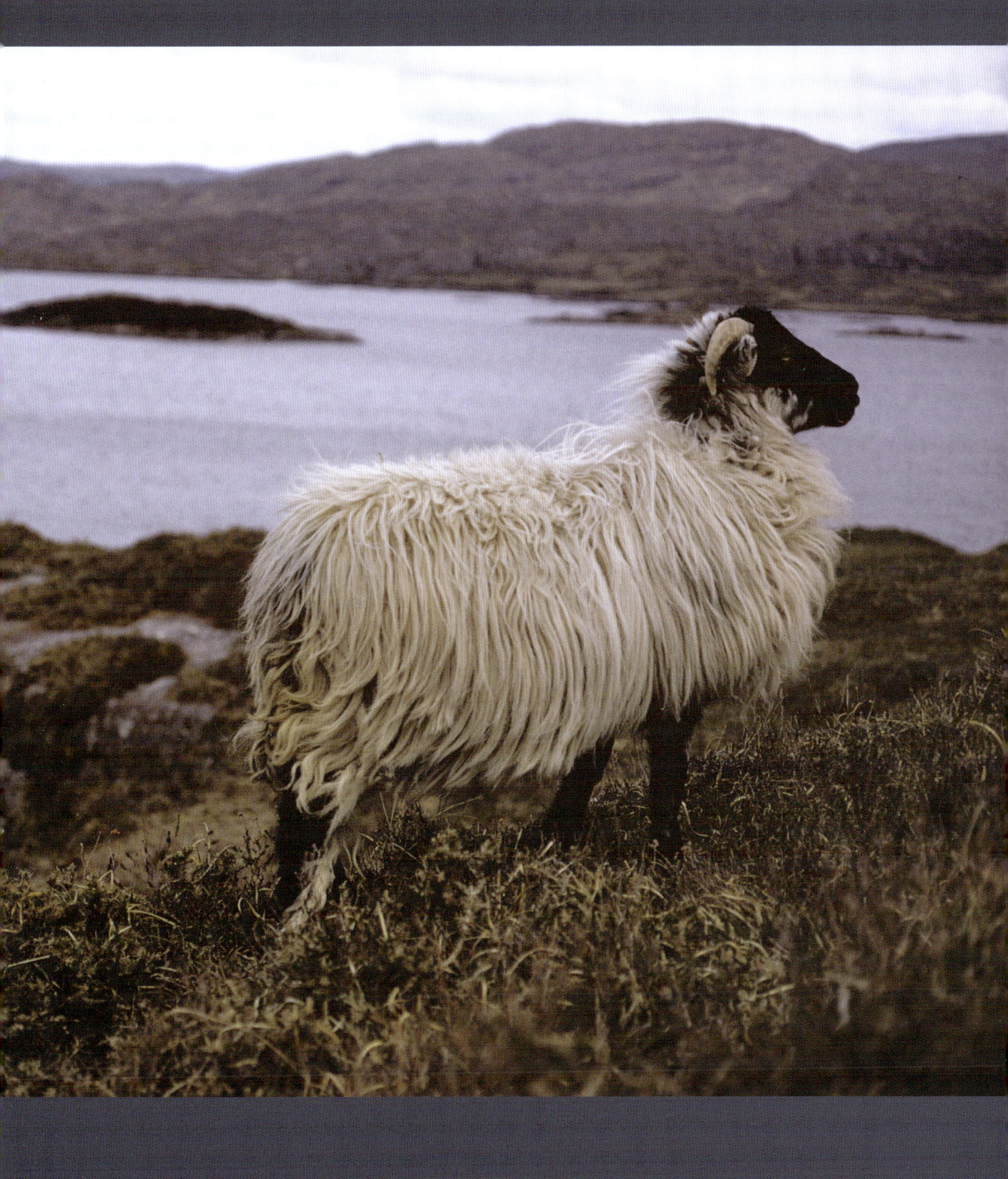

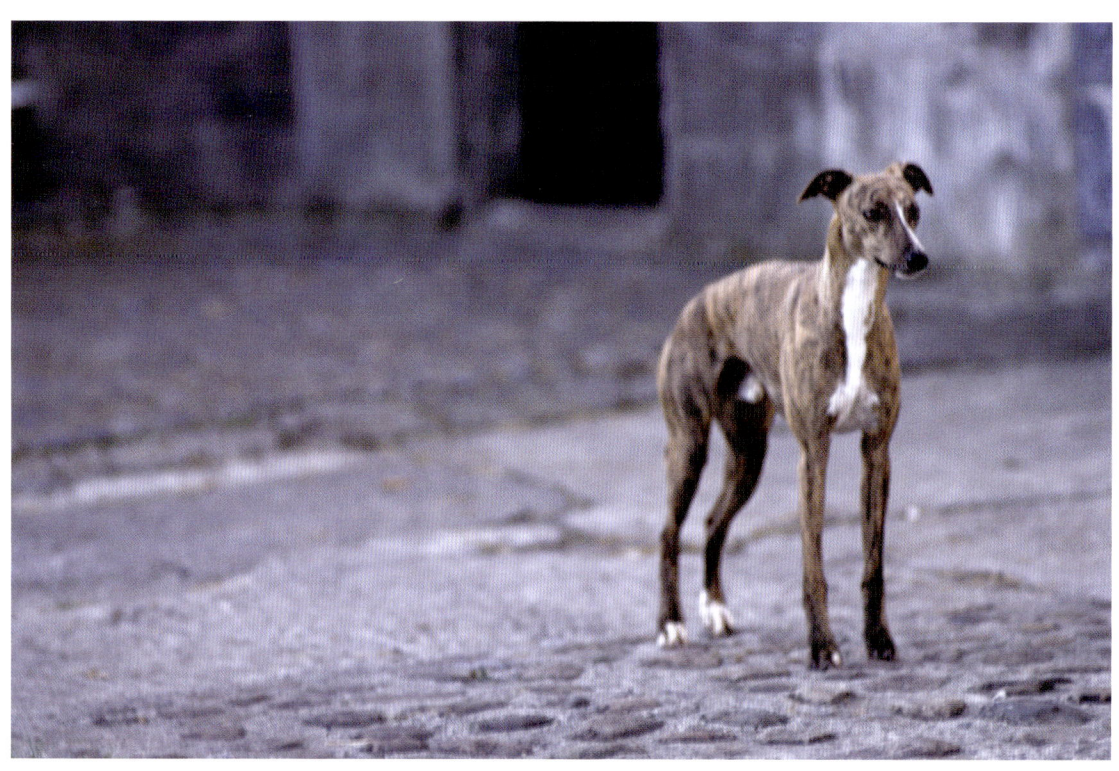

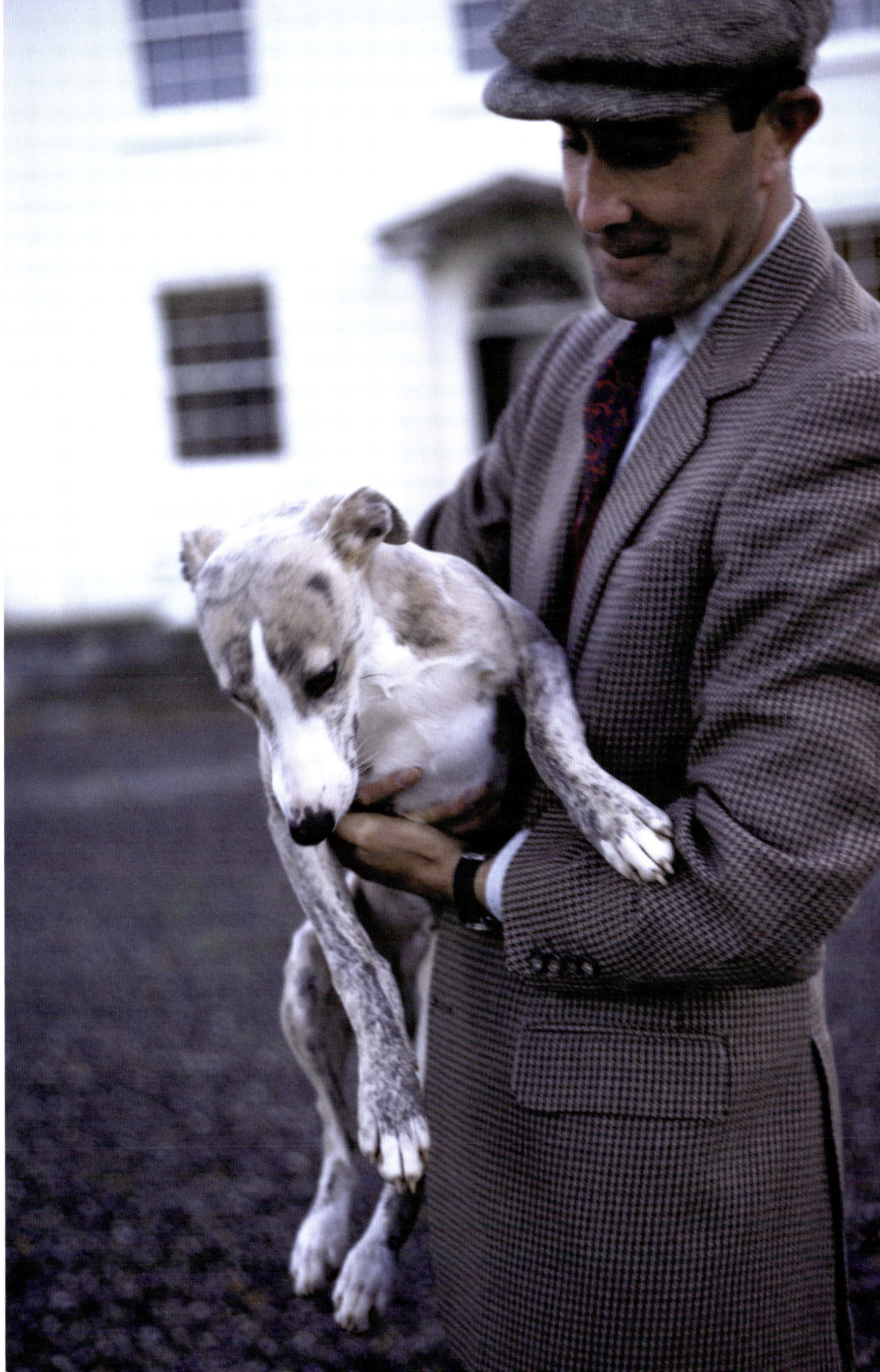

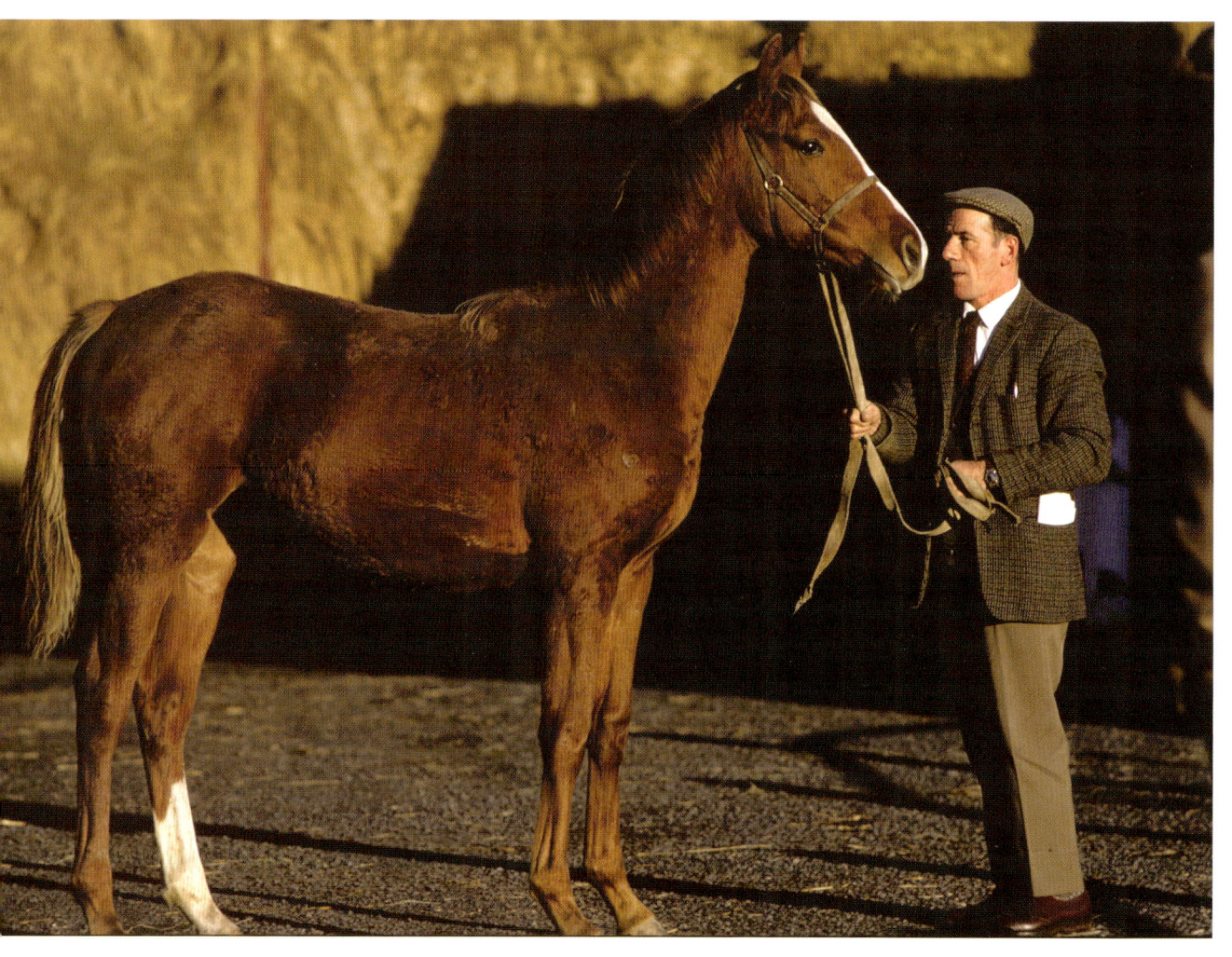

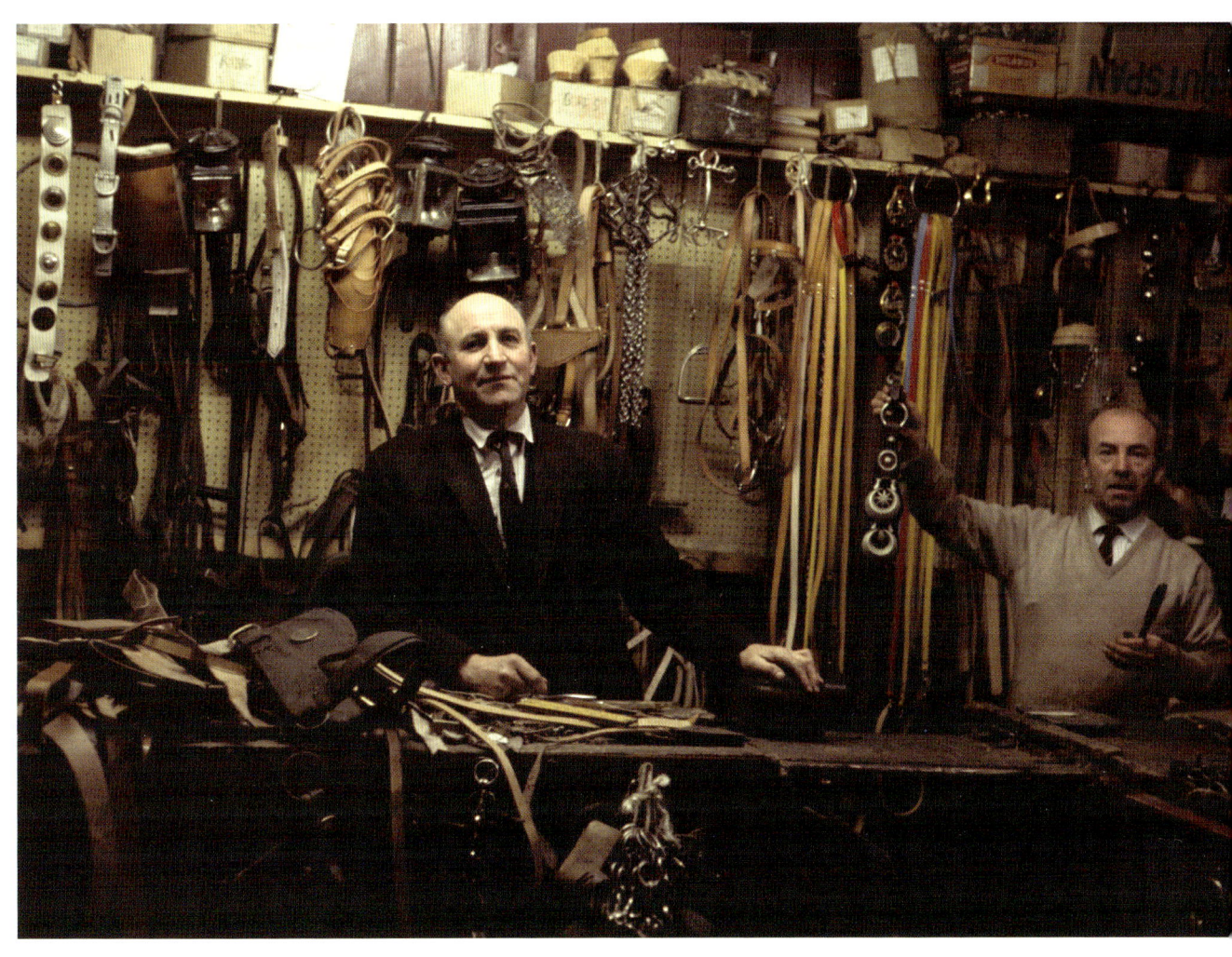

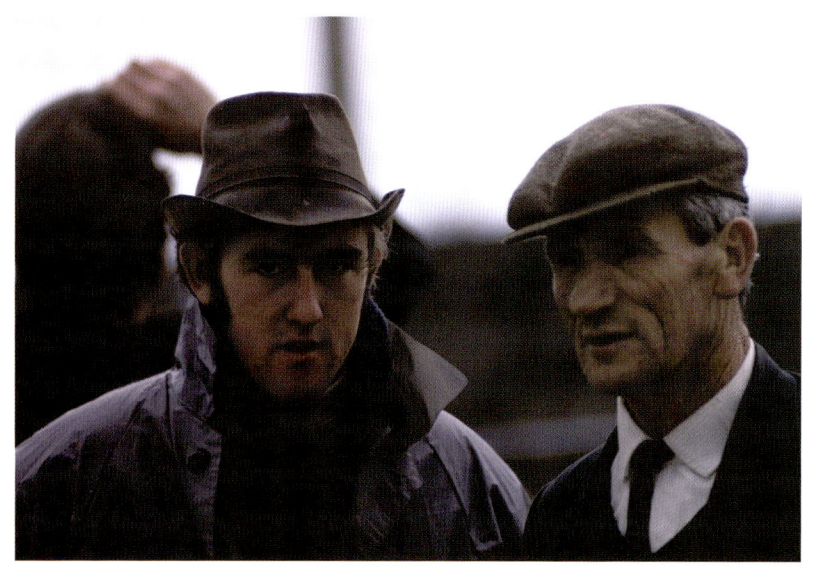
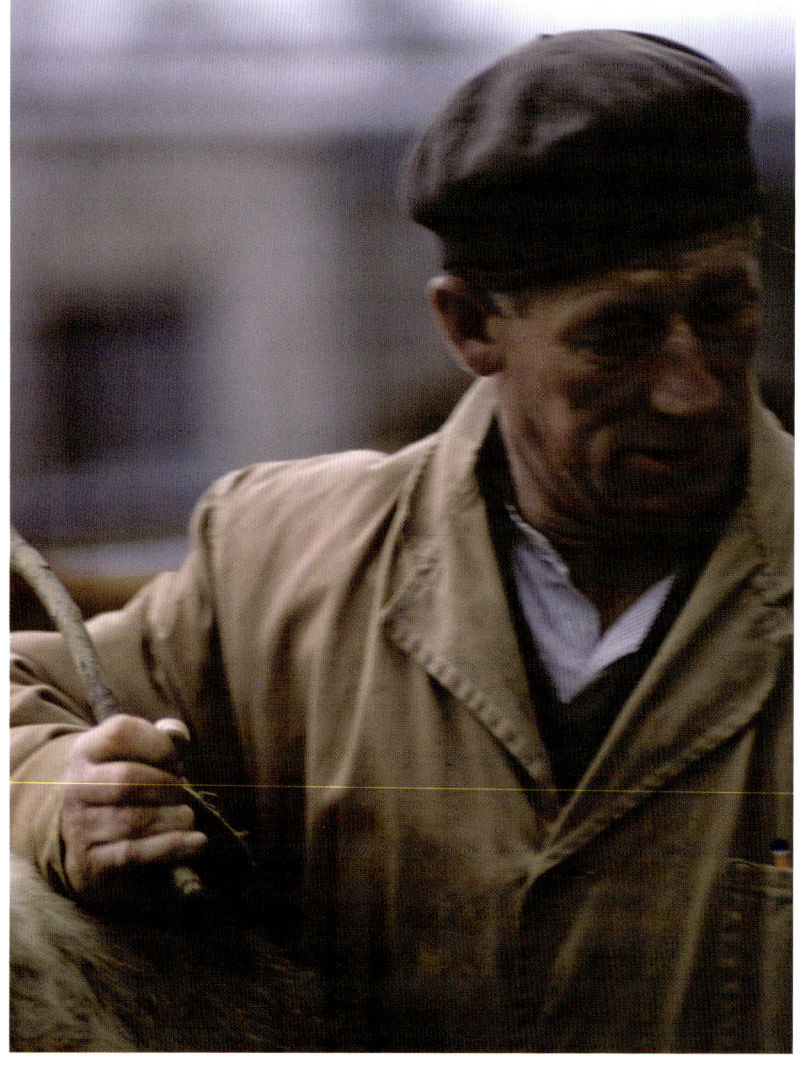
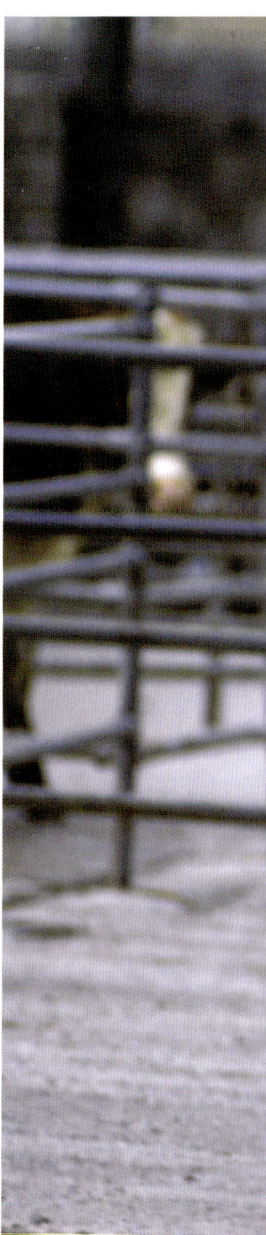

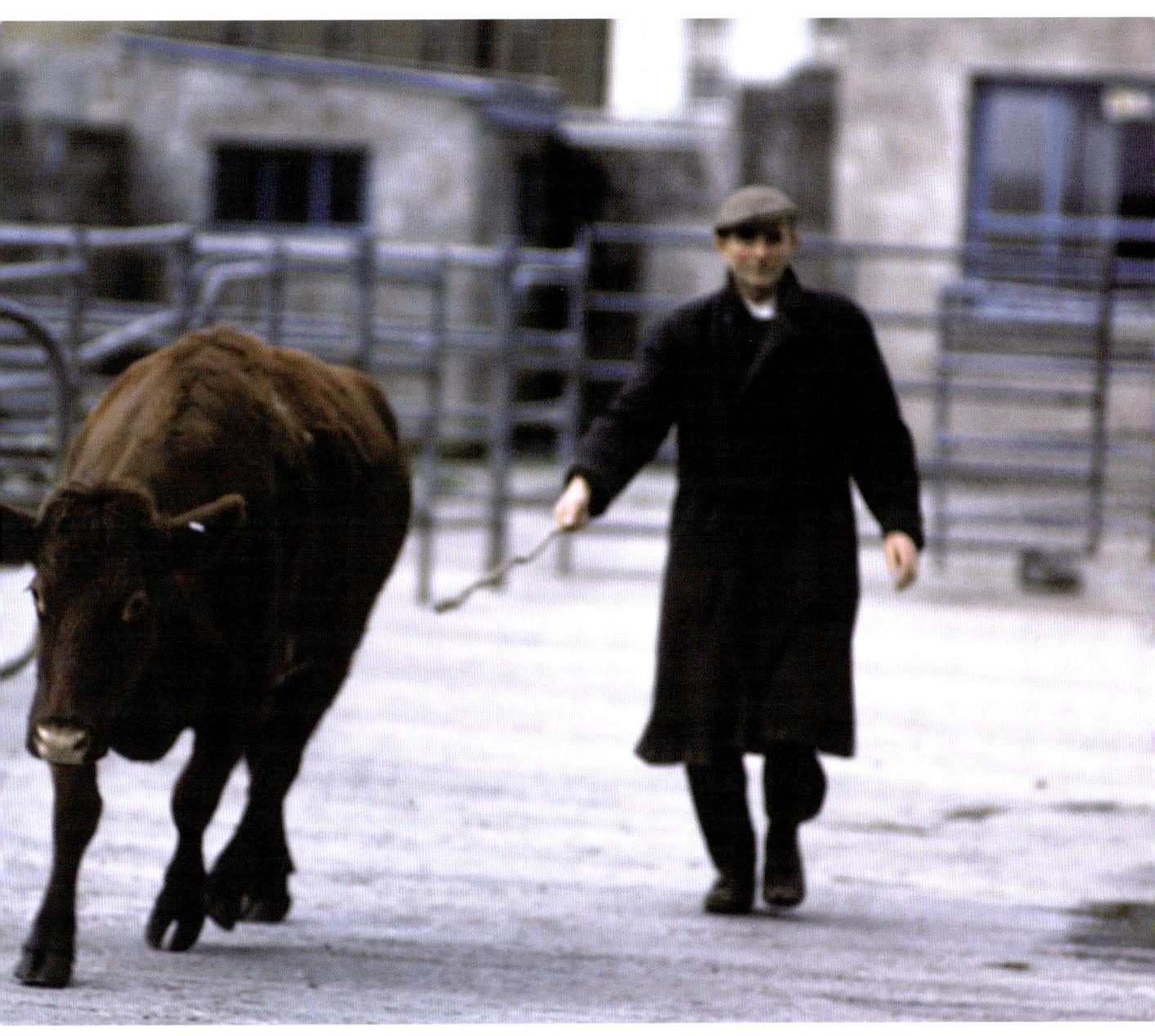

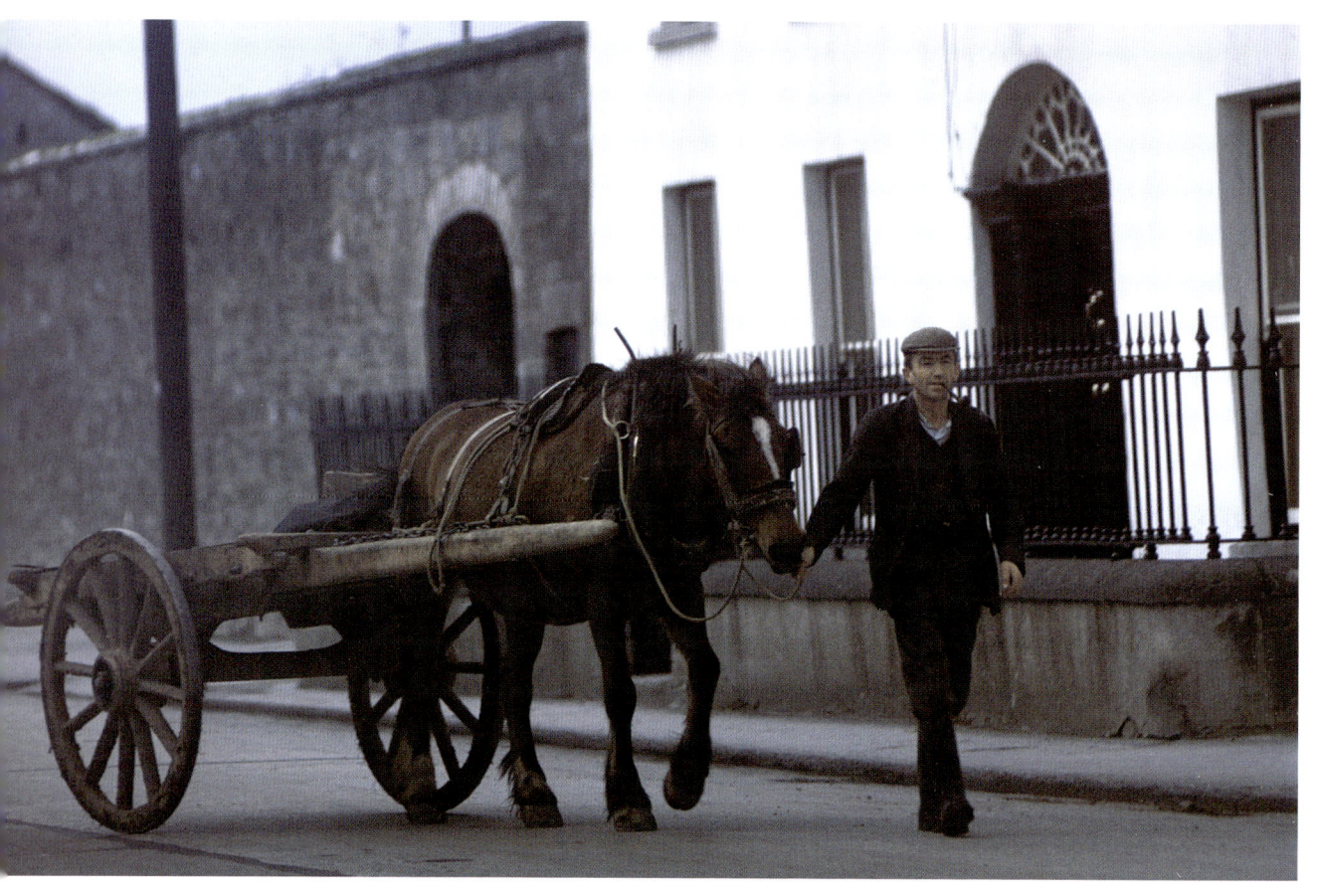

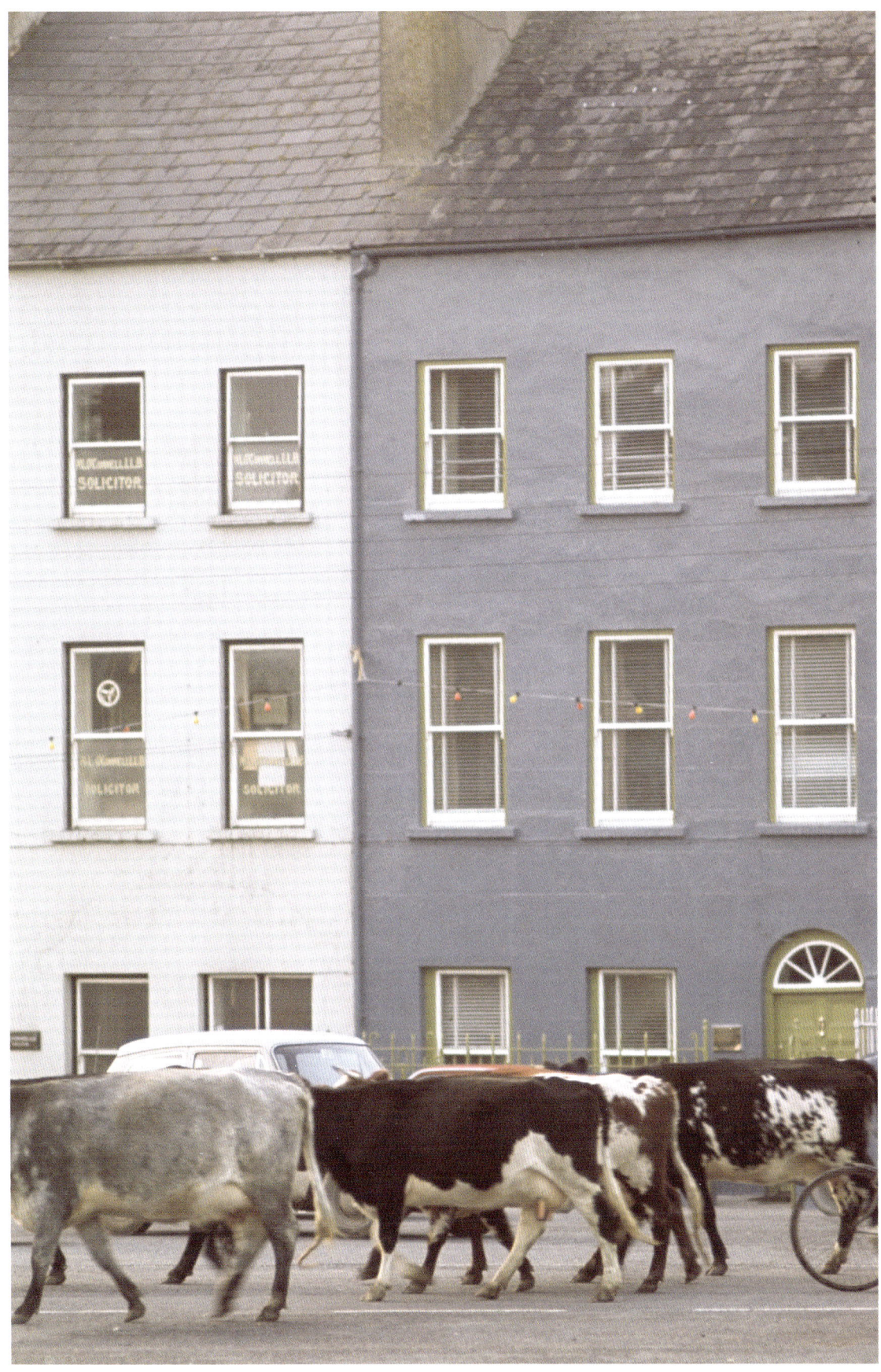

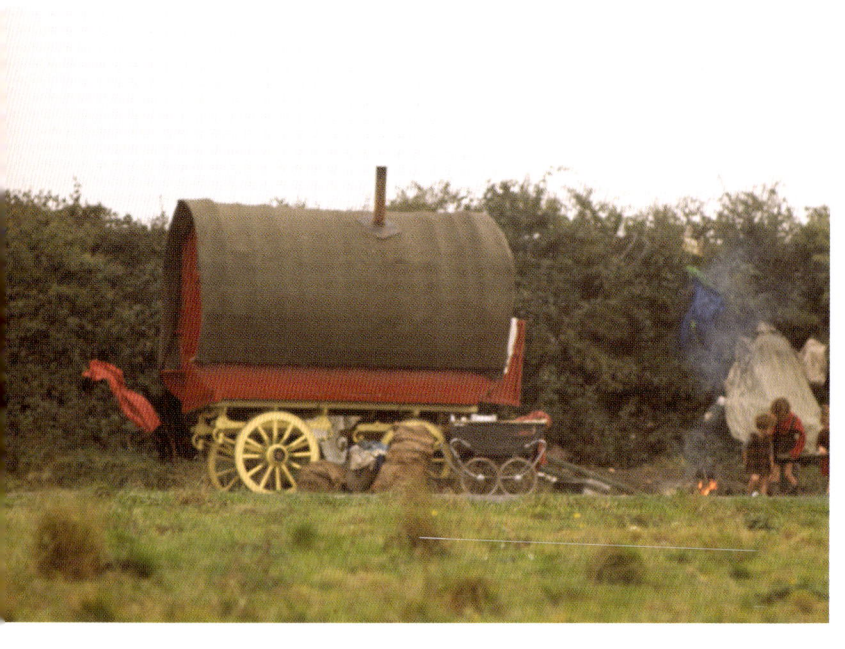
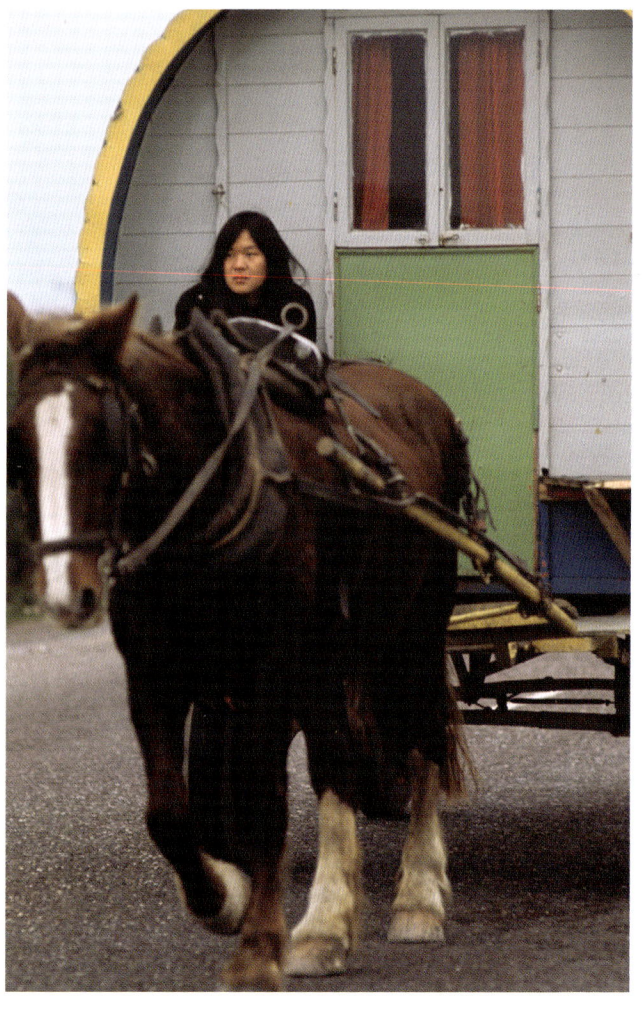
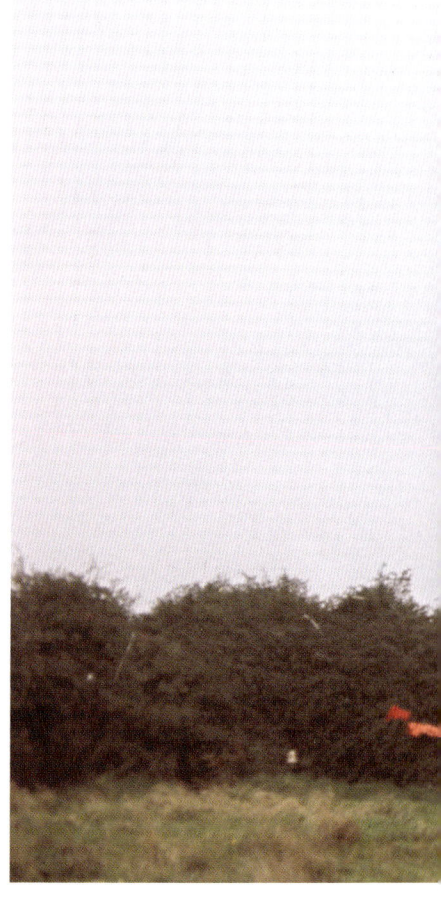

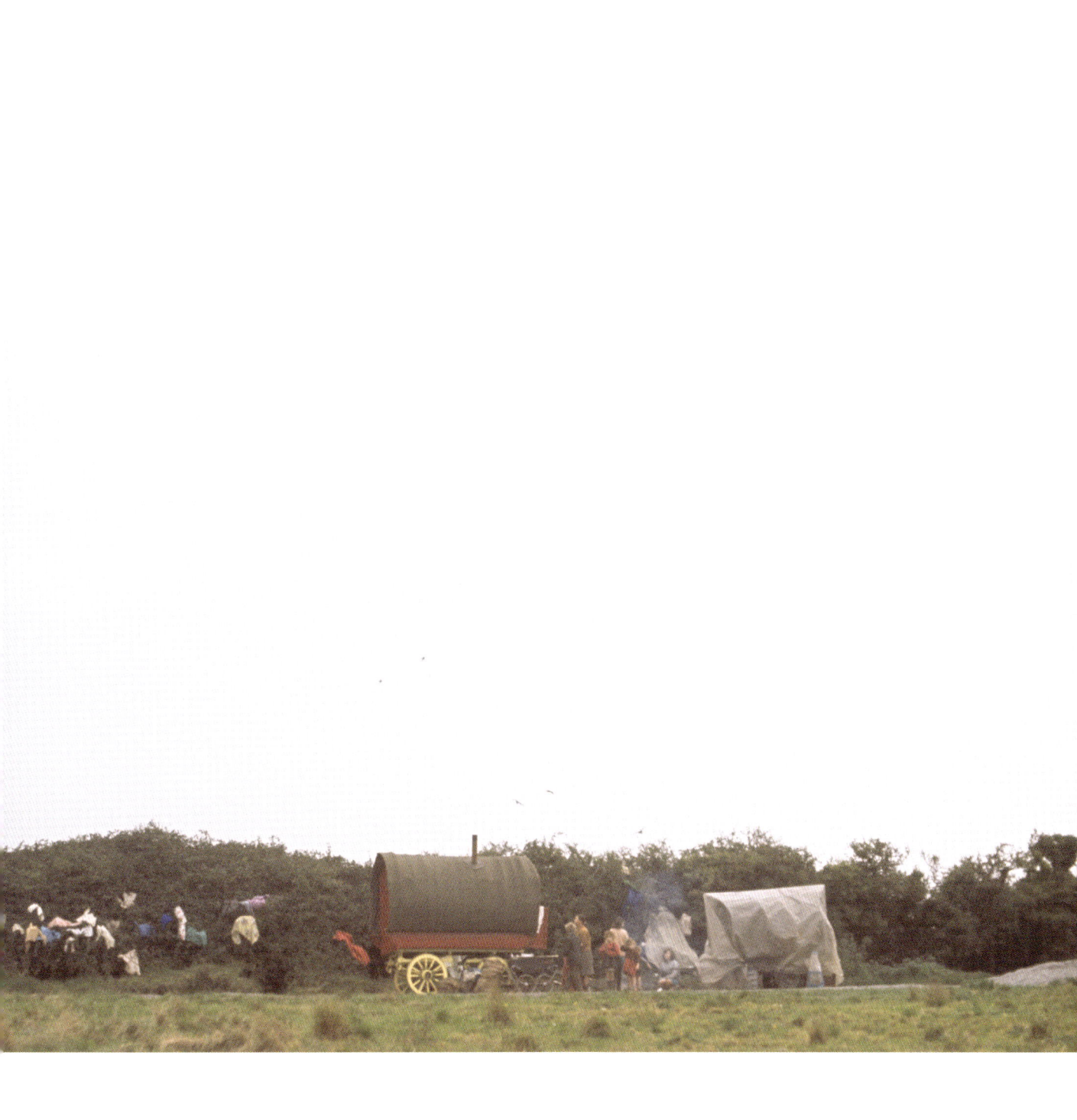

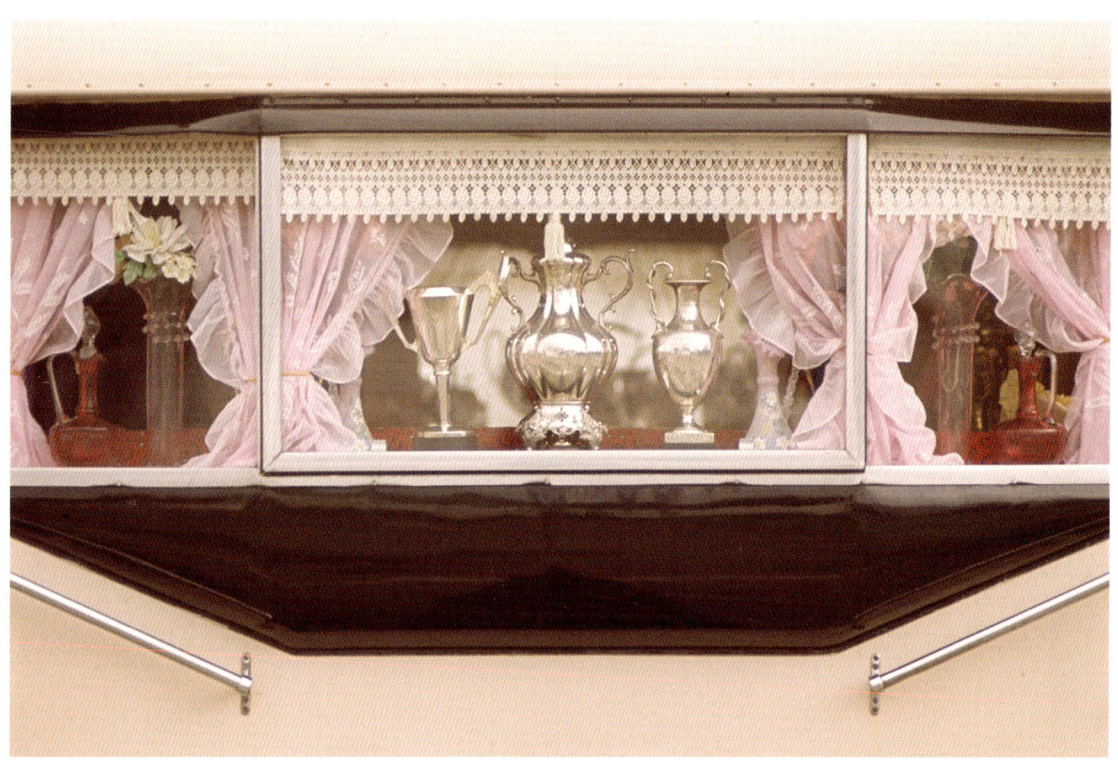

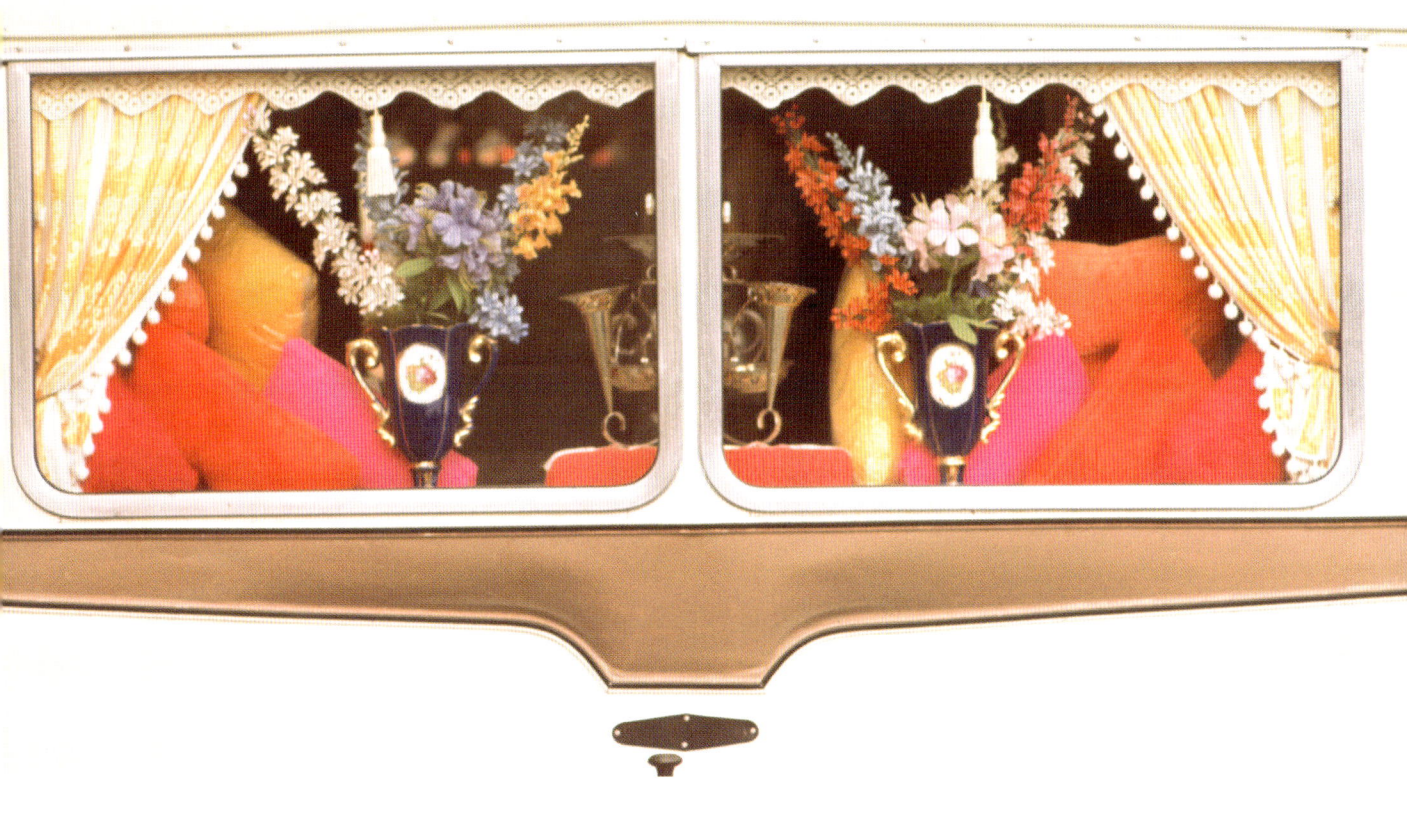

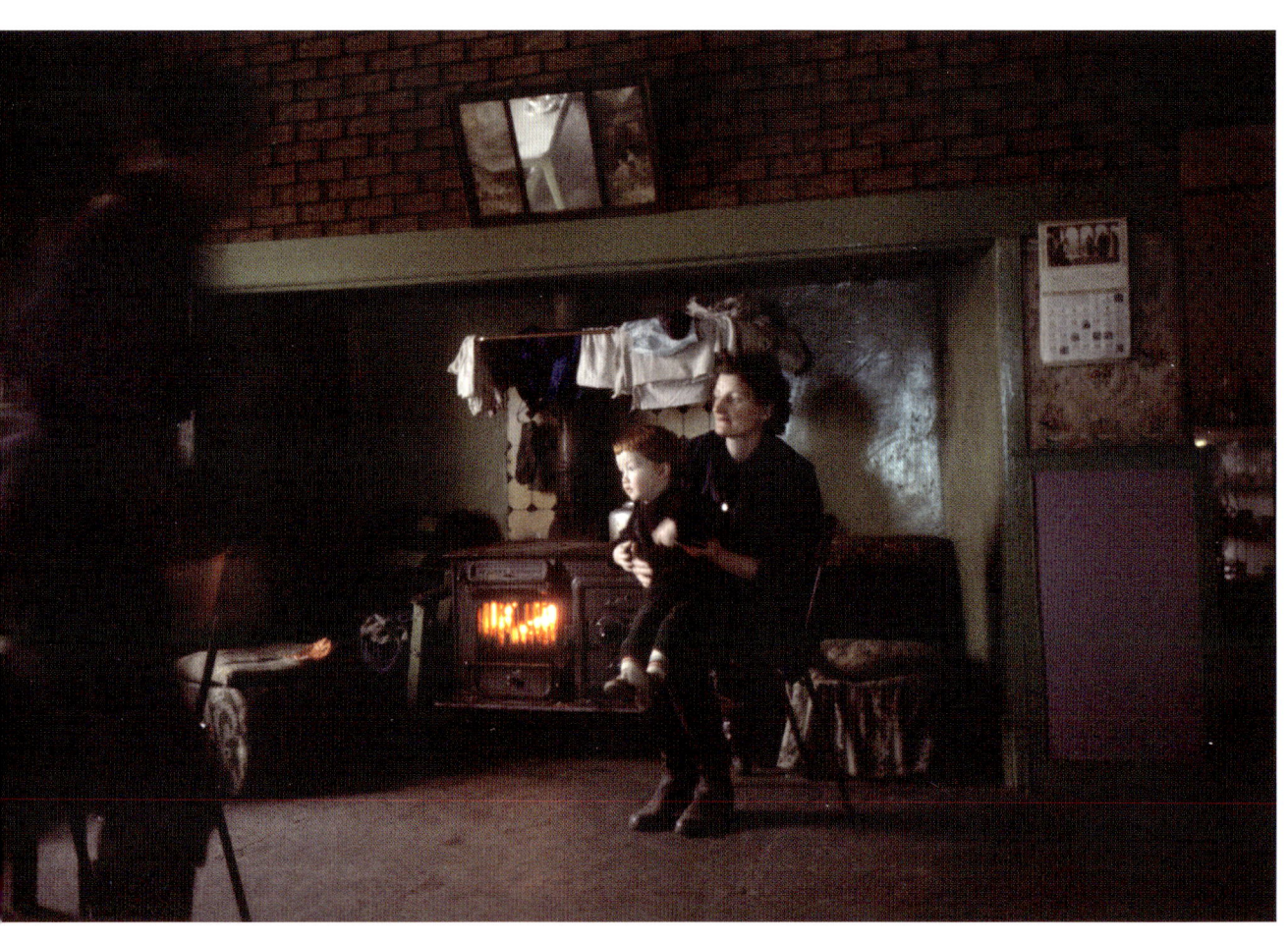

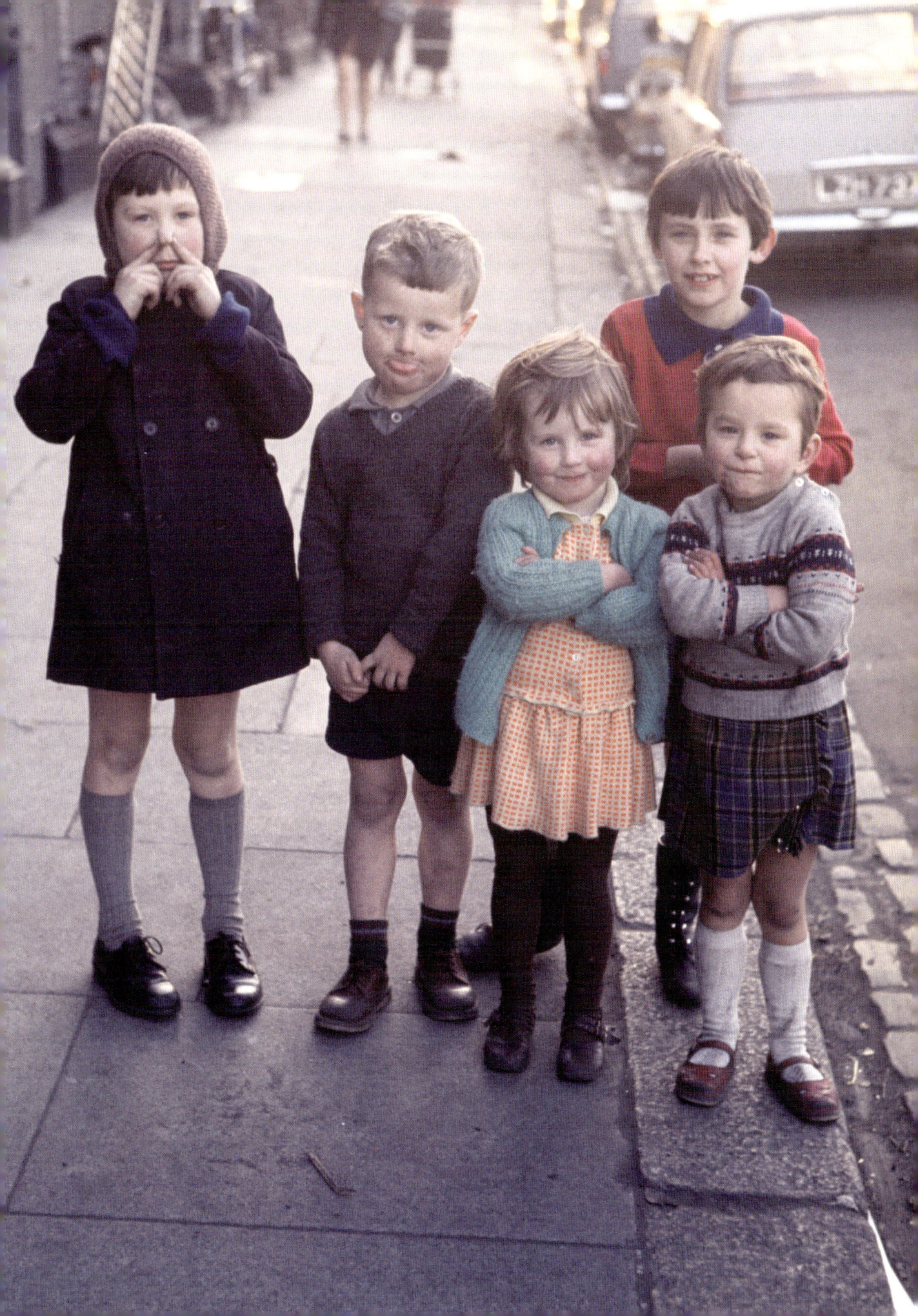

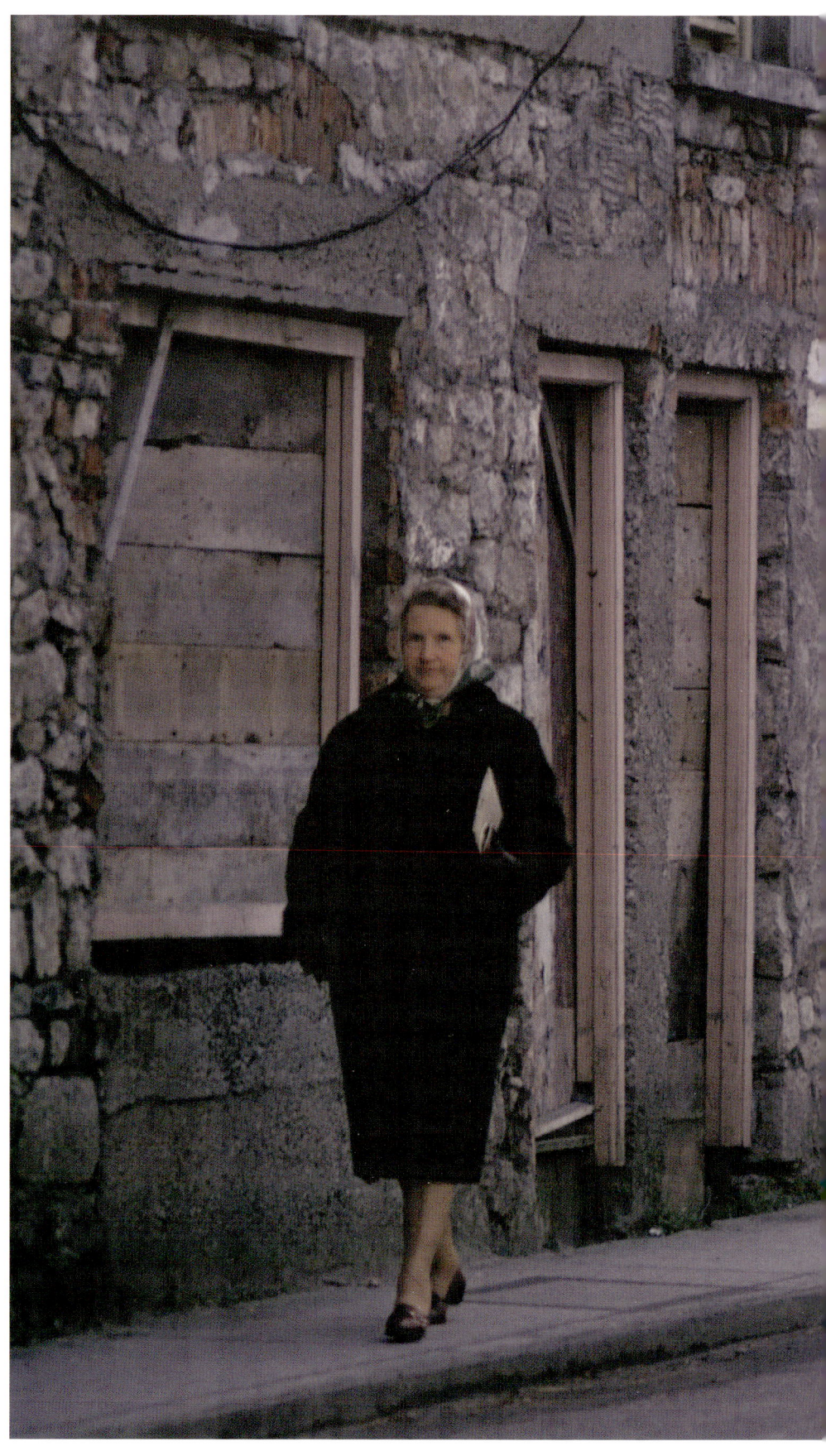

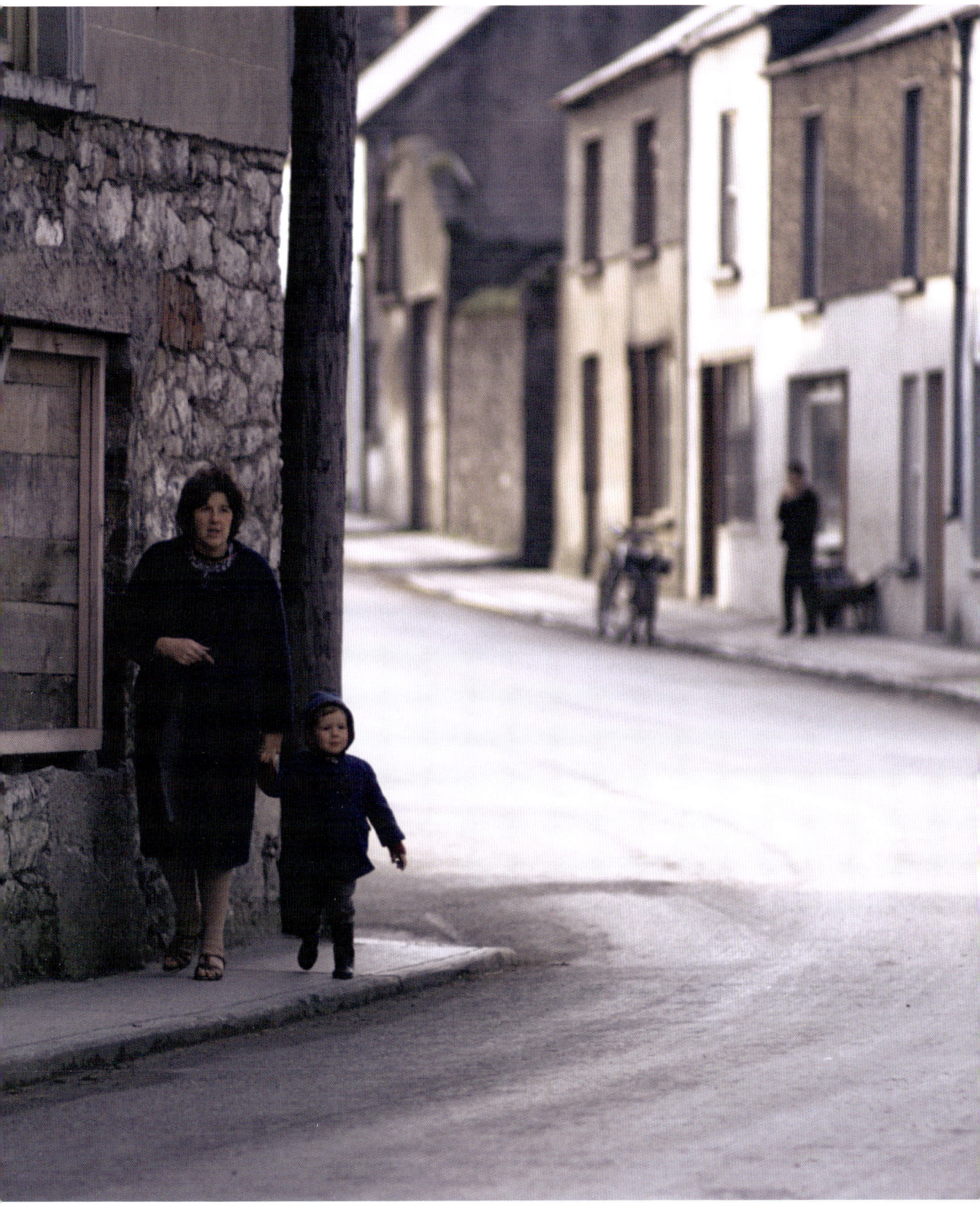

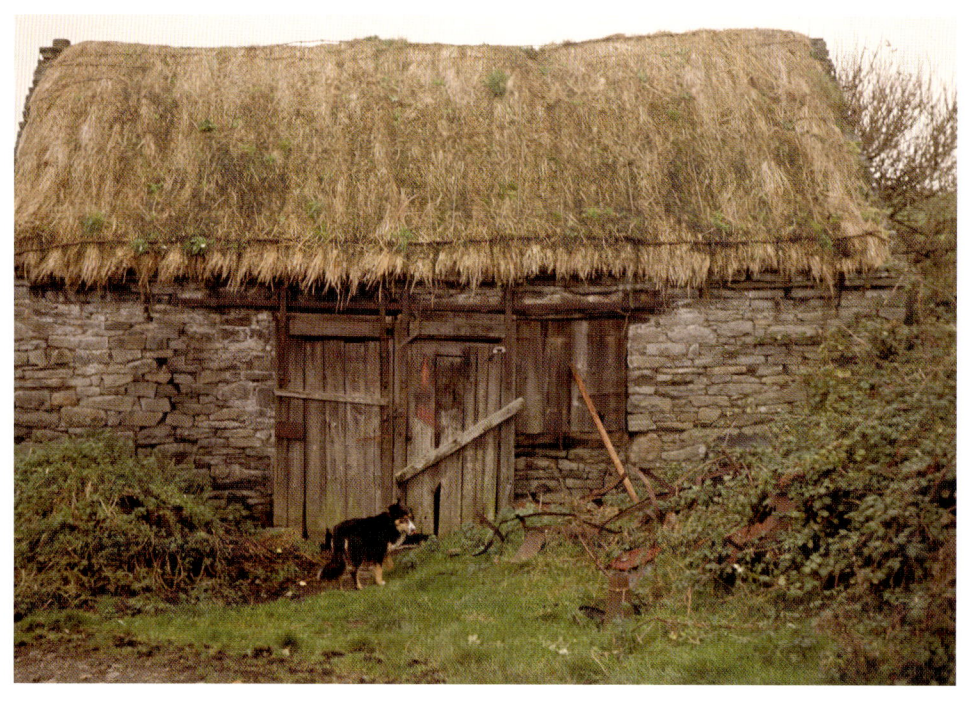
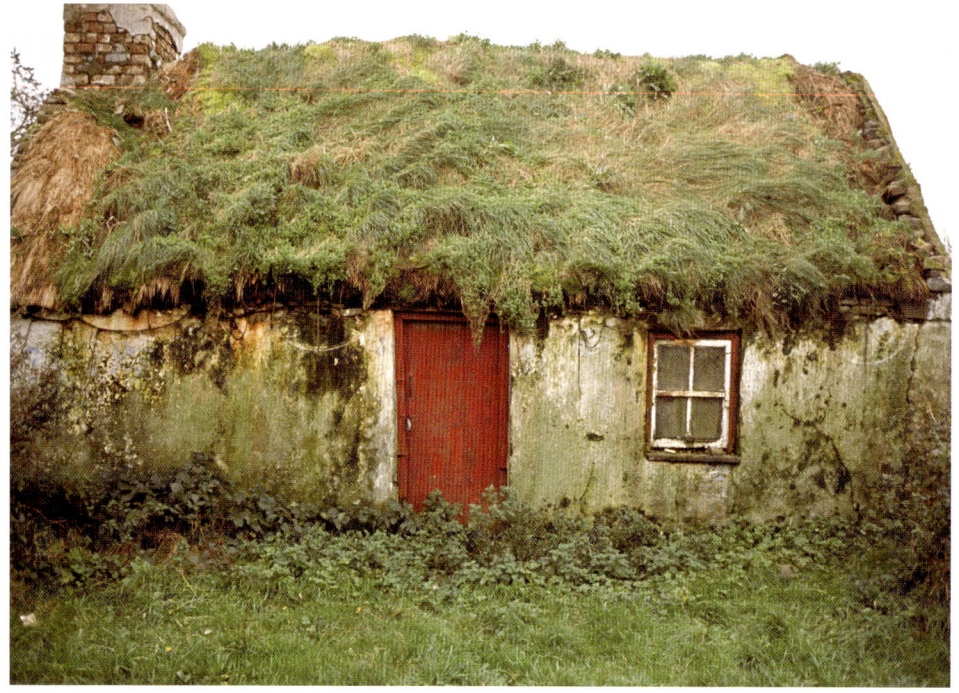

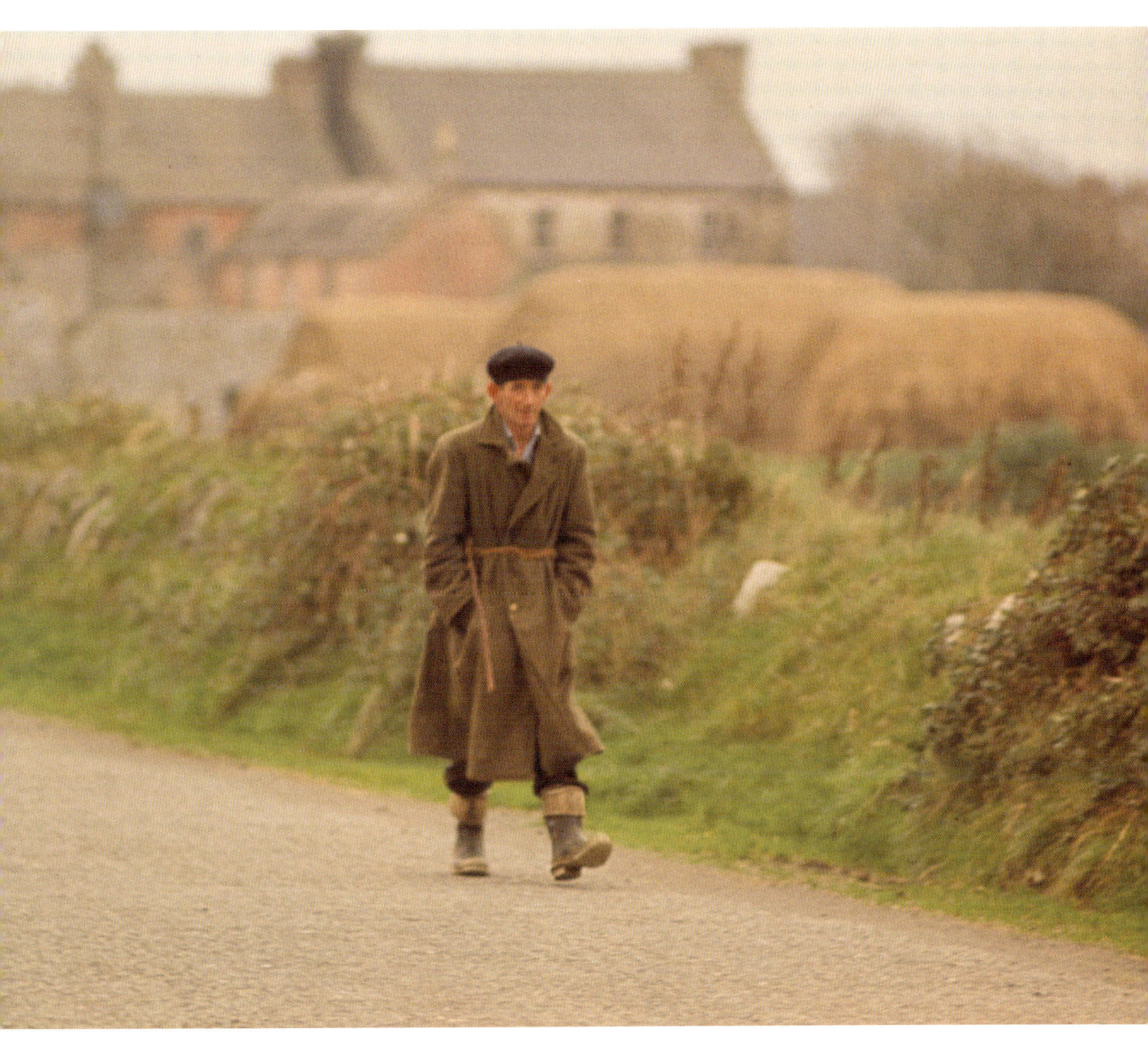

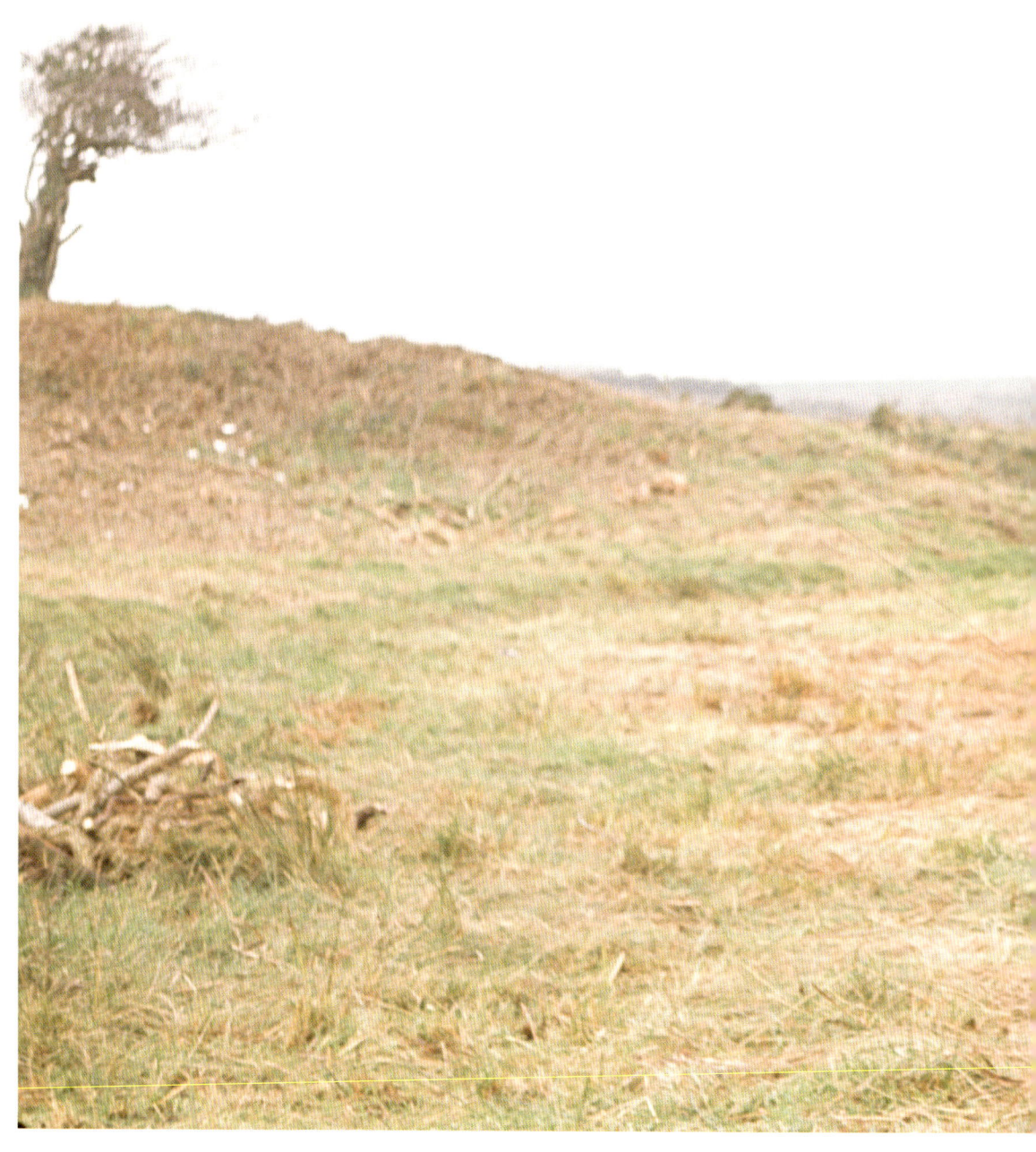

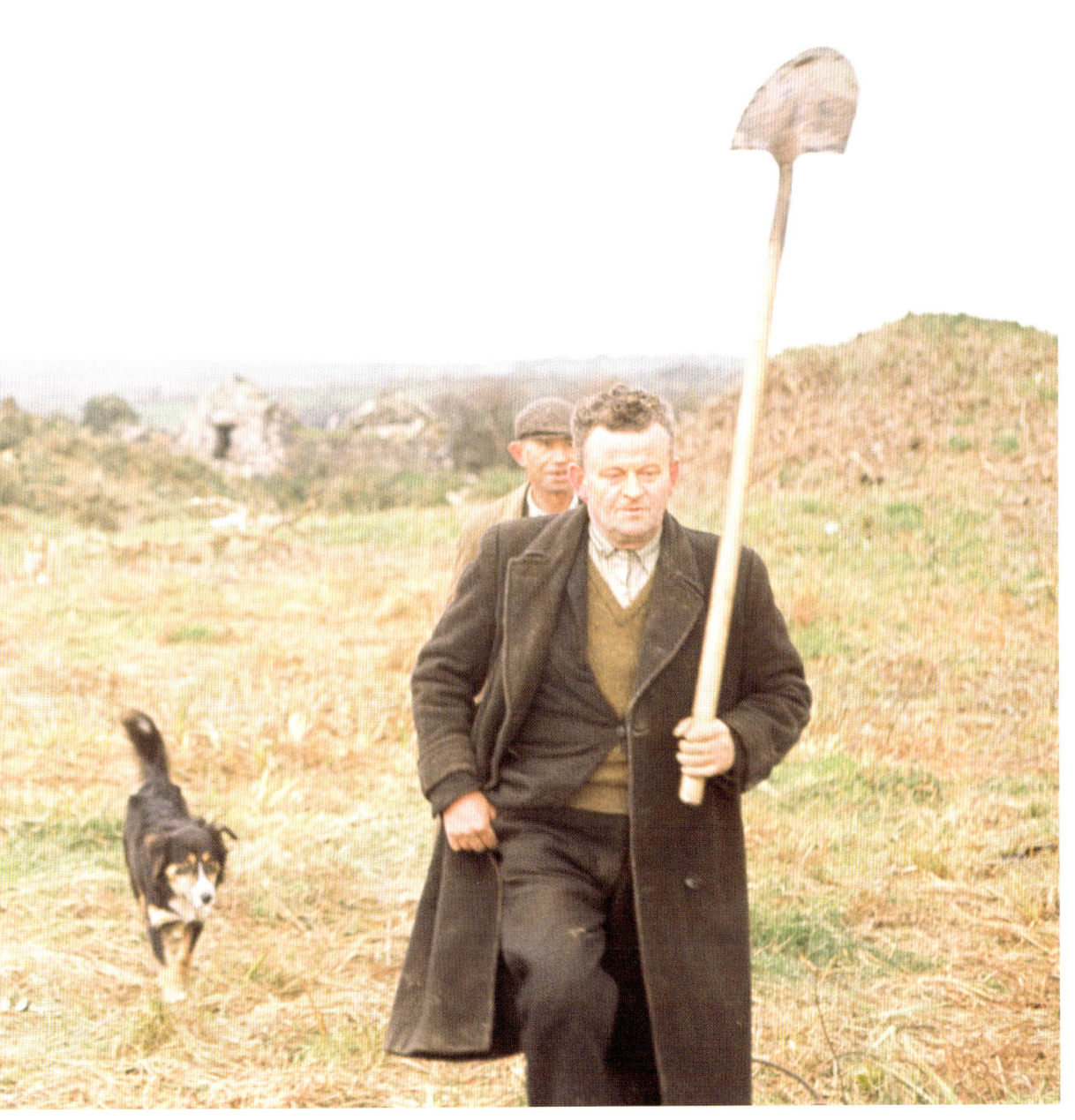

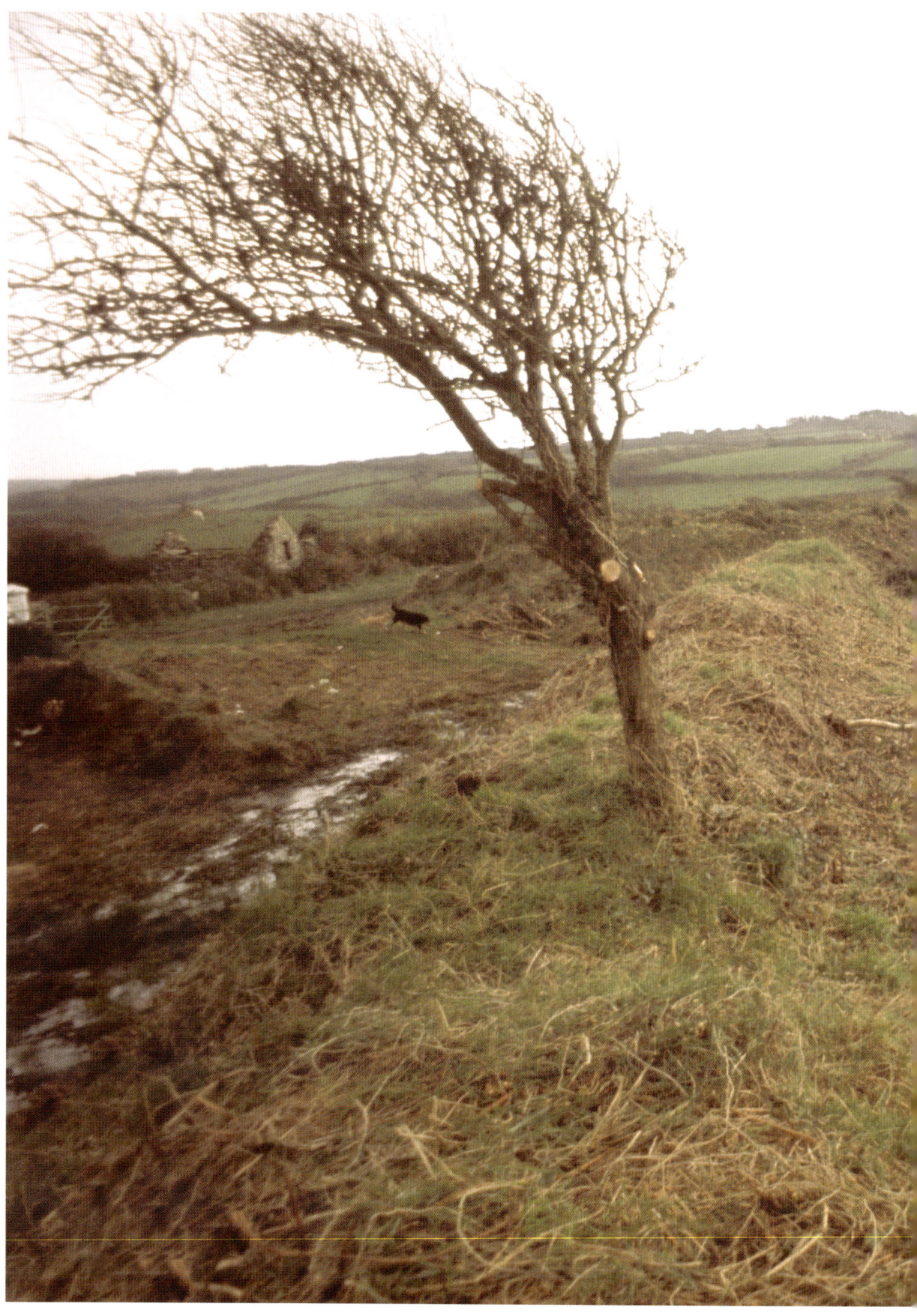

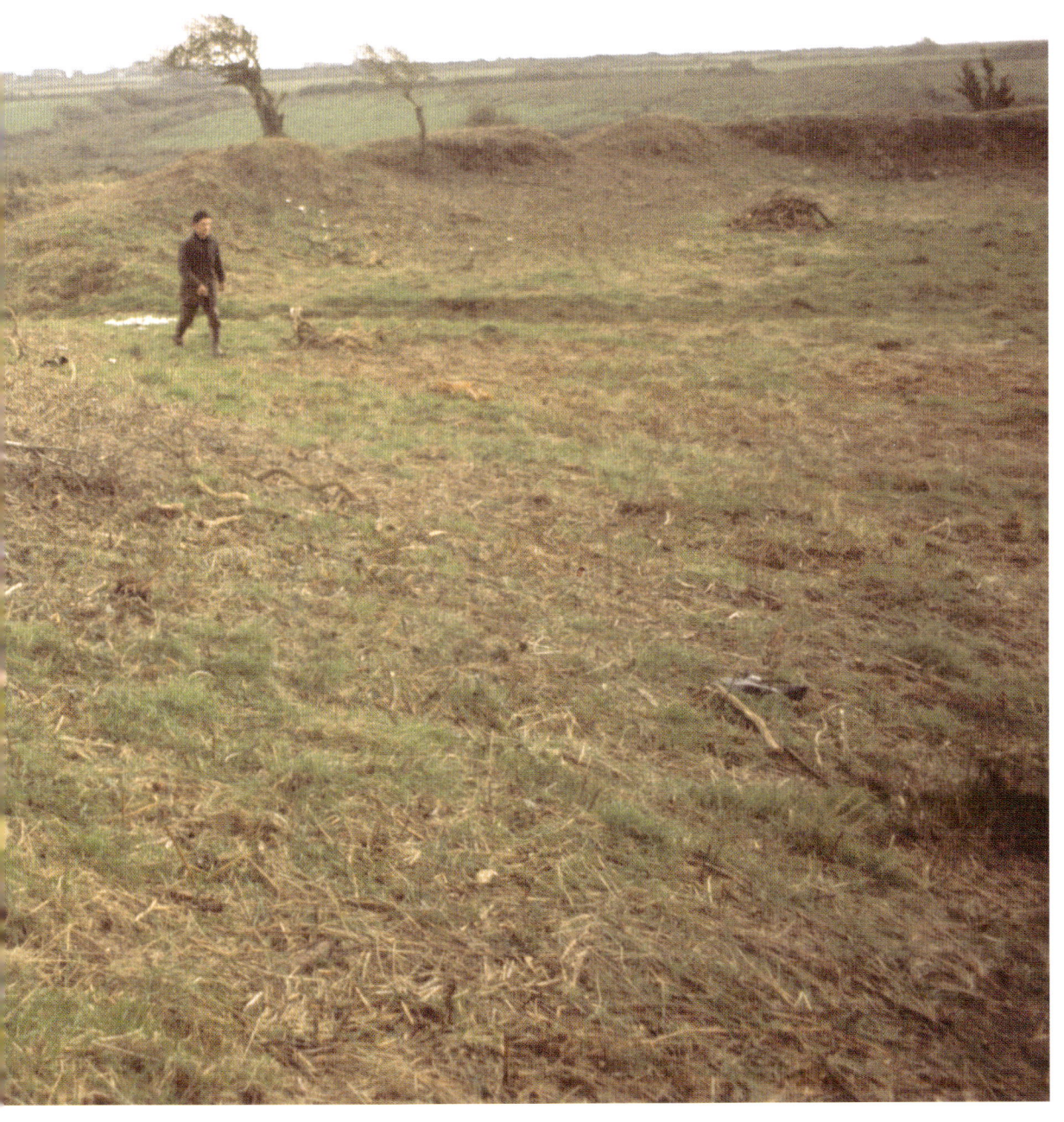

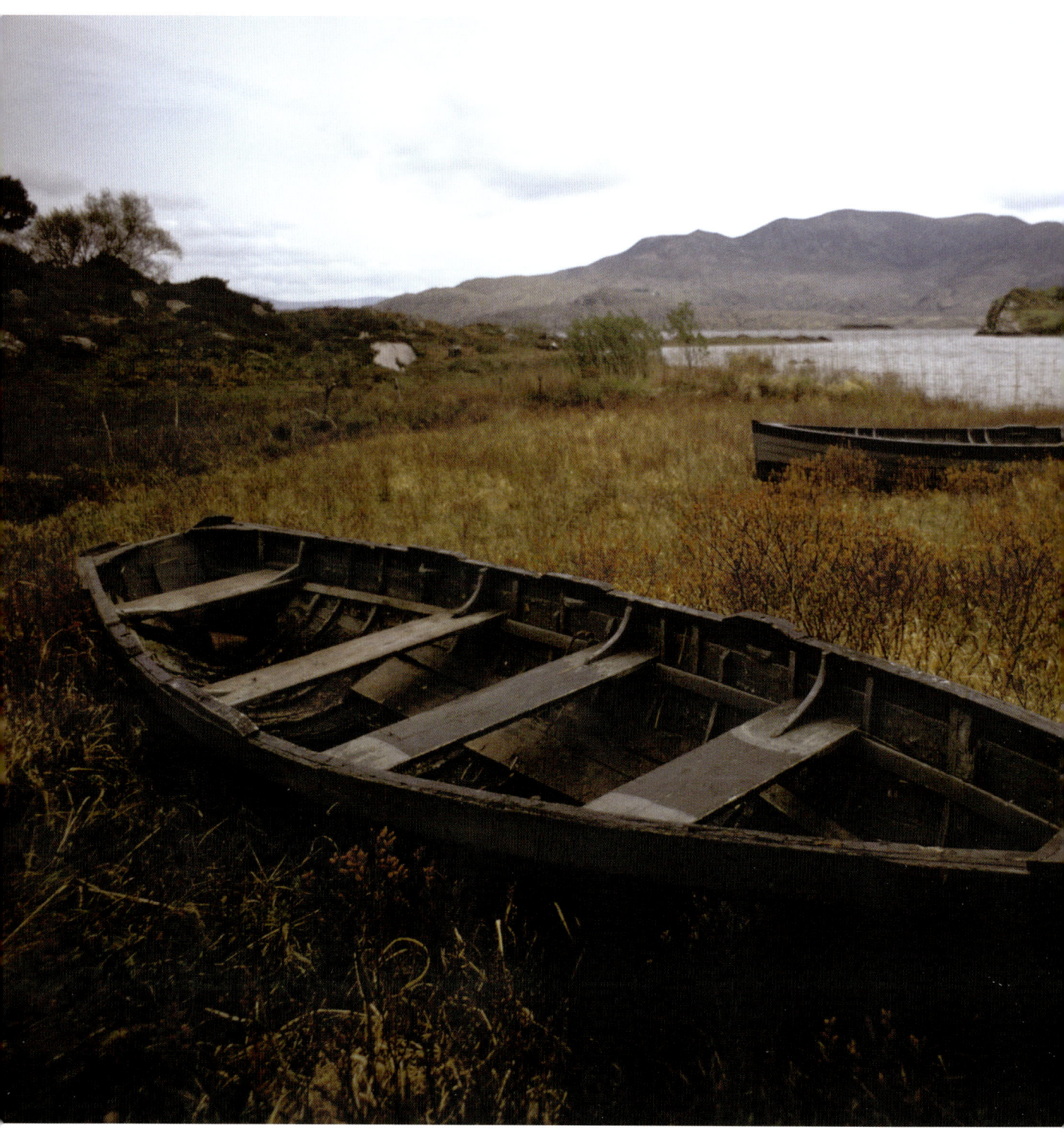

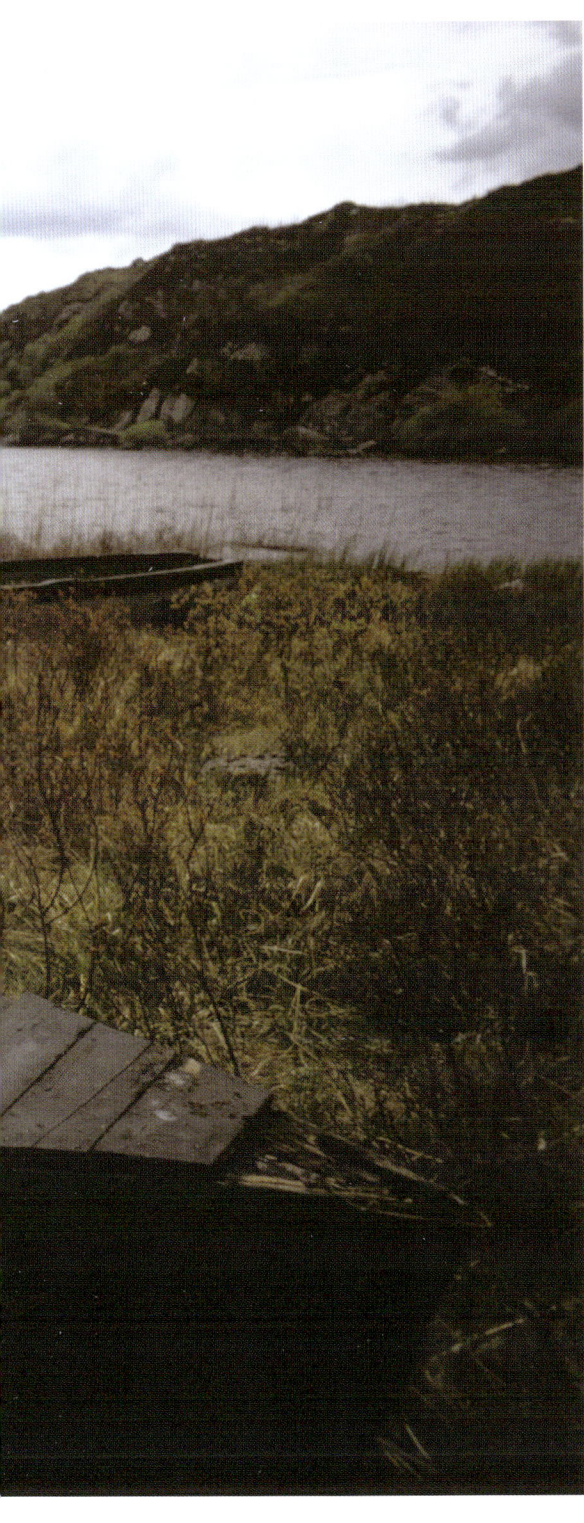

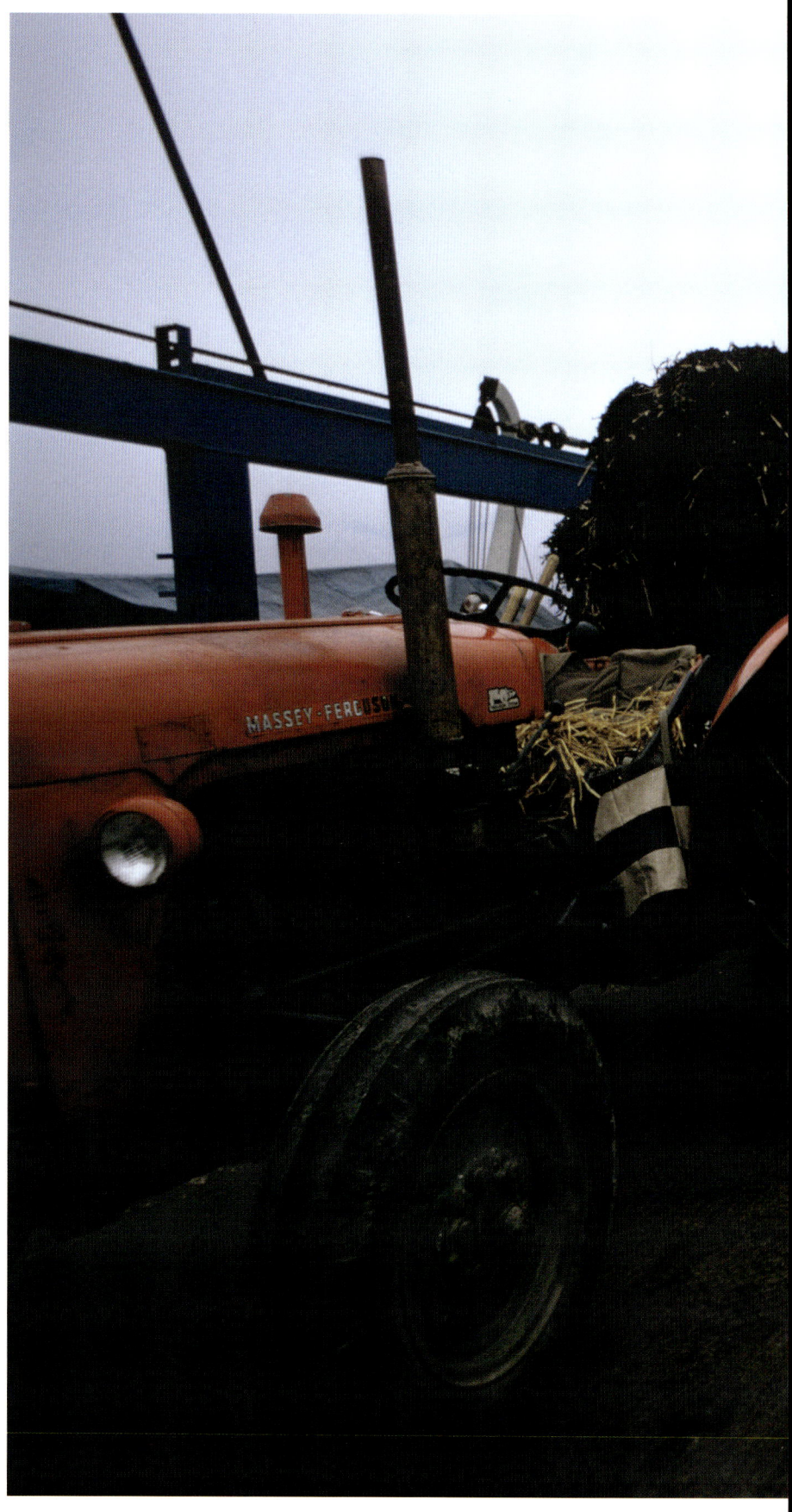

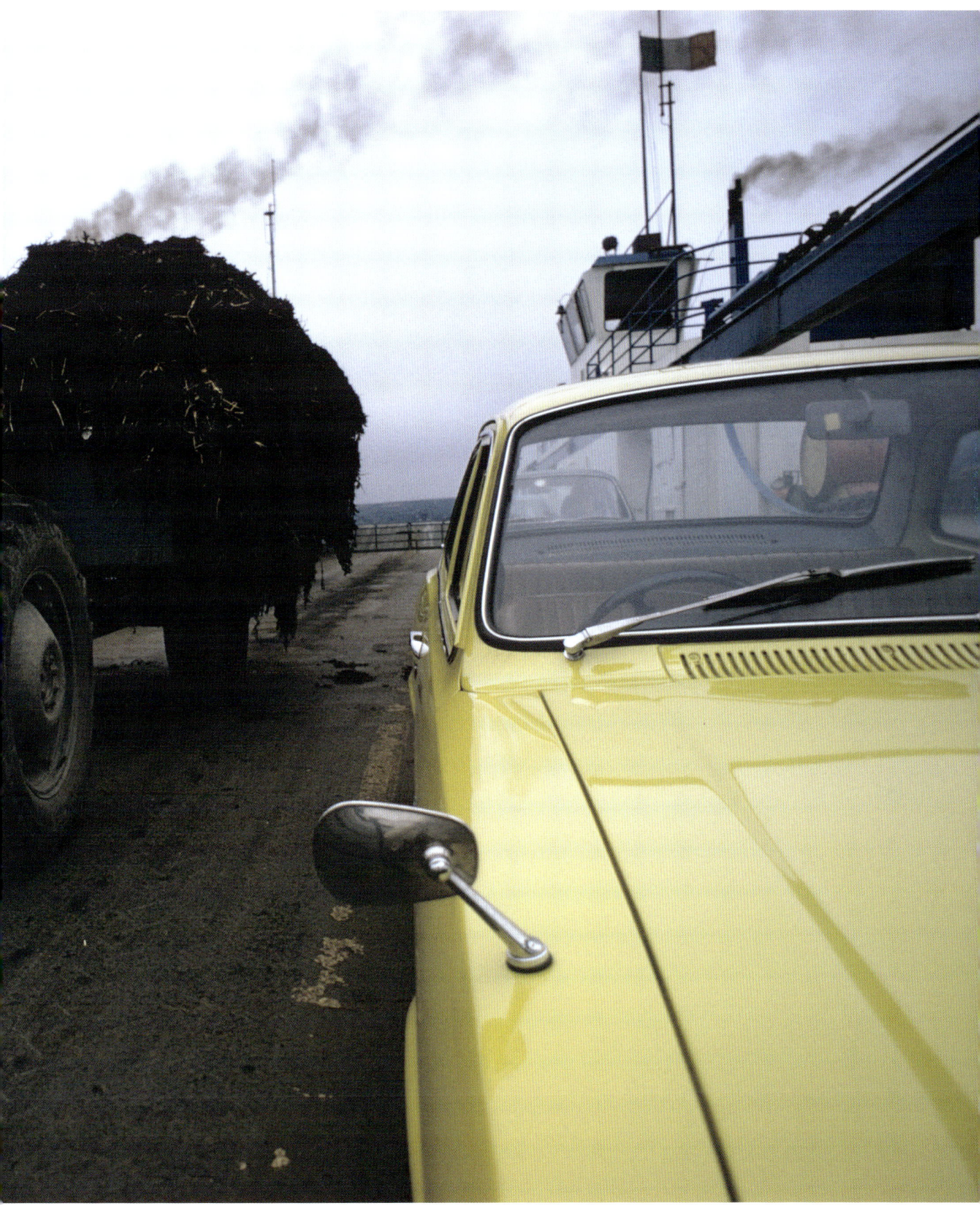

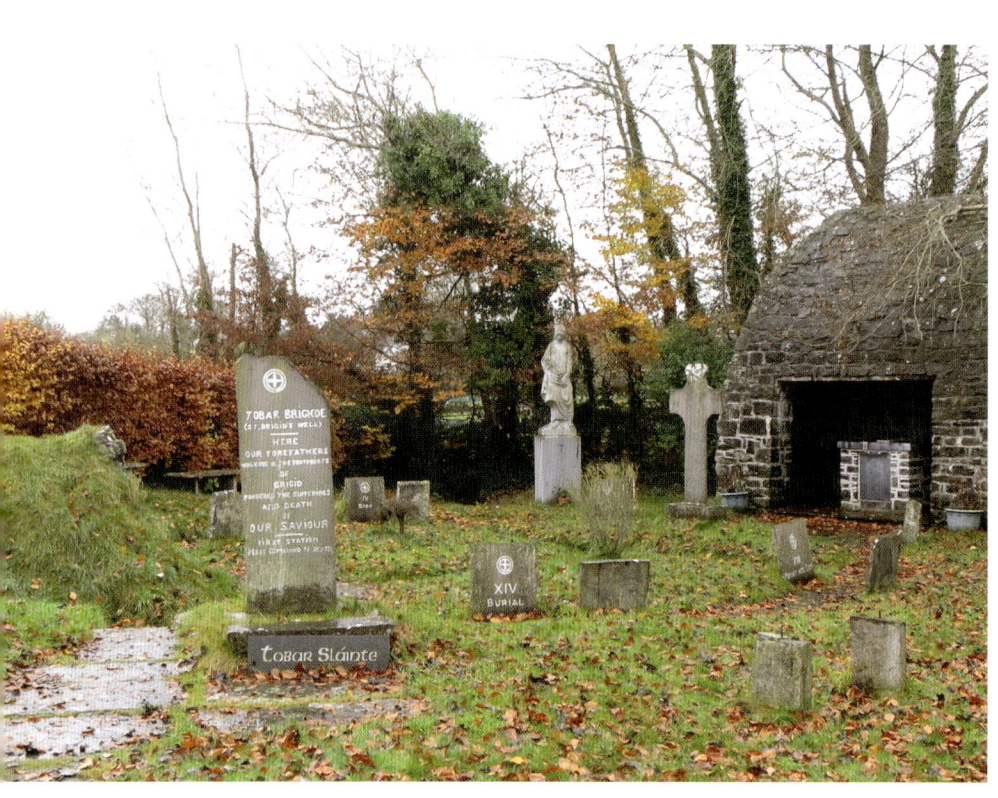
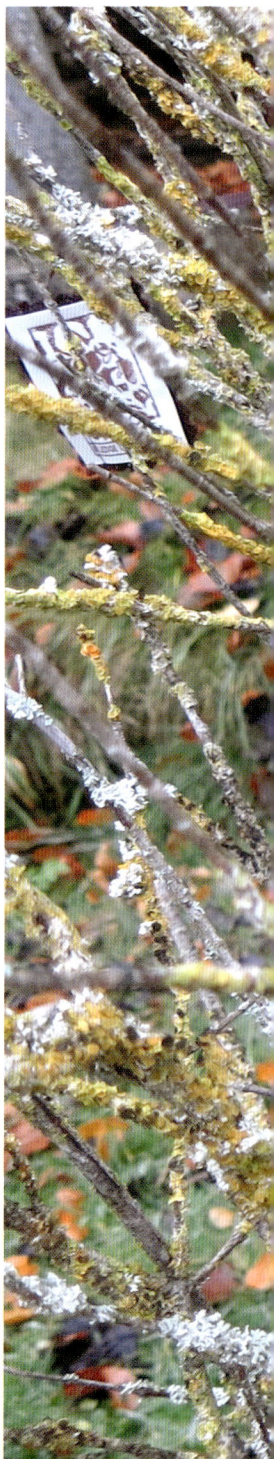

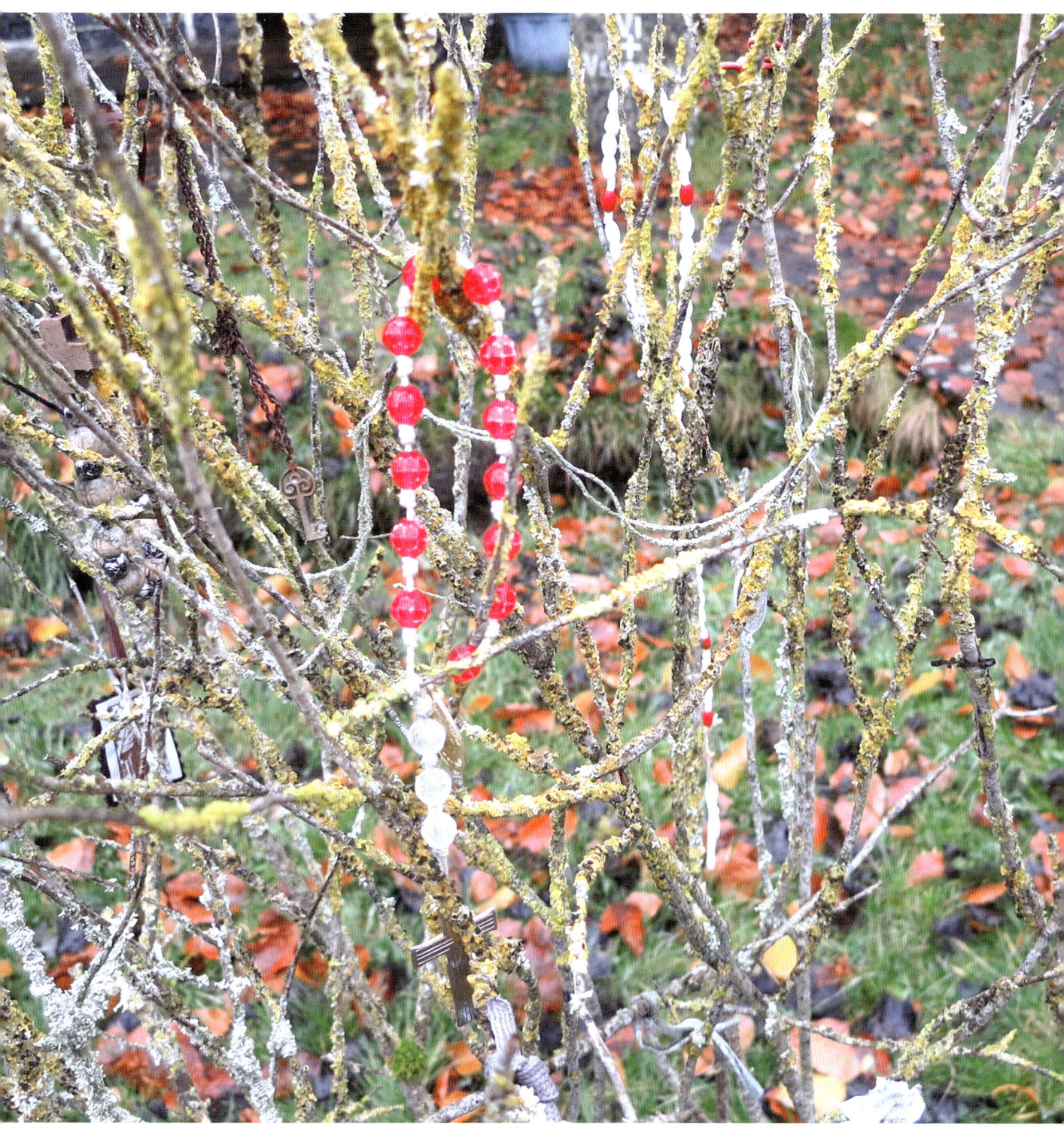

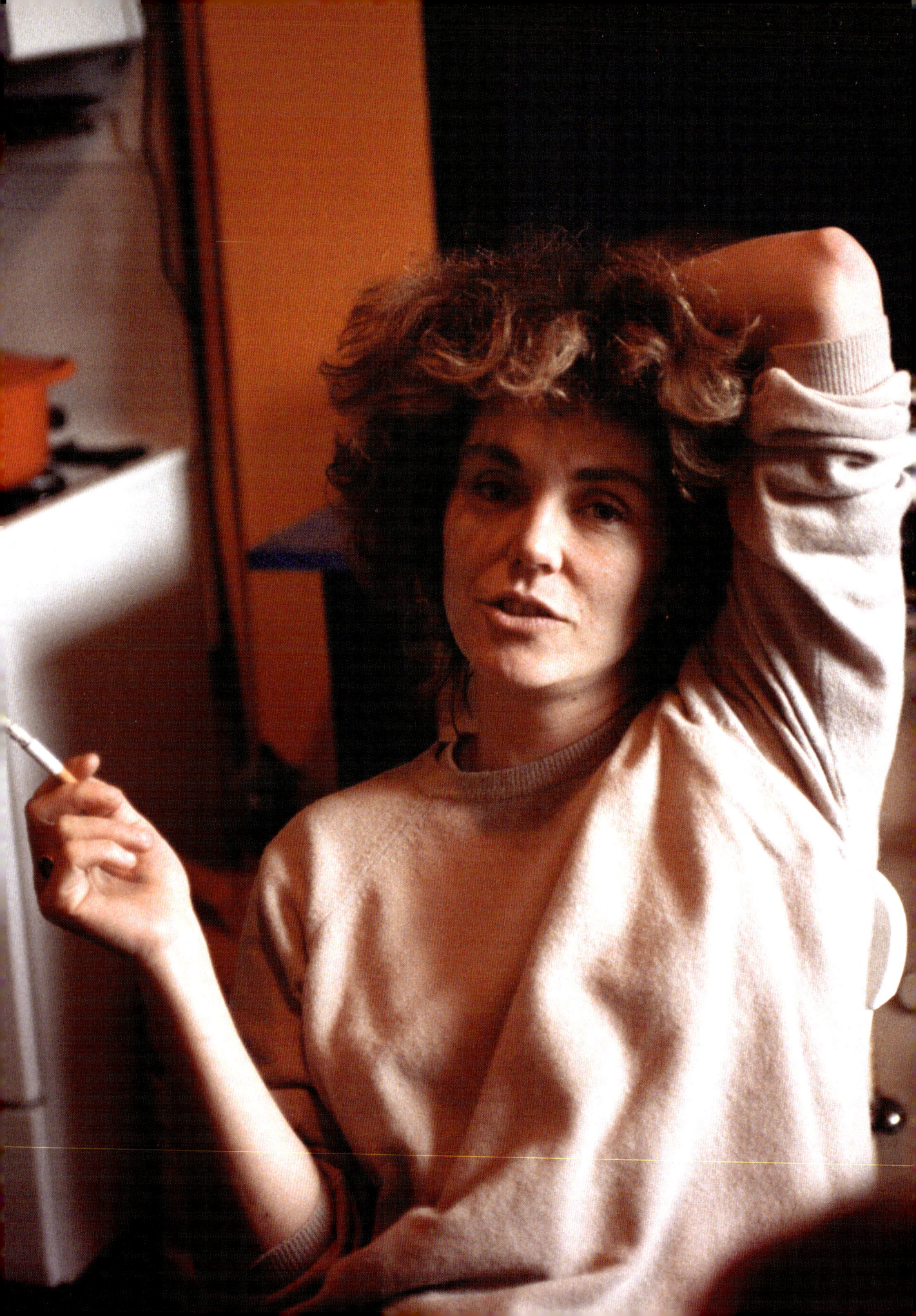

Marina Guinness,
Family & Friends

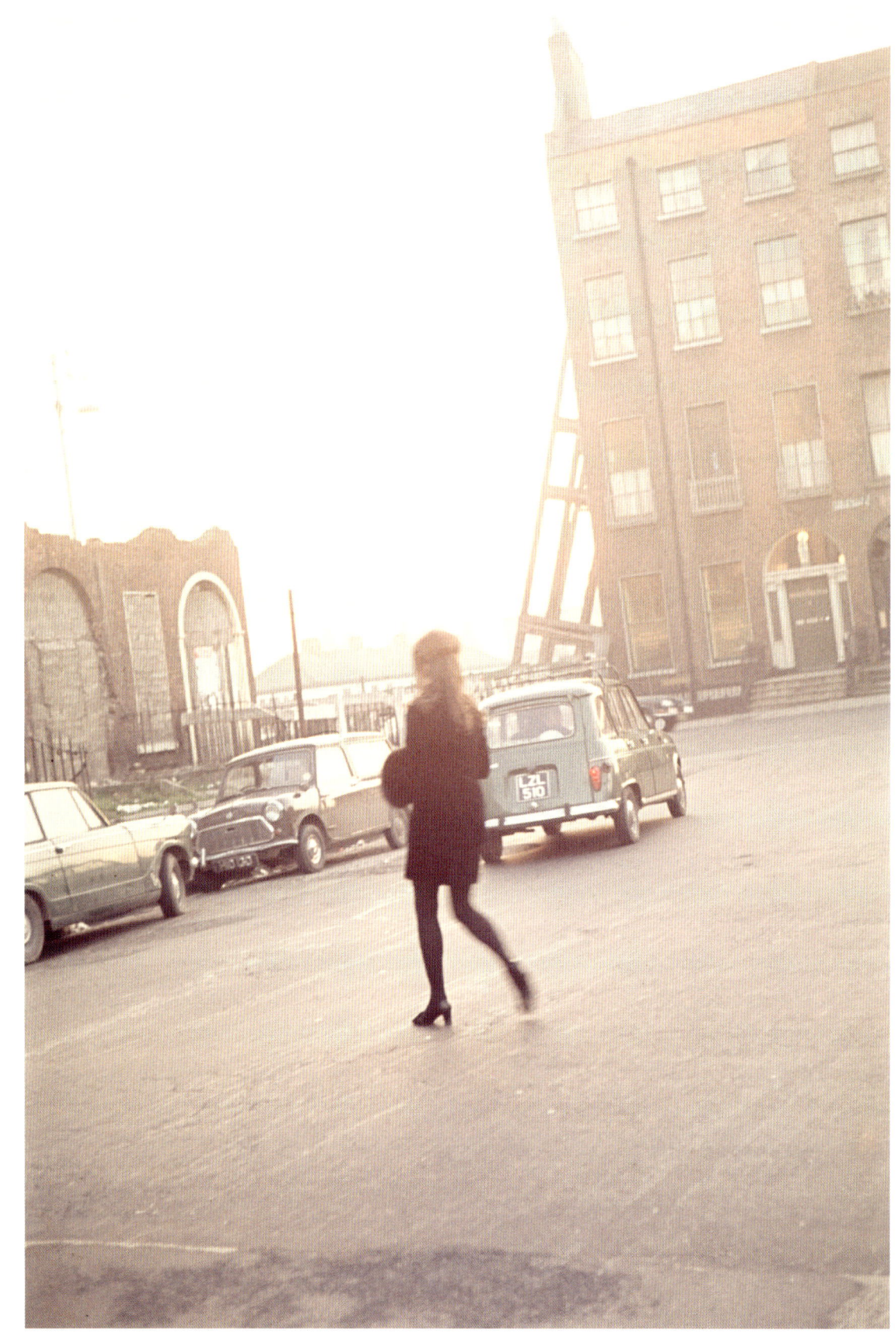

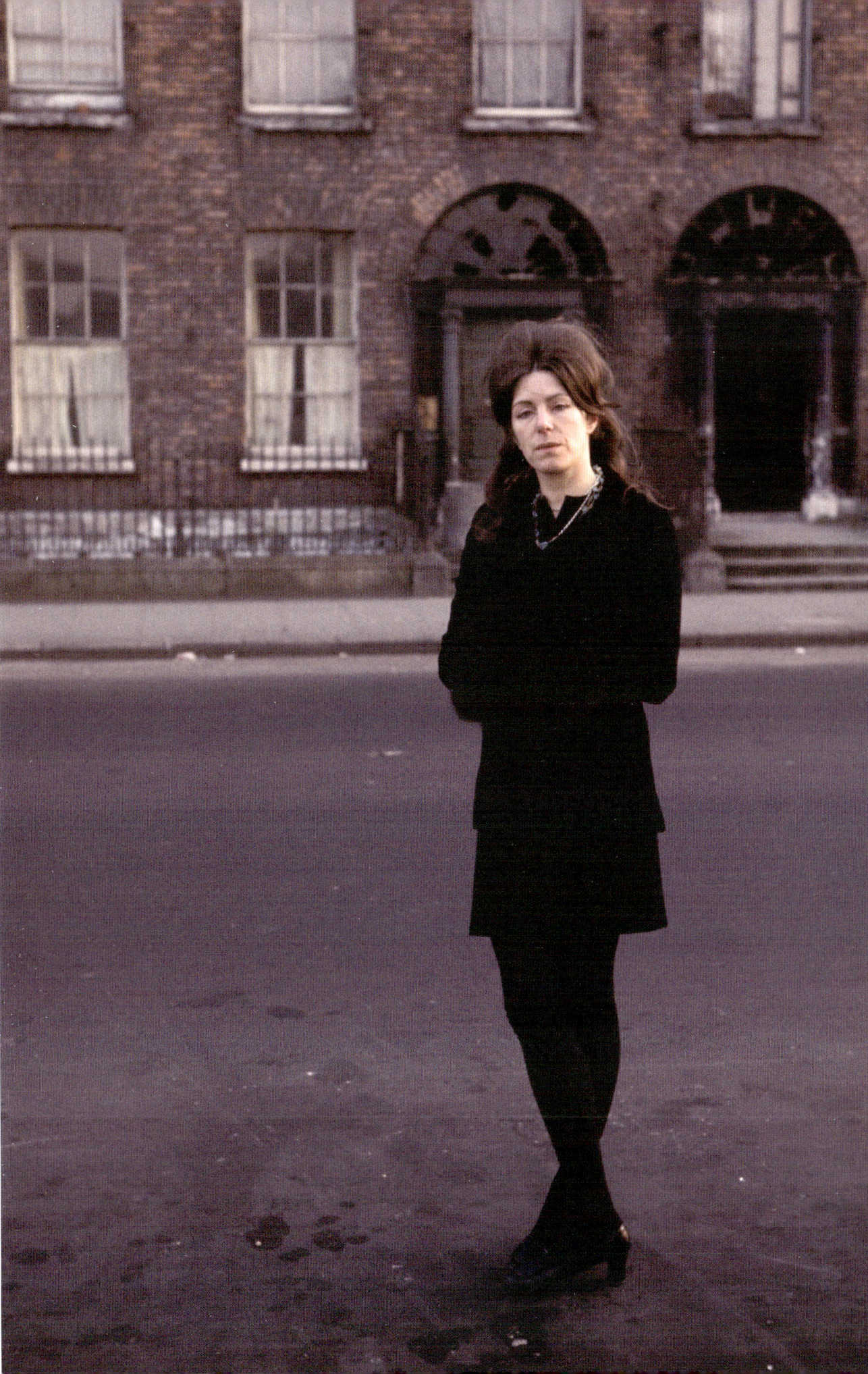

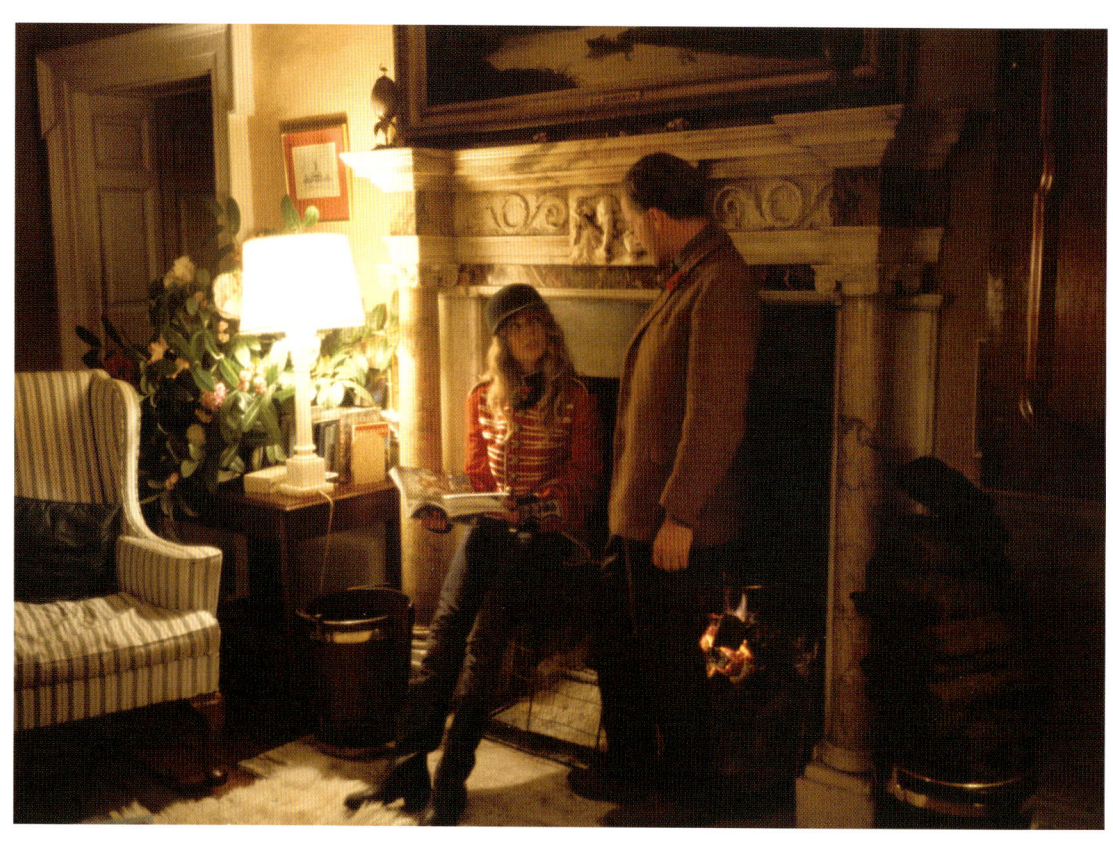

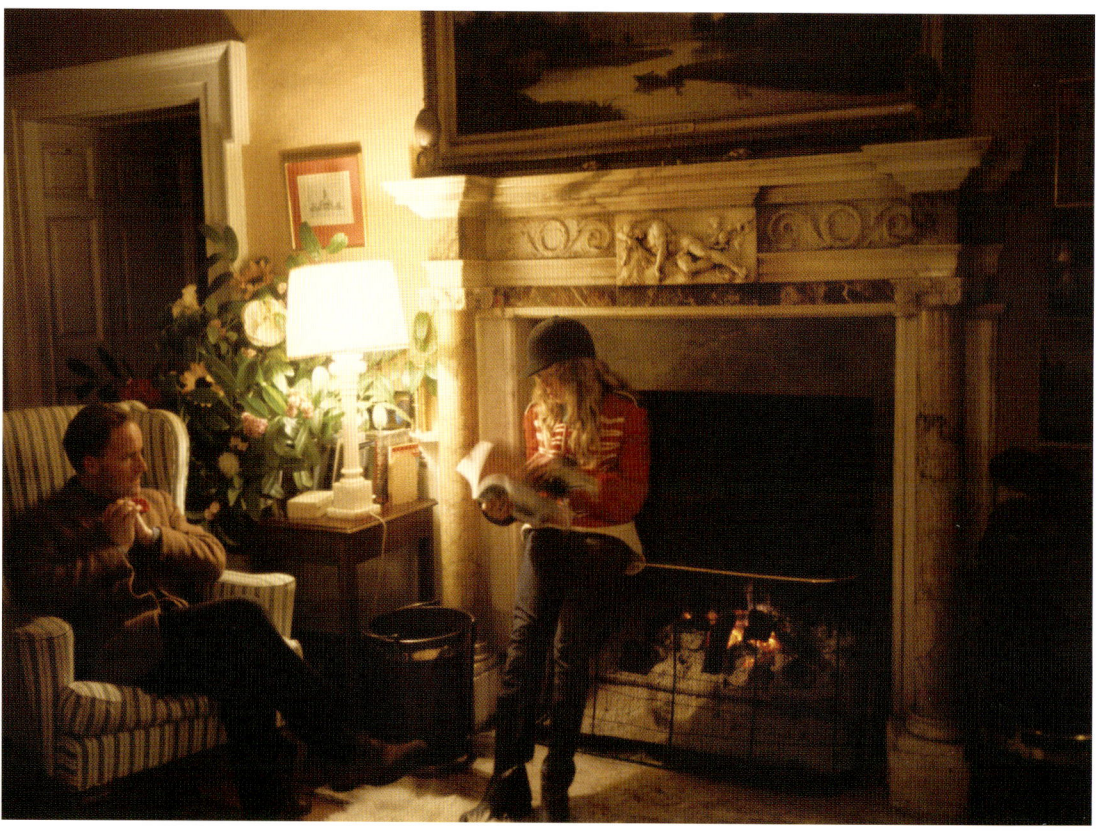

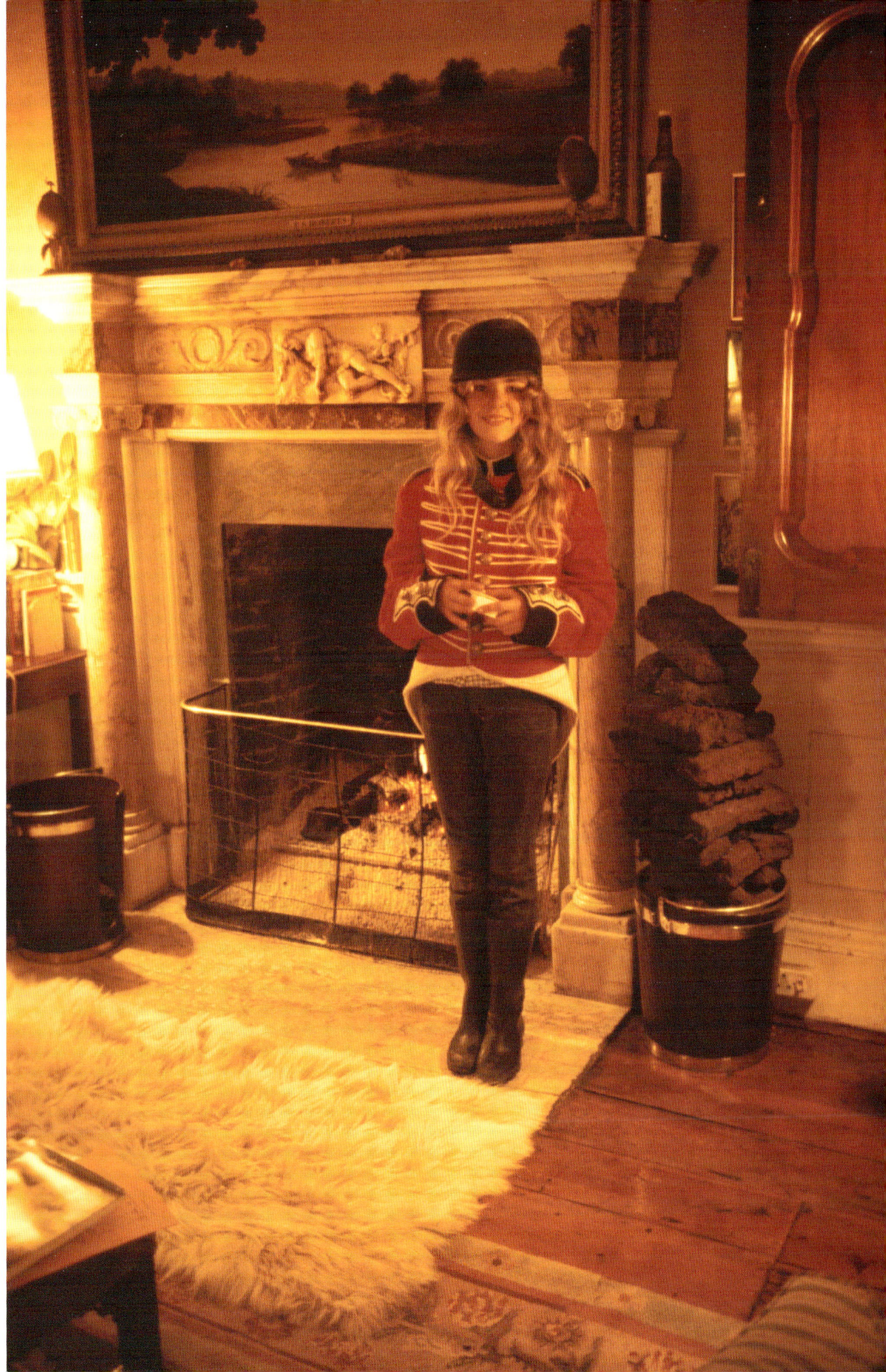

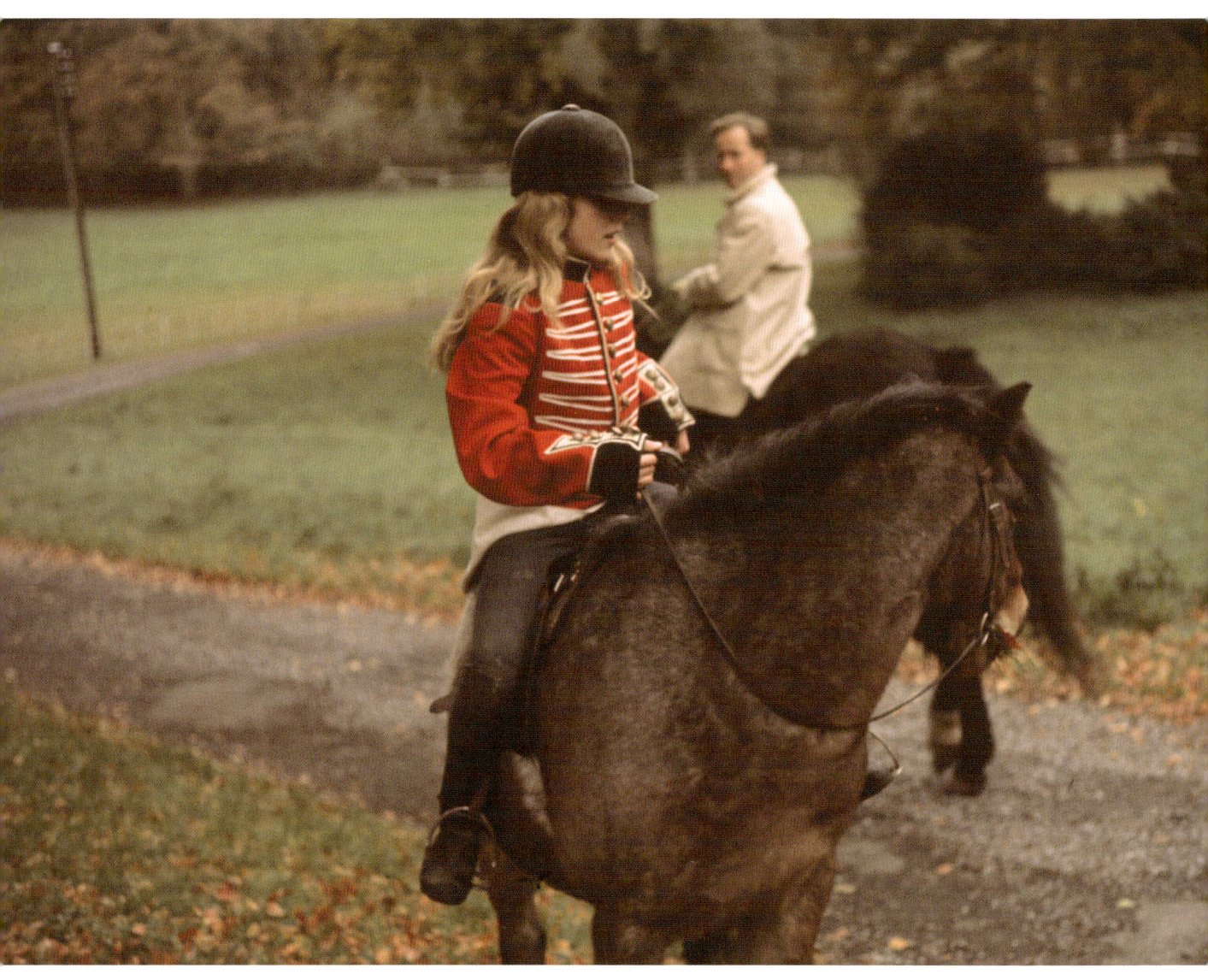

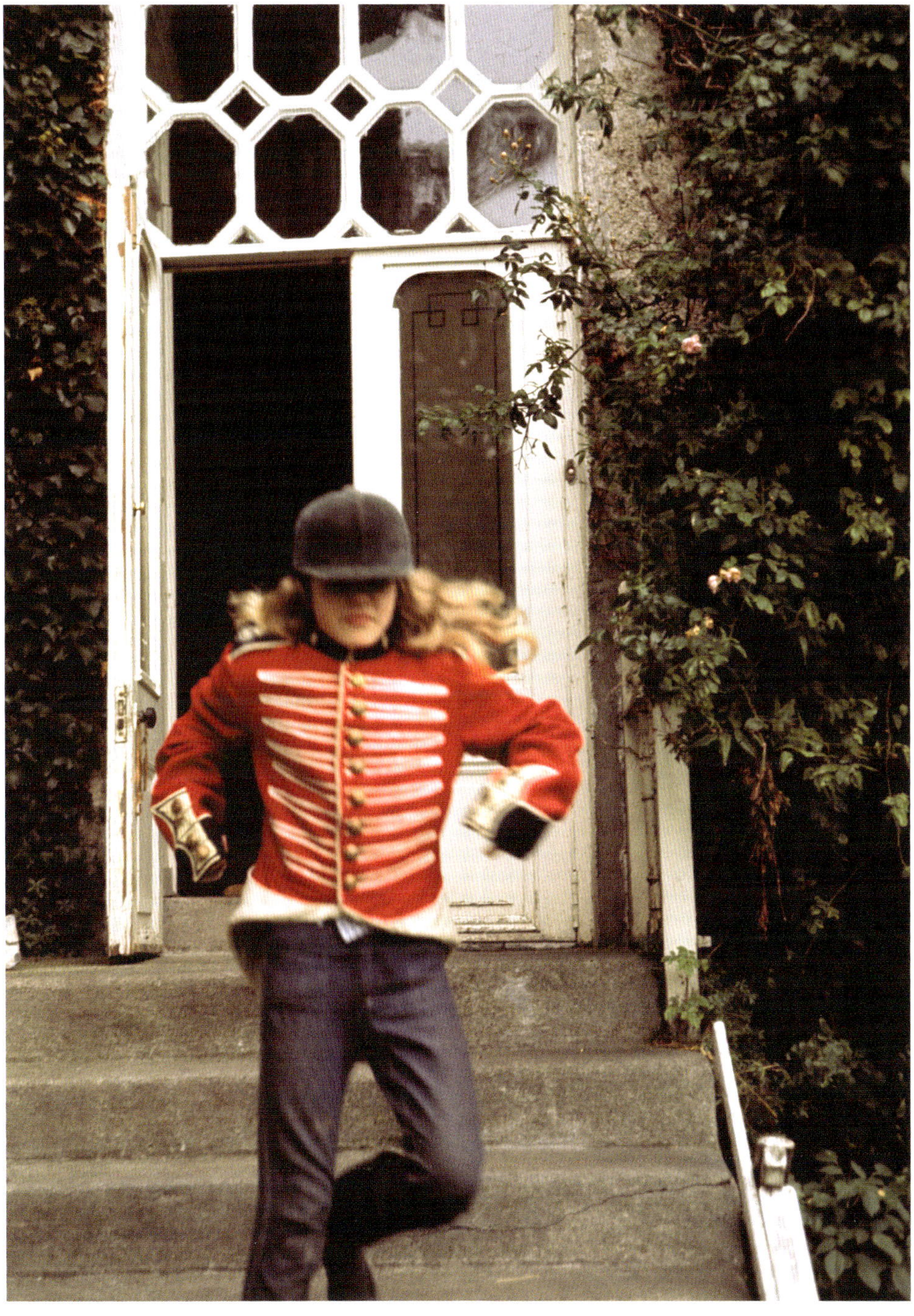

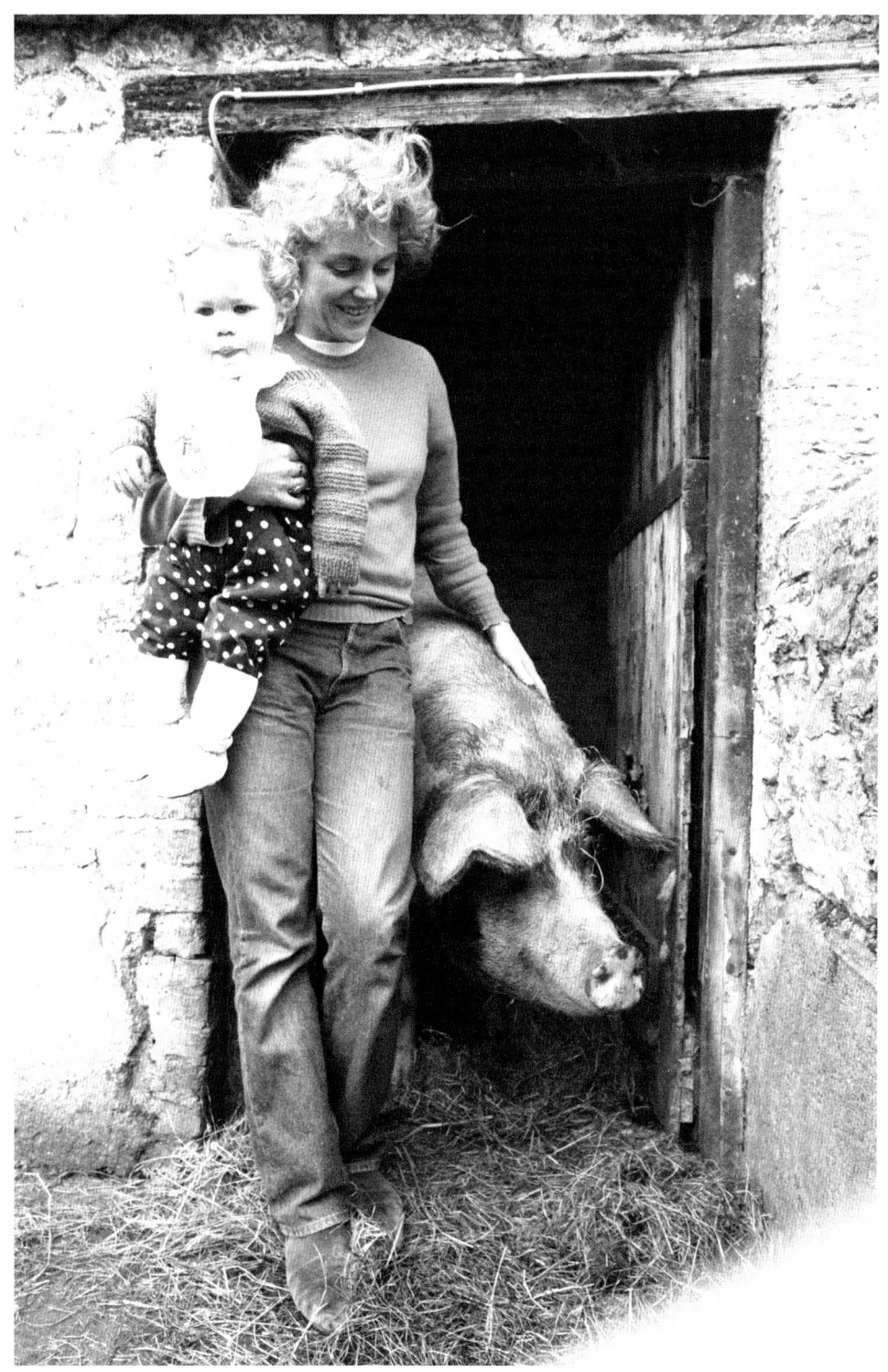

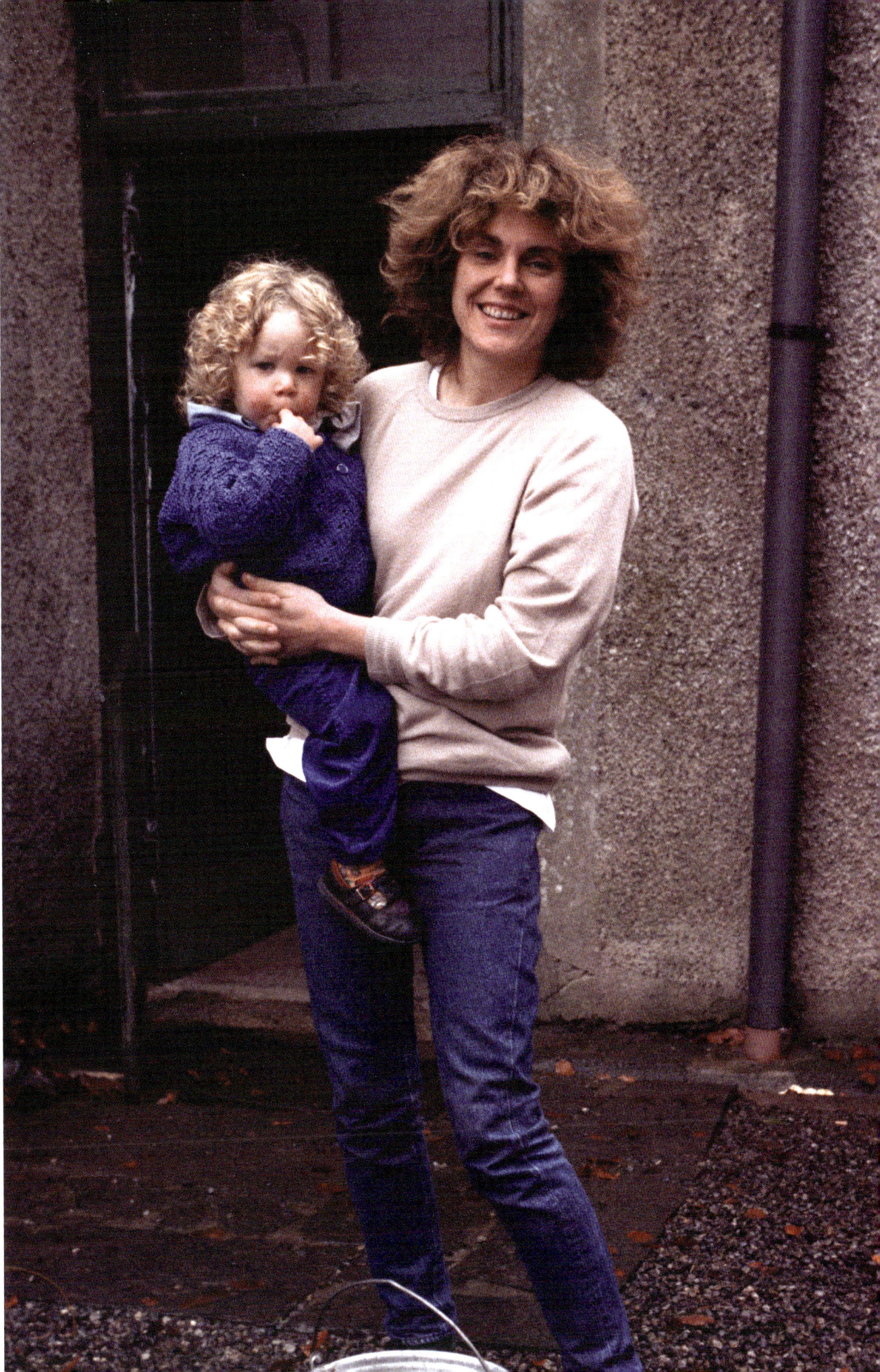

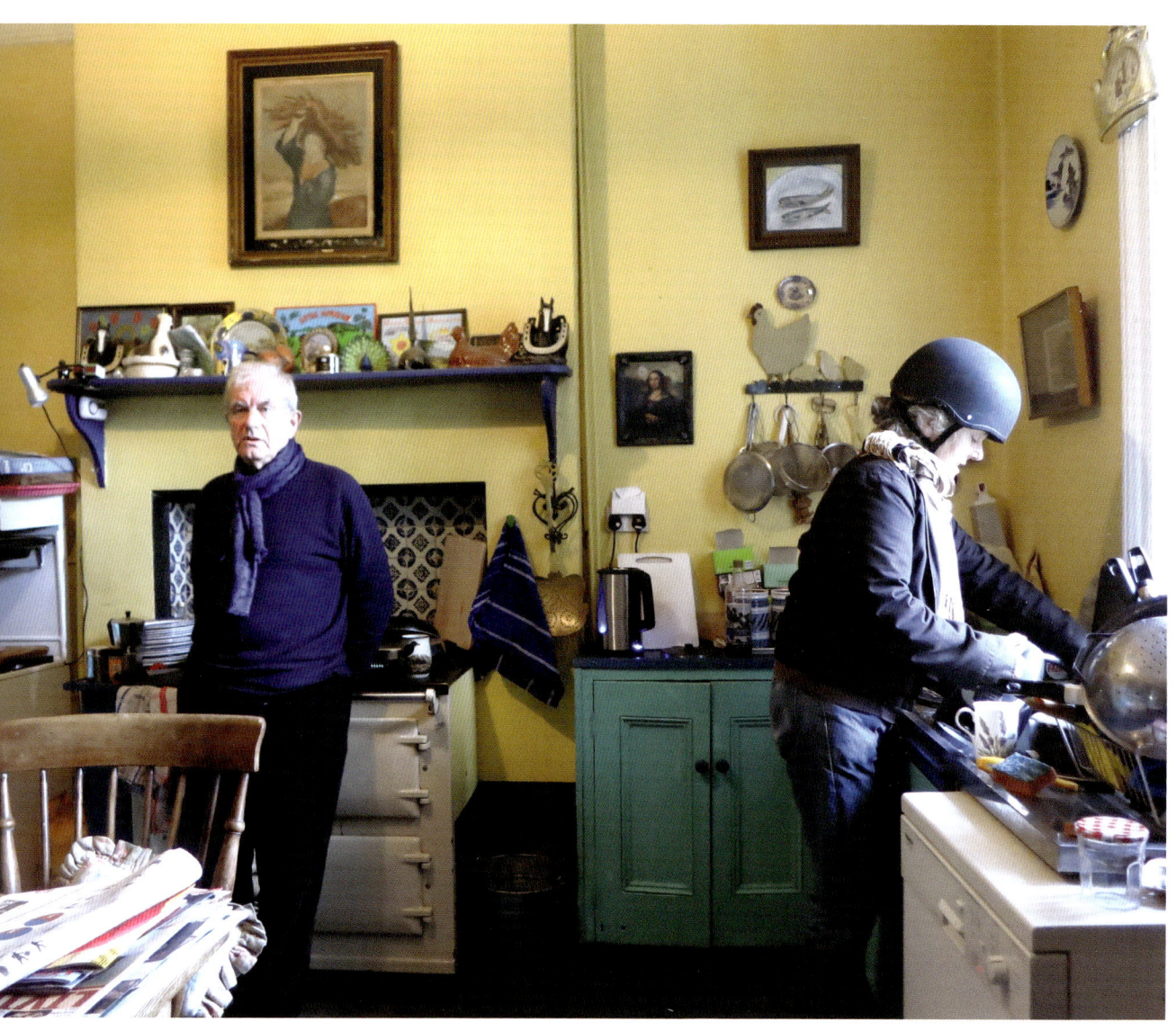

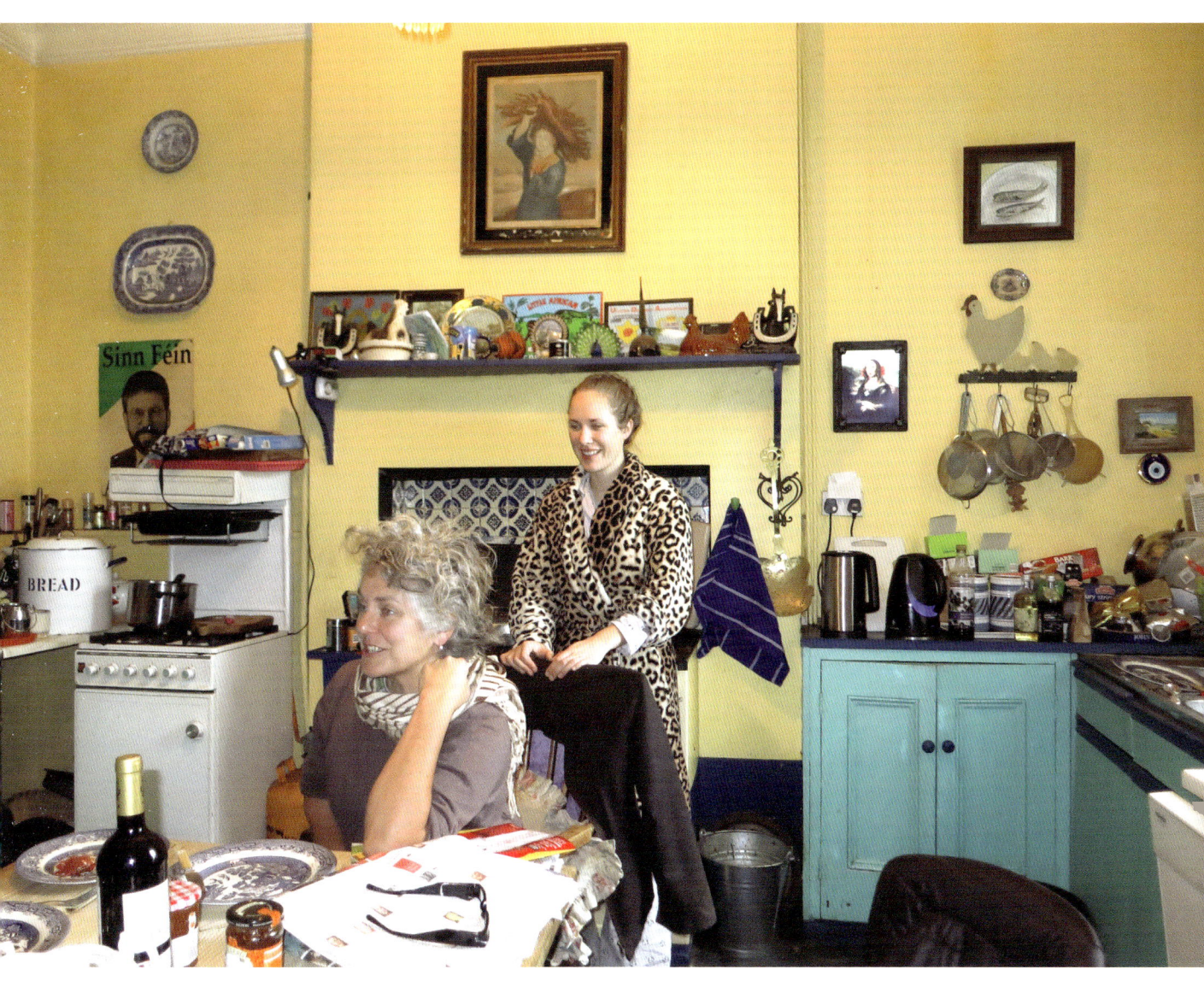

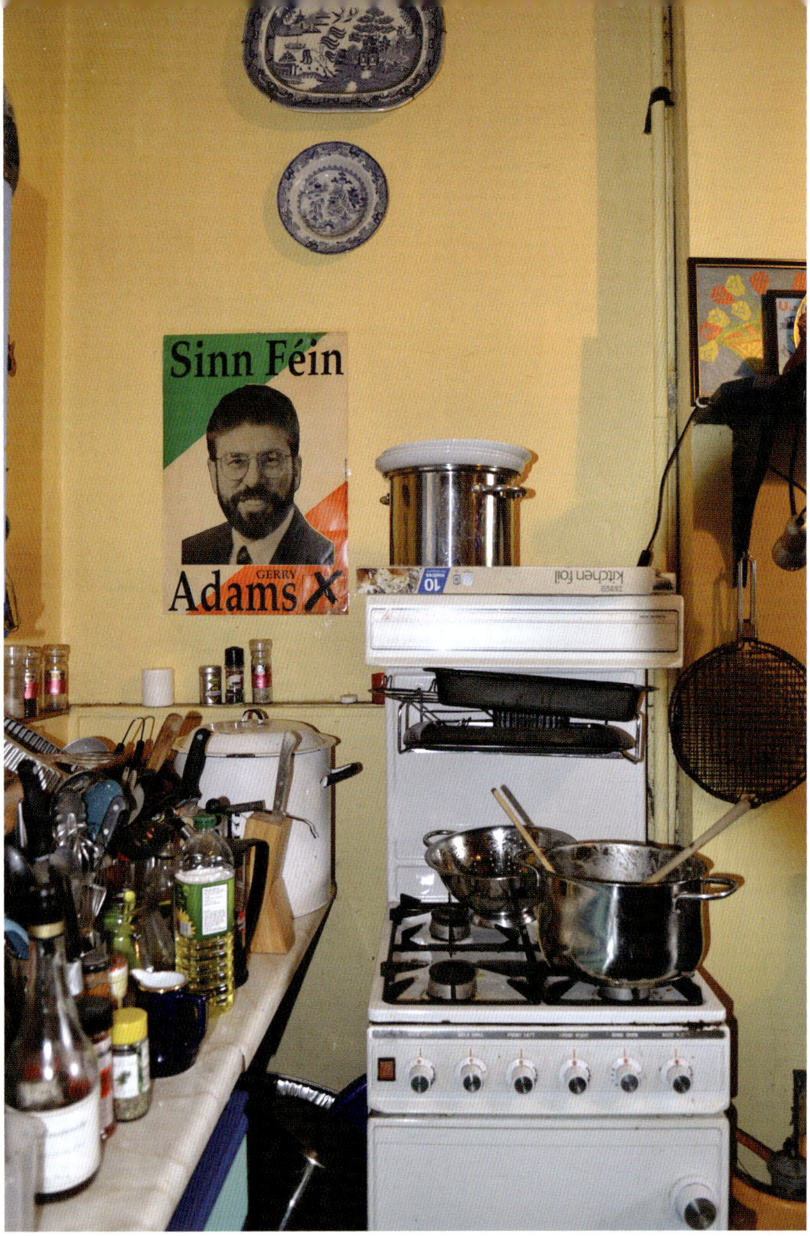

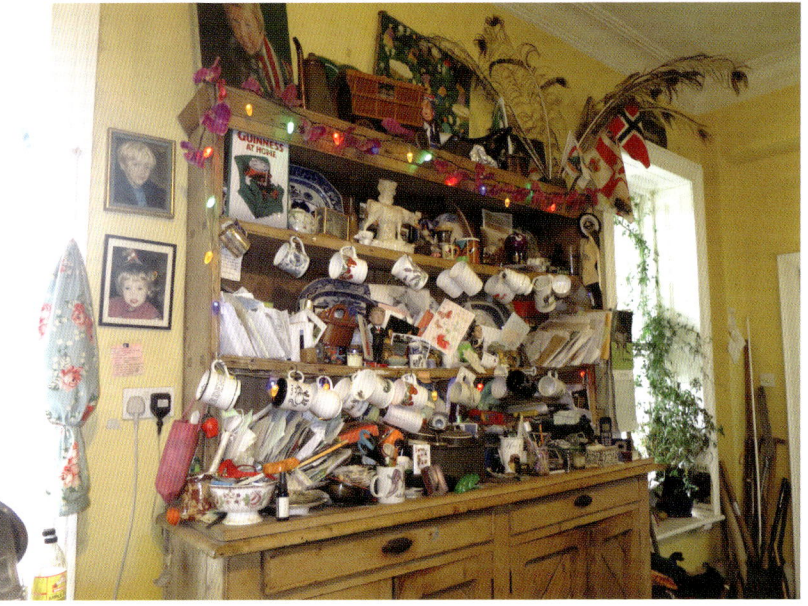

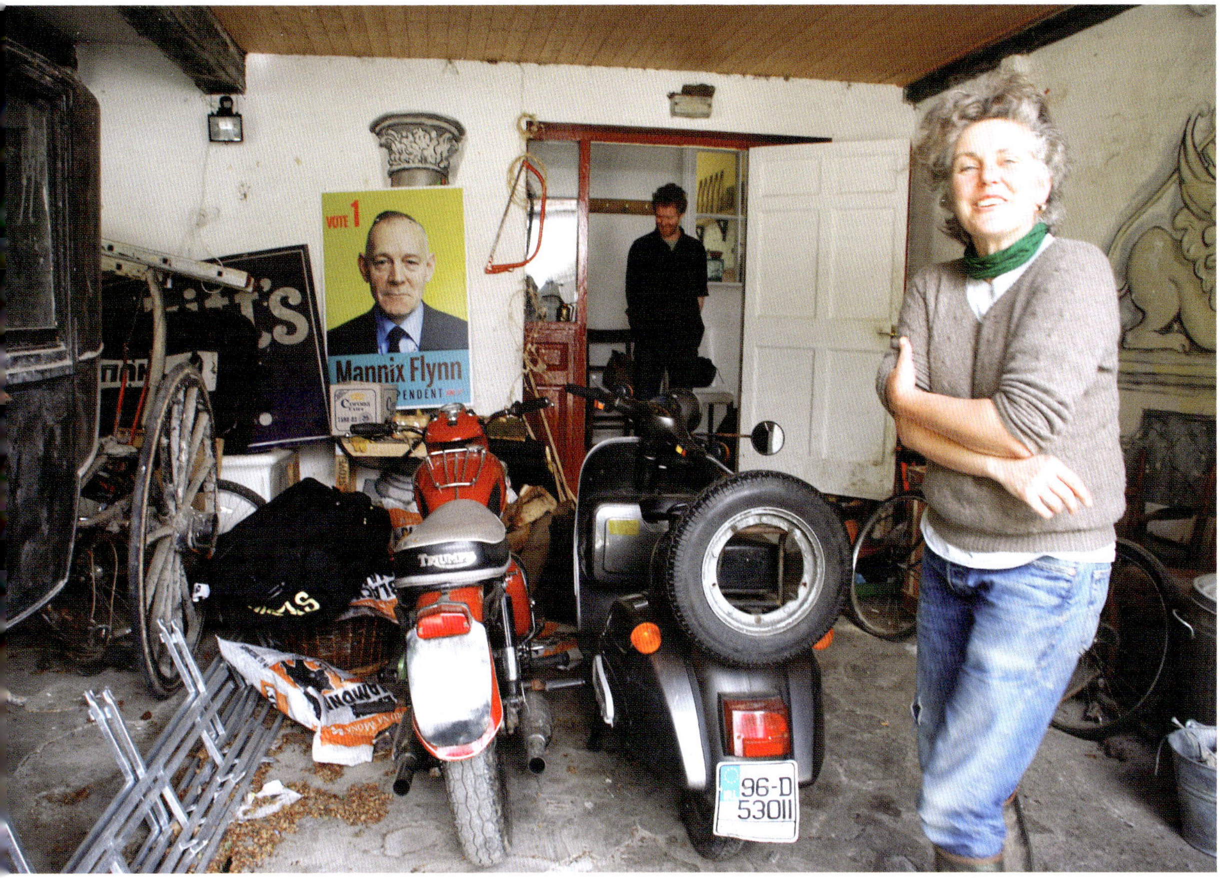

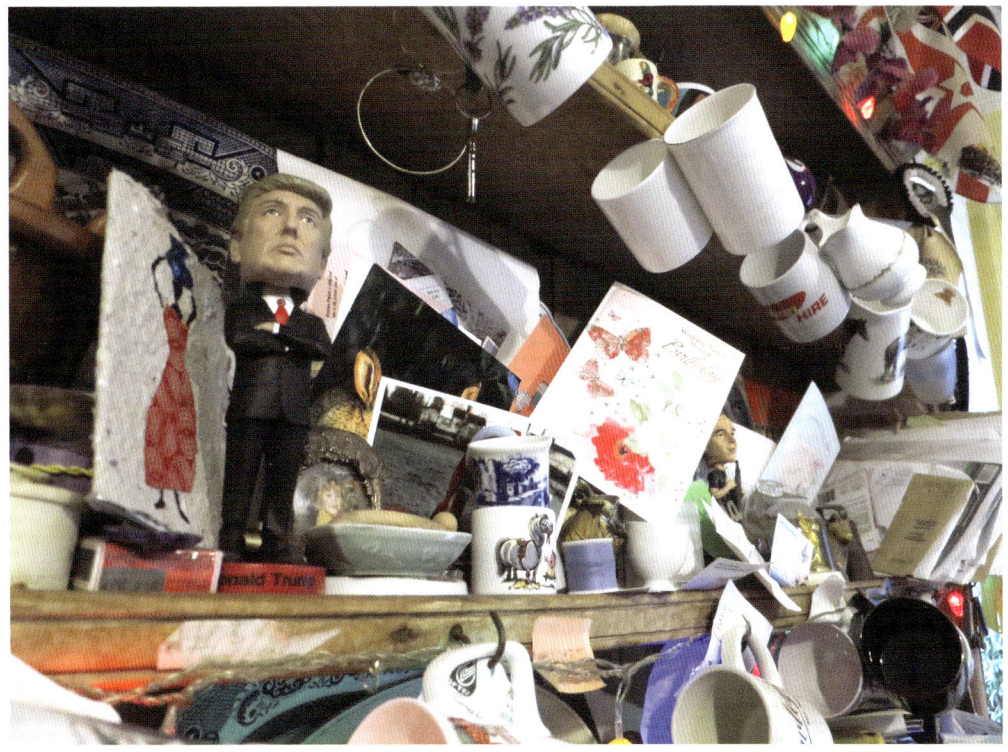

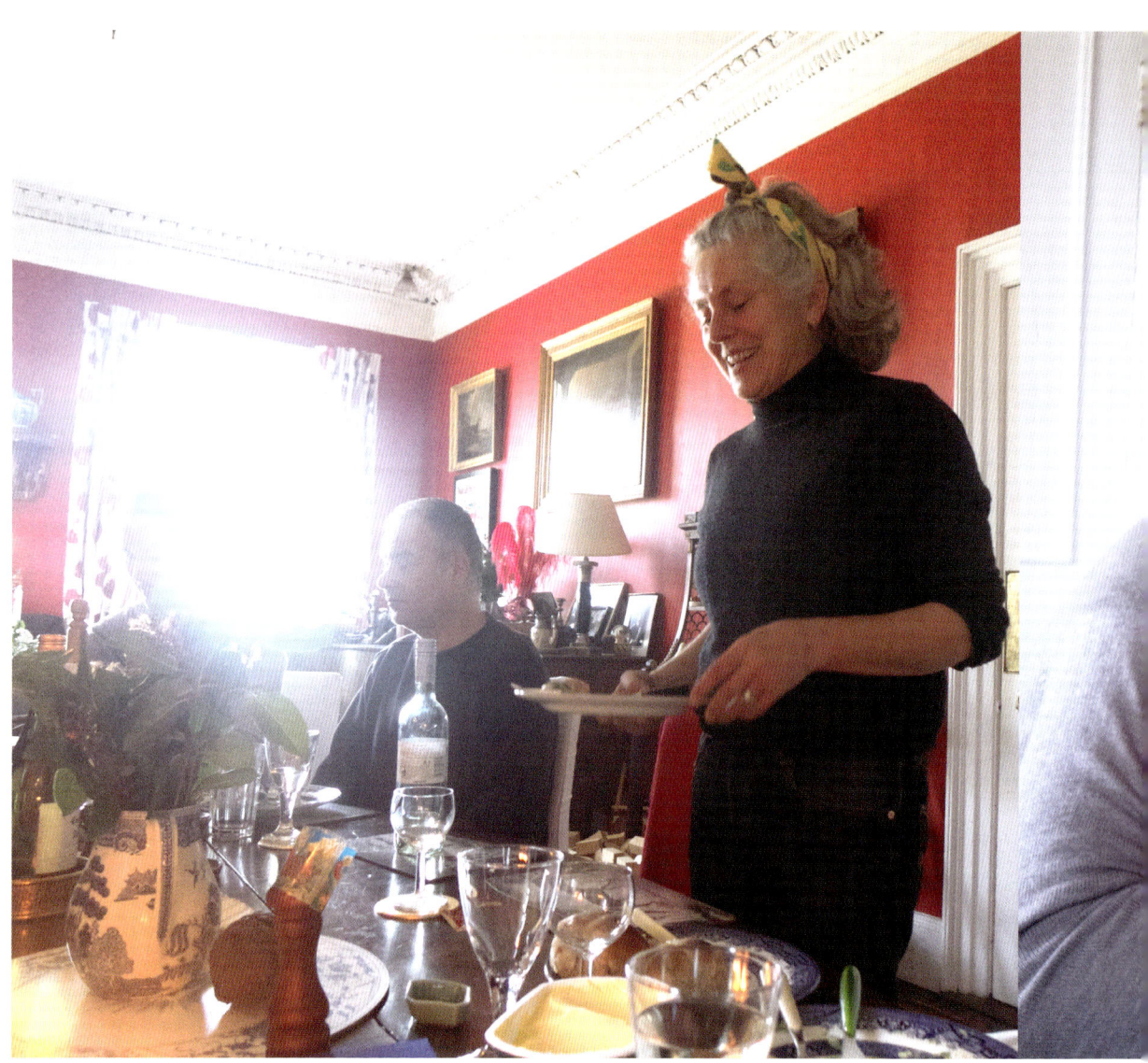

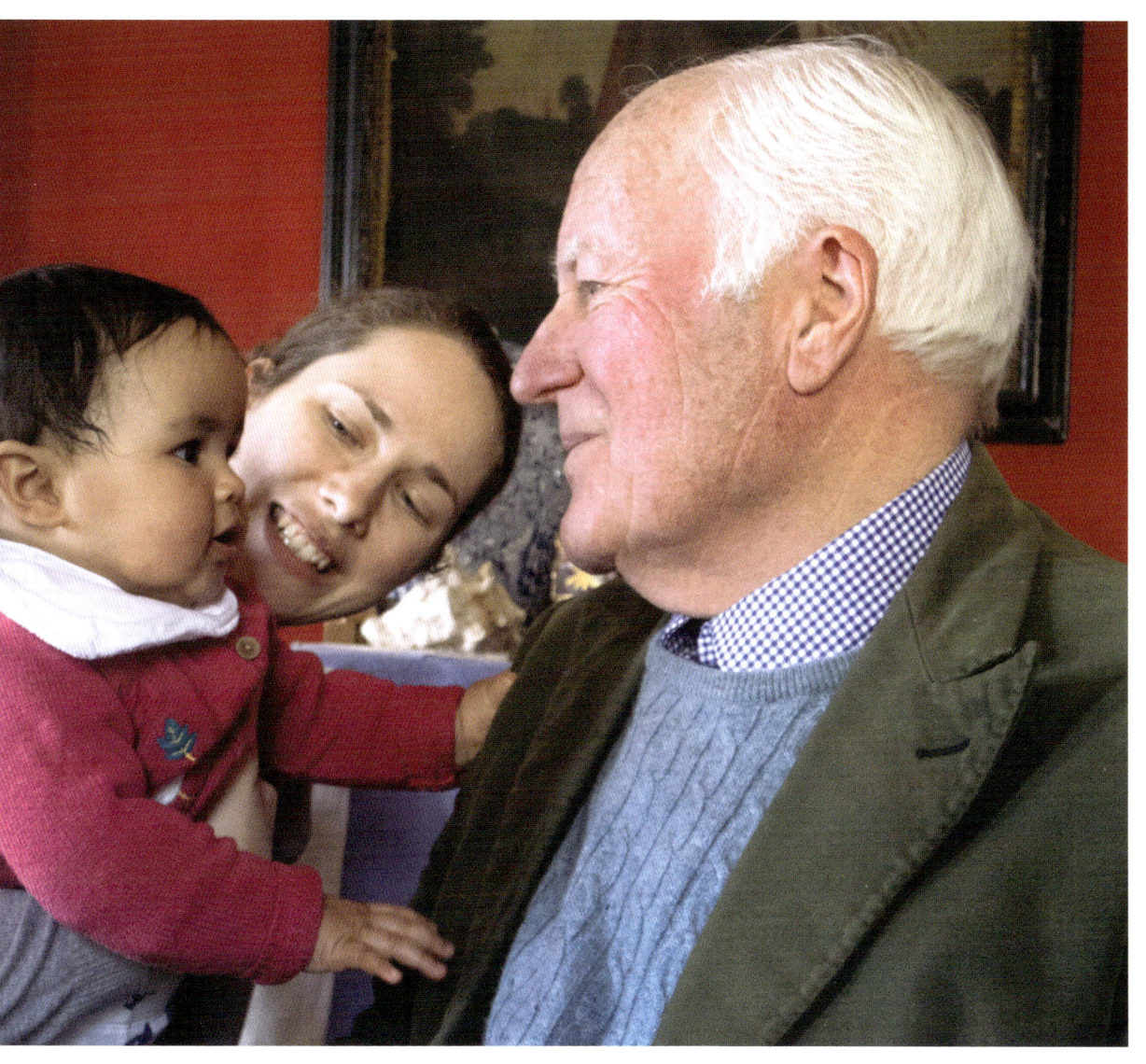

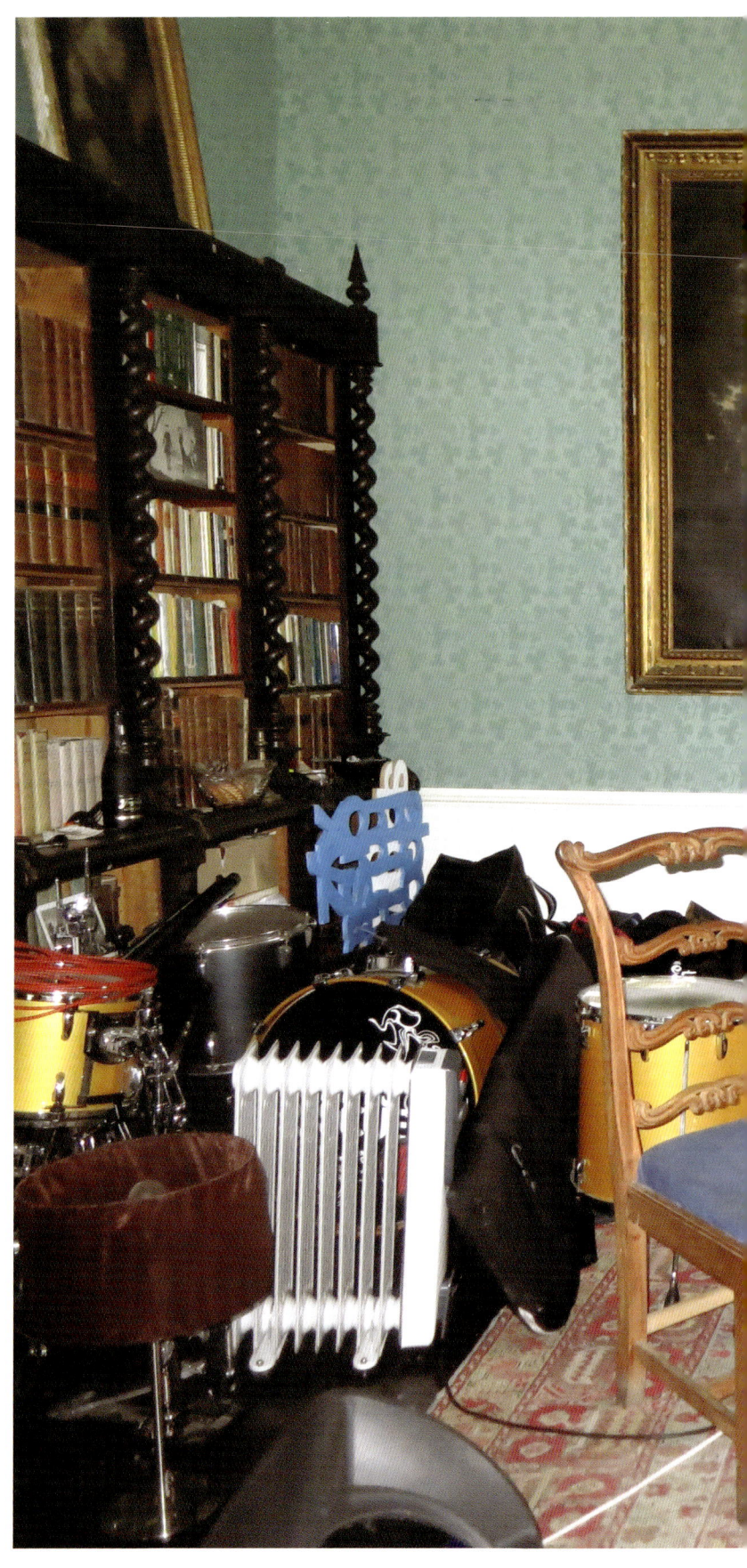

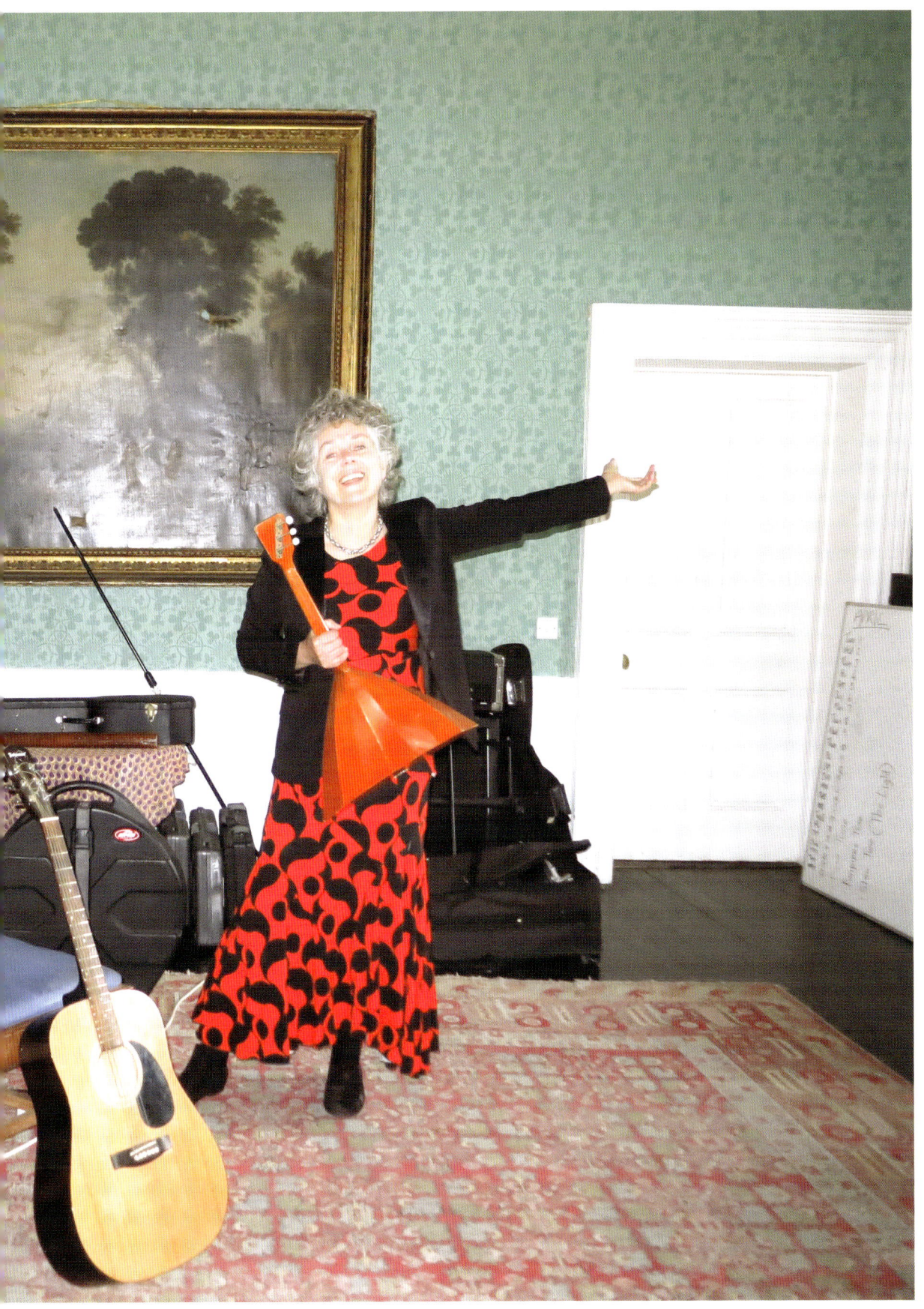

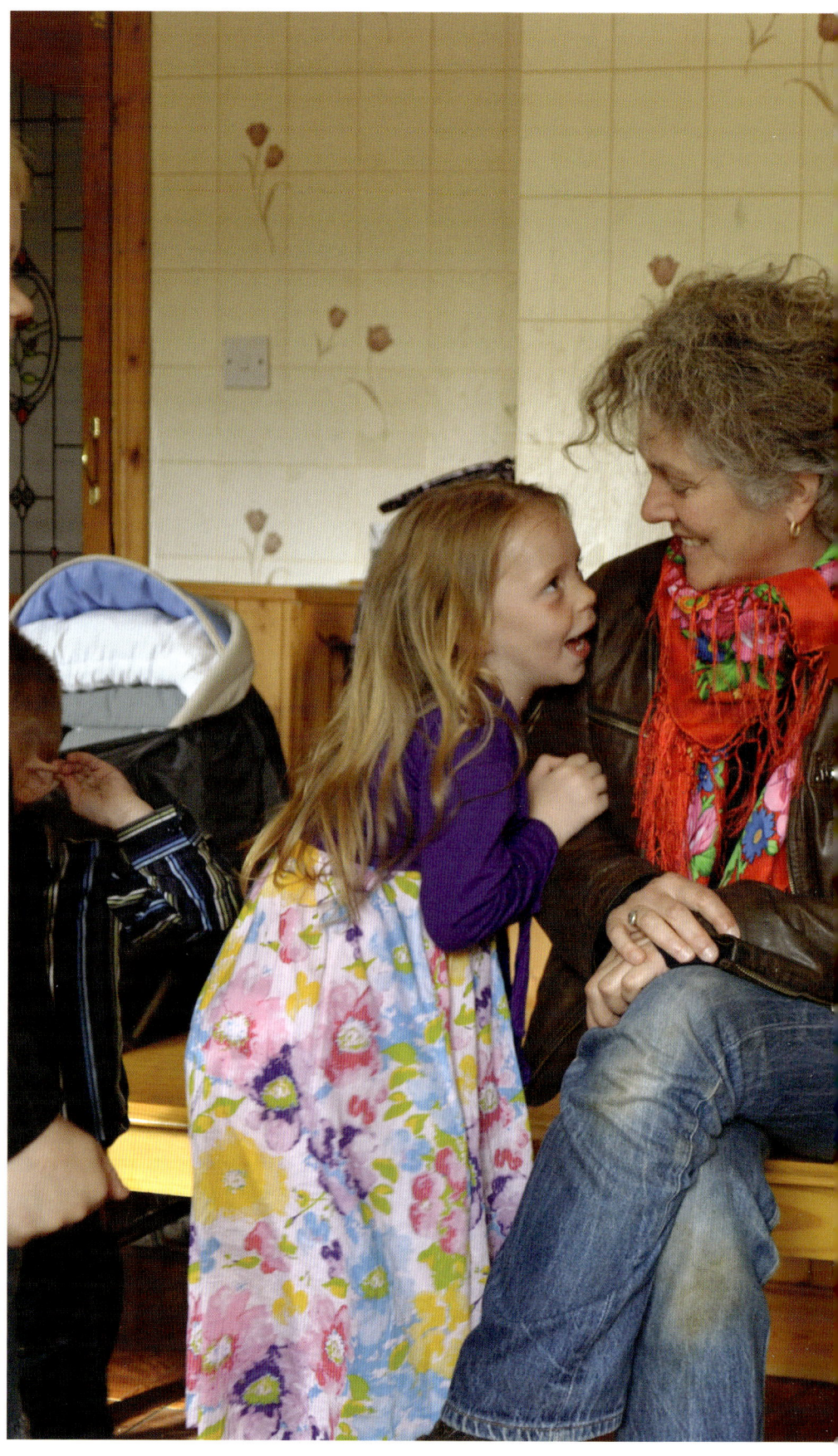

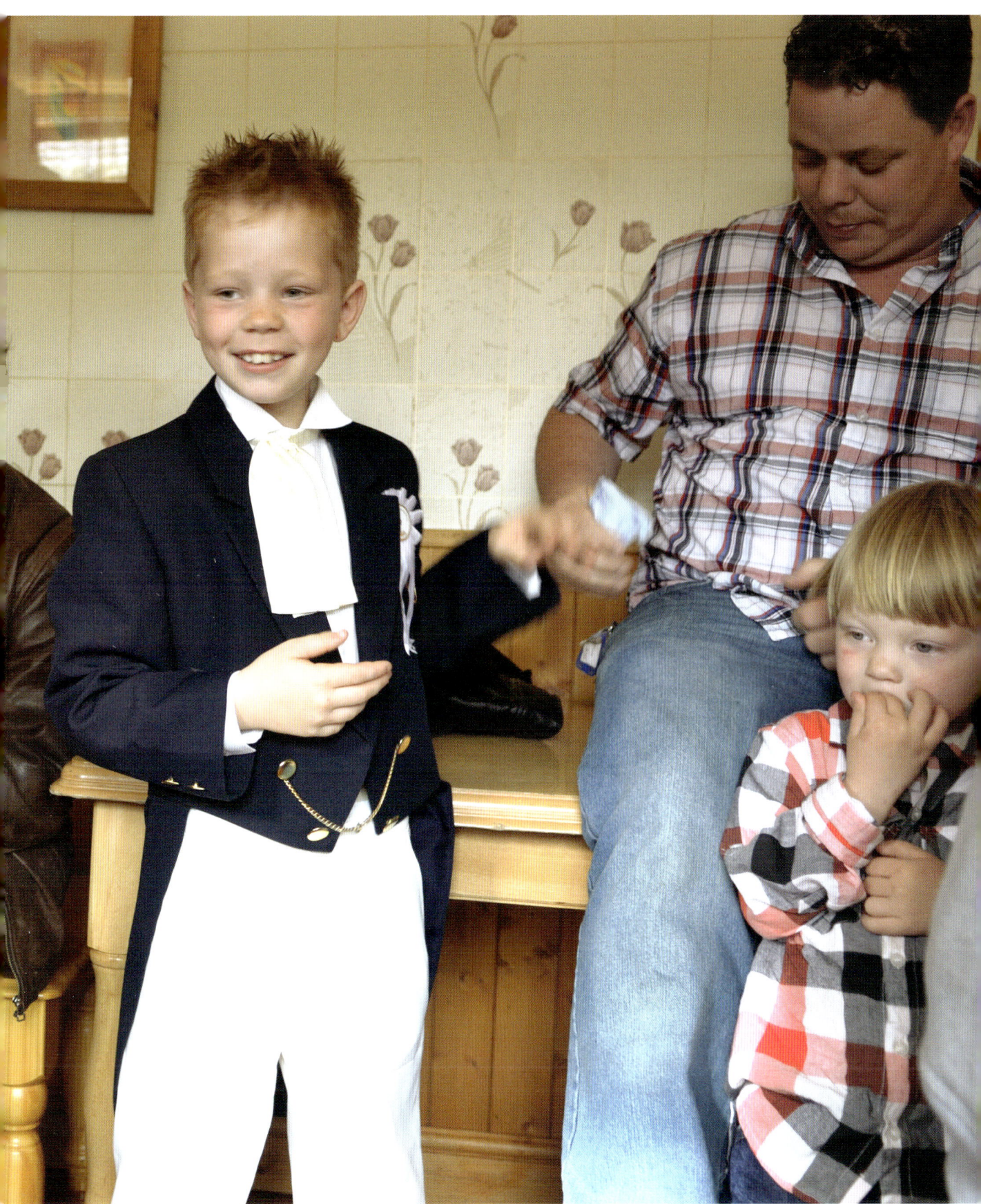

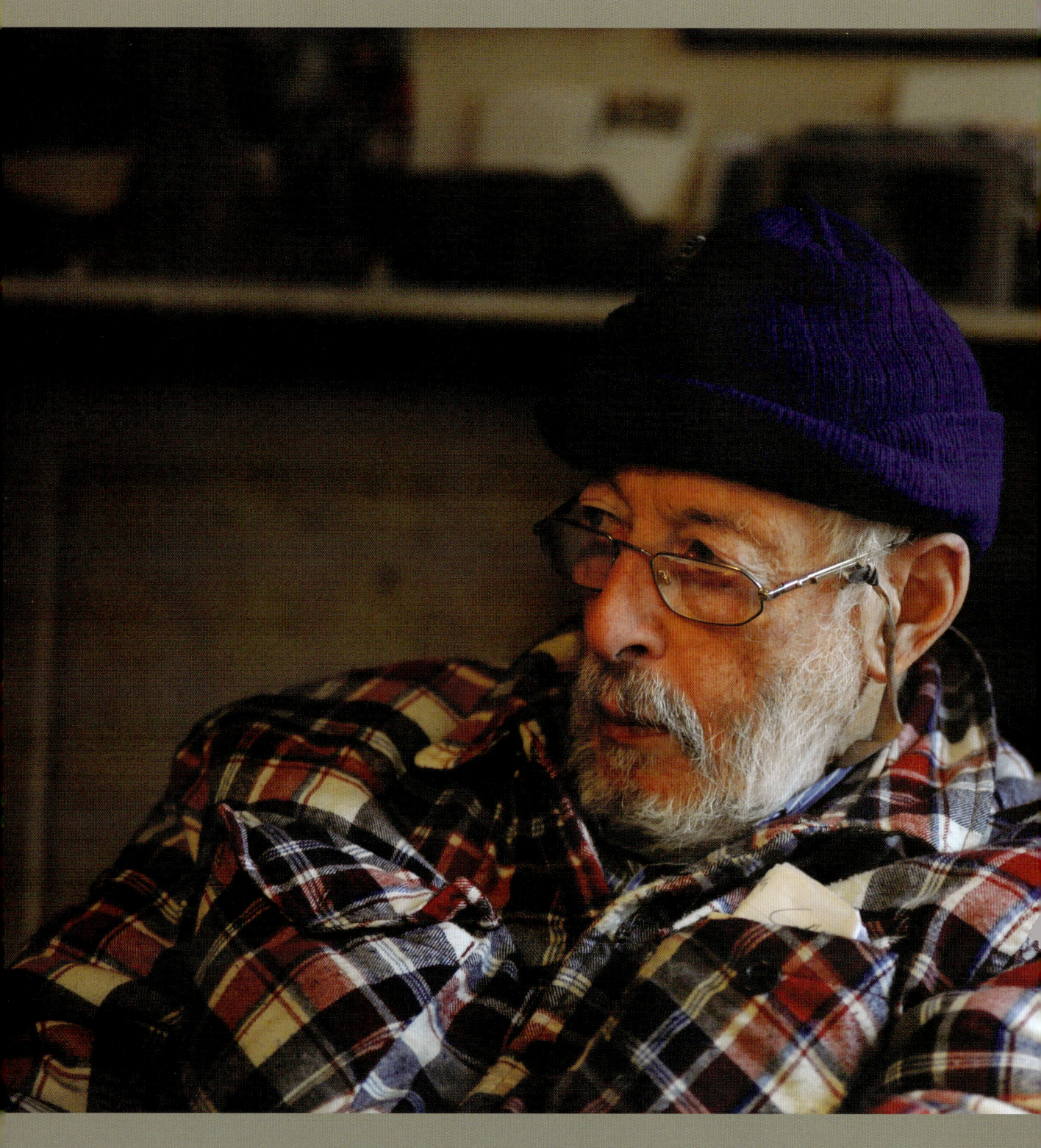

JP Donleavy

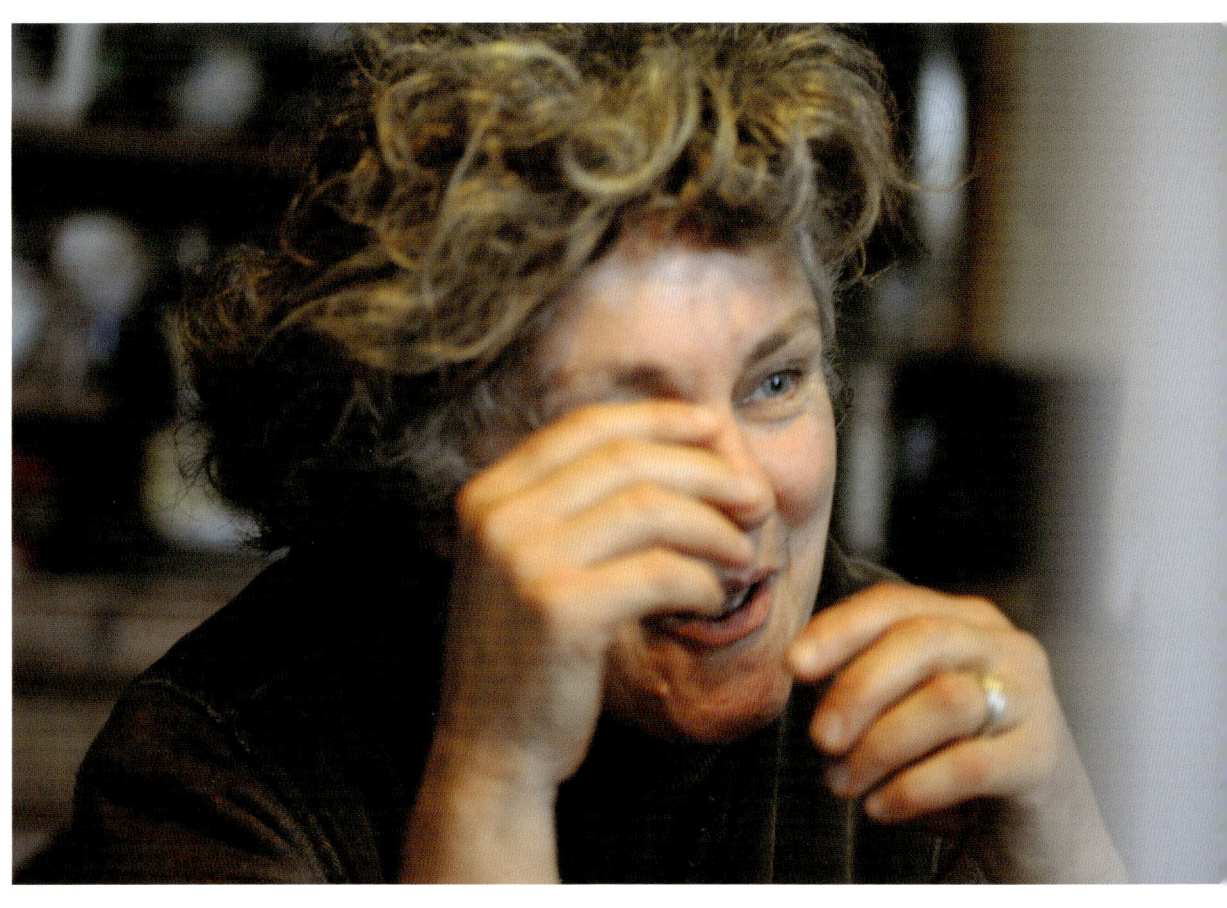

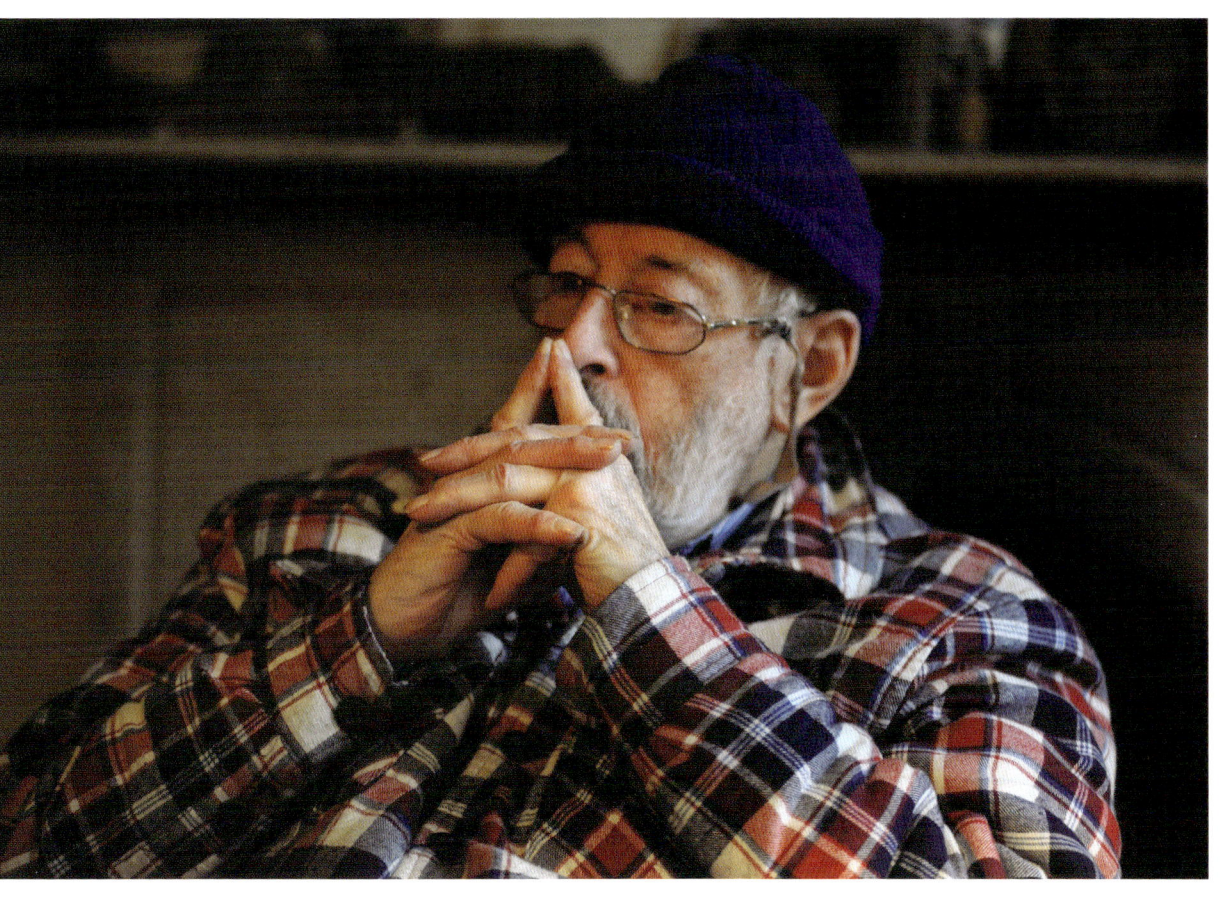

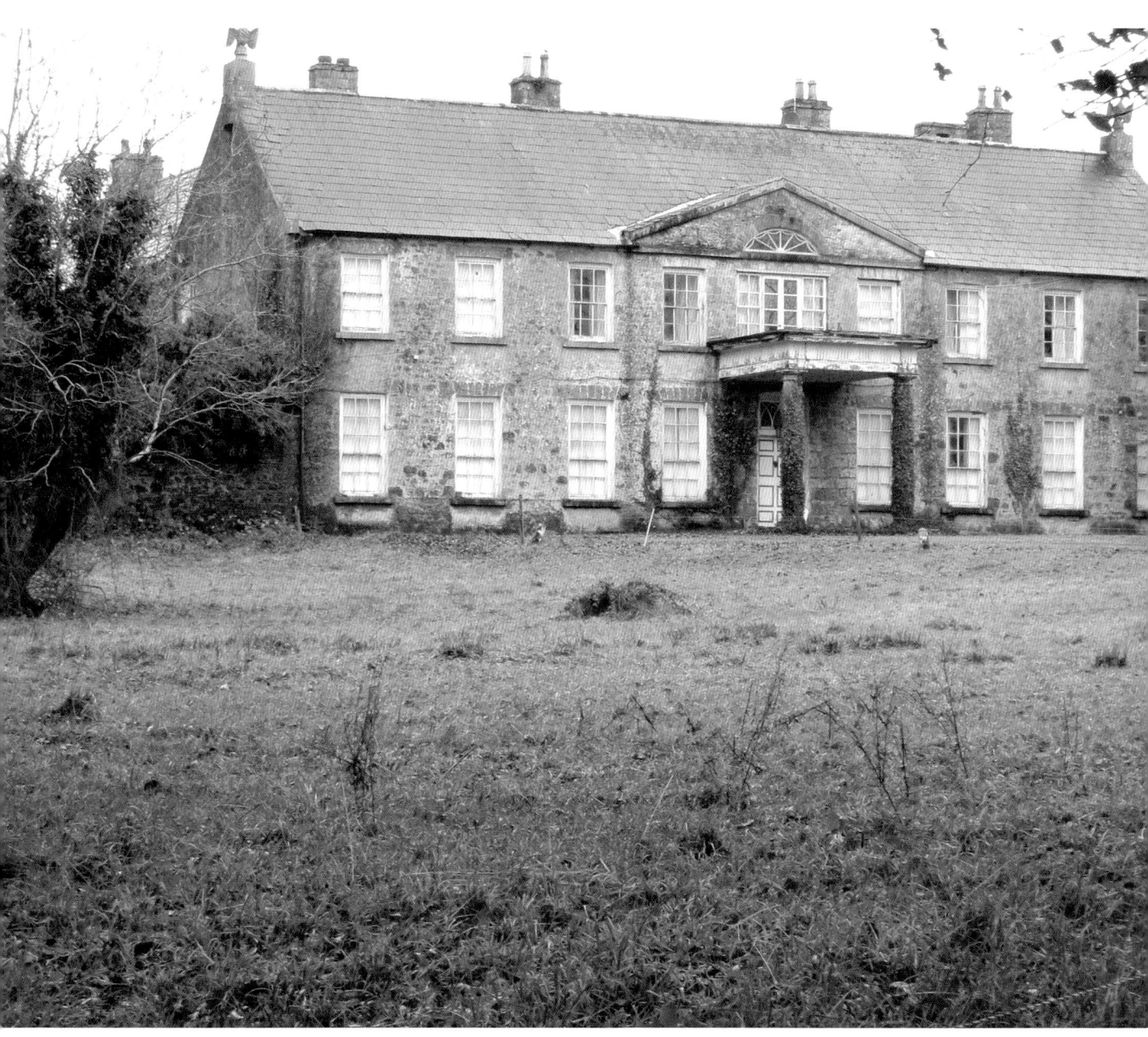

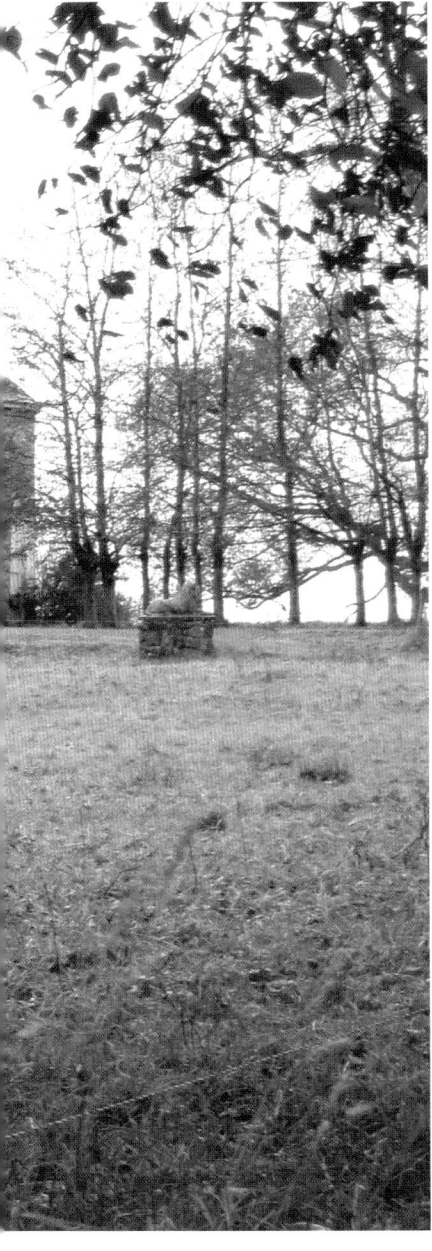
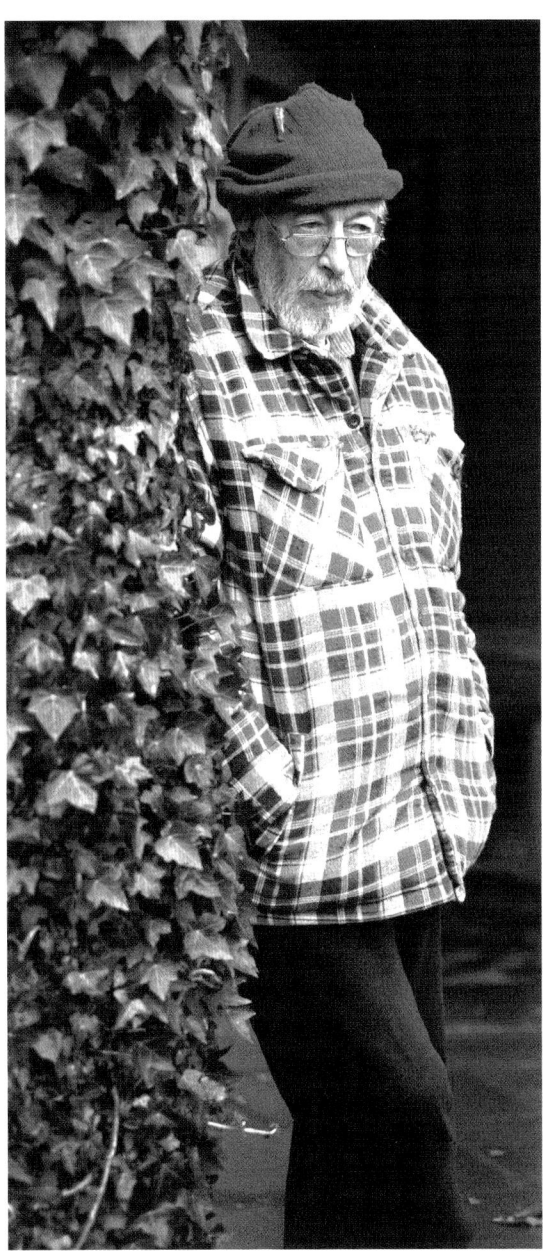

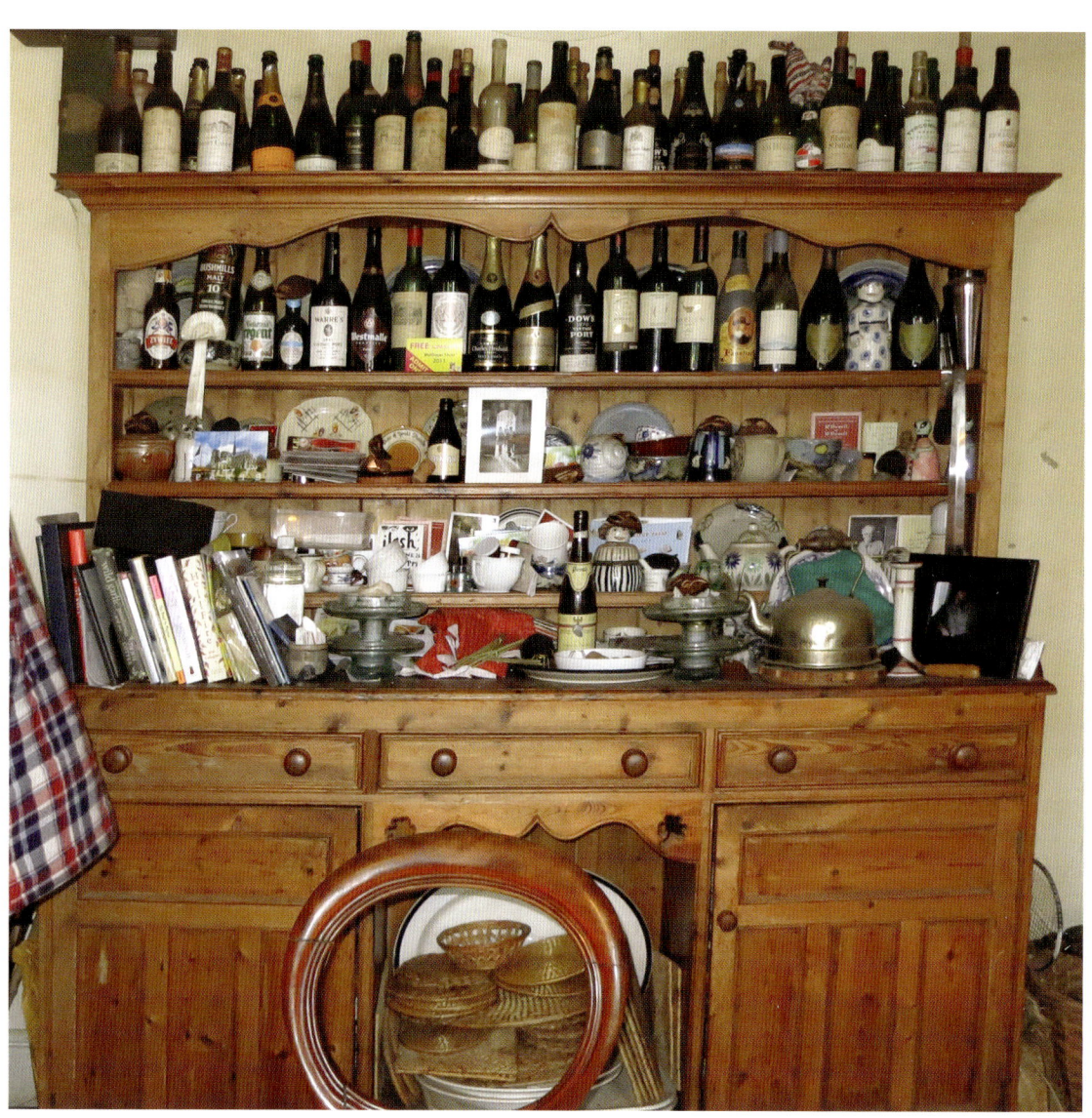

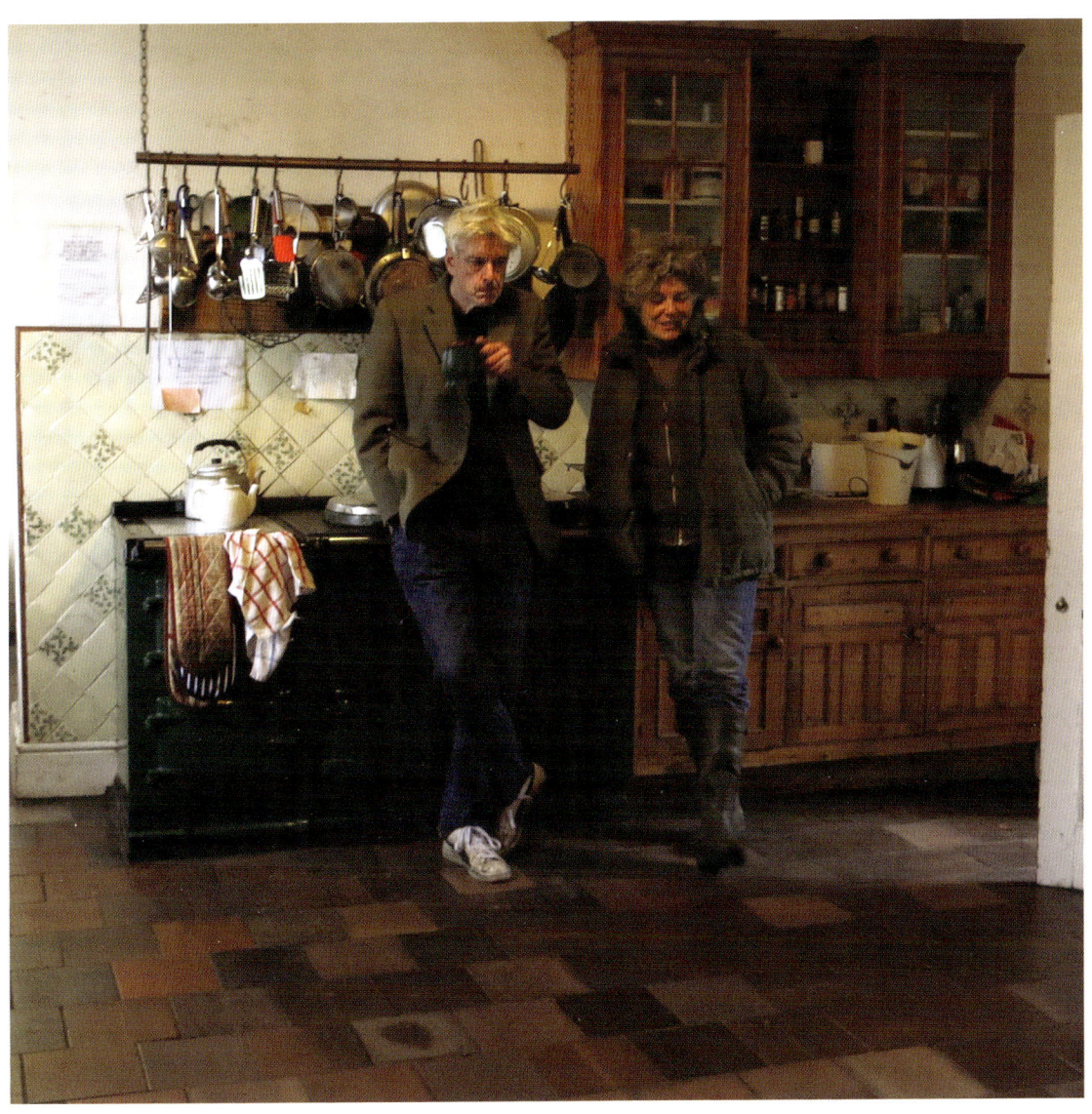

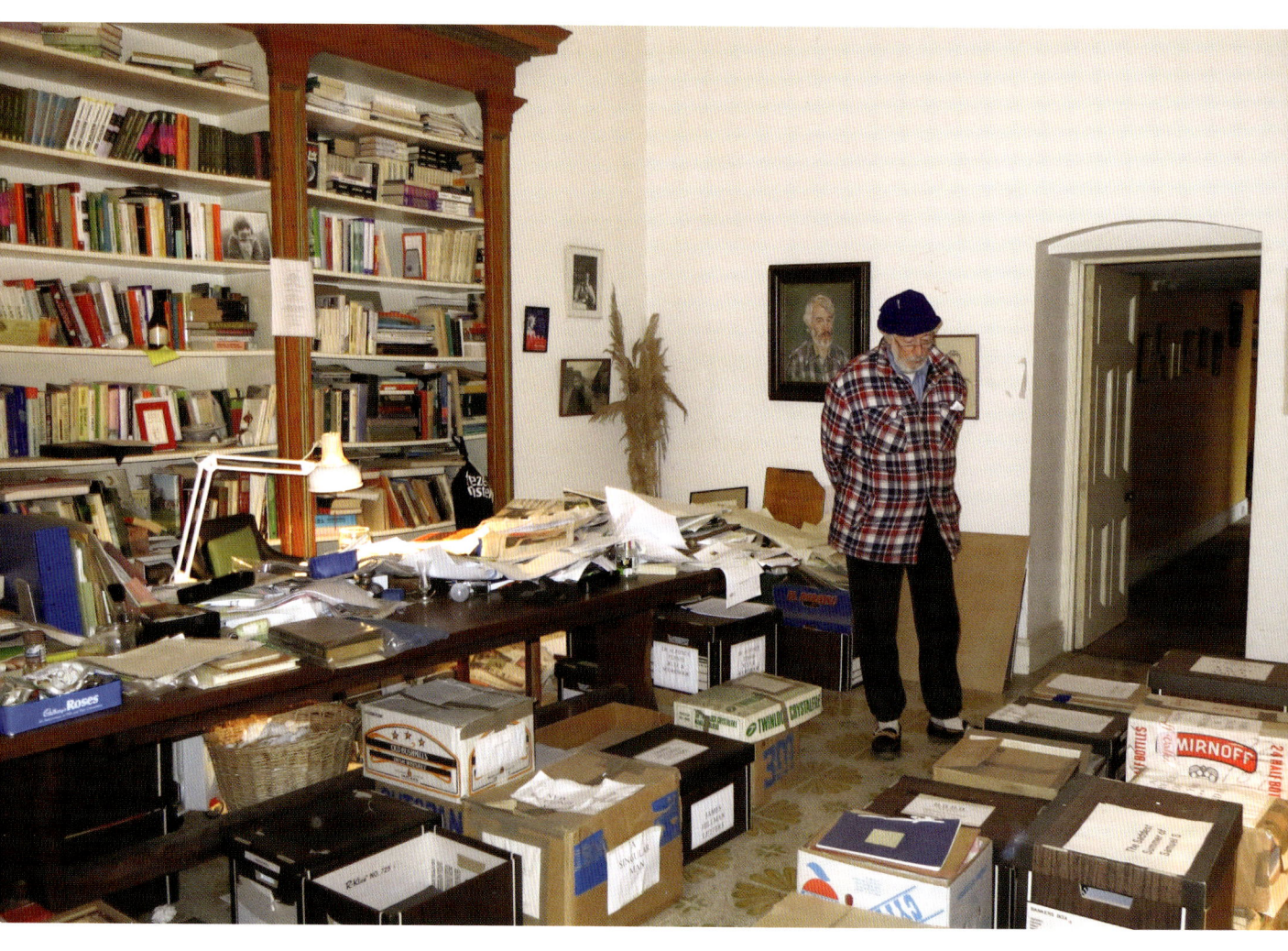

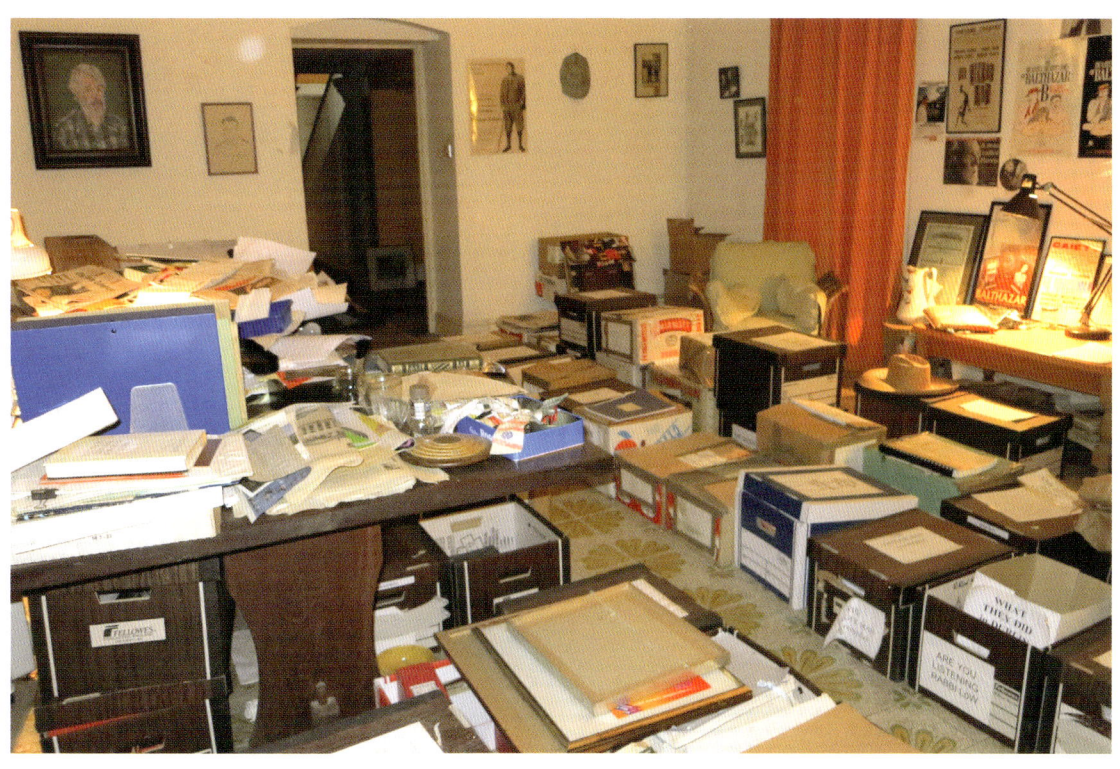

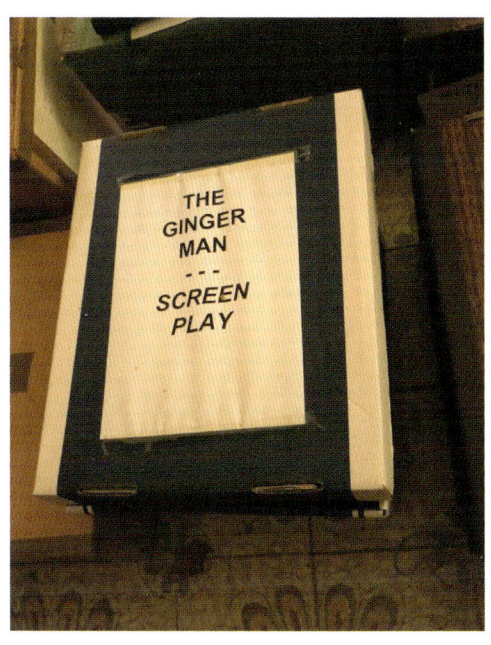

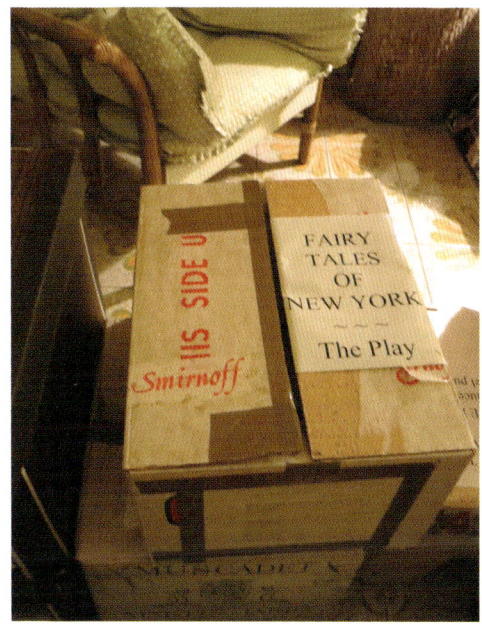

Tim Pat Coogan

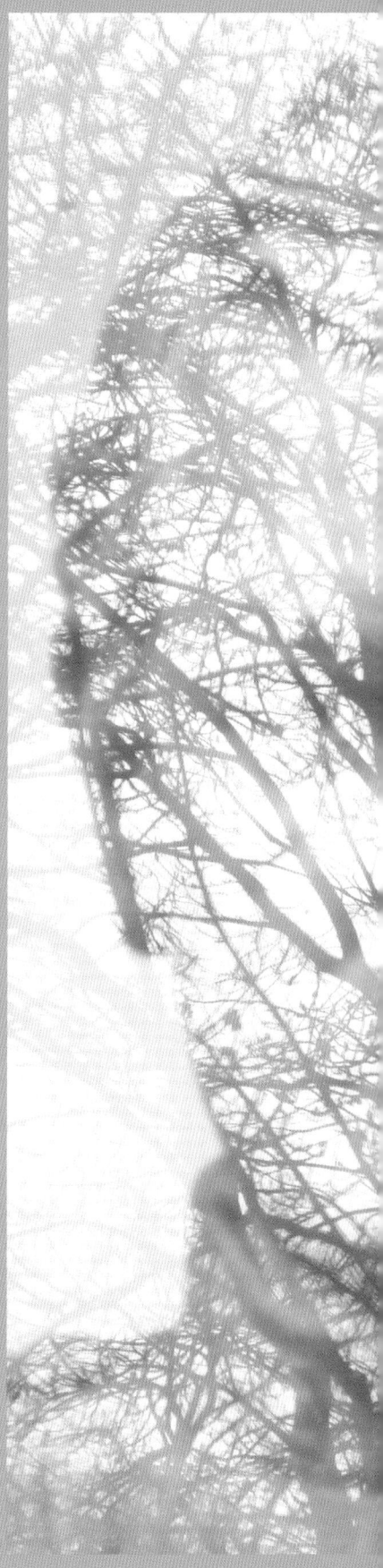

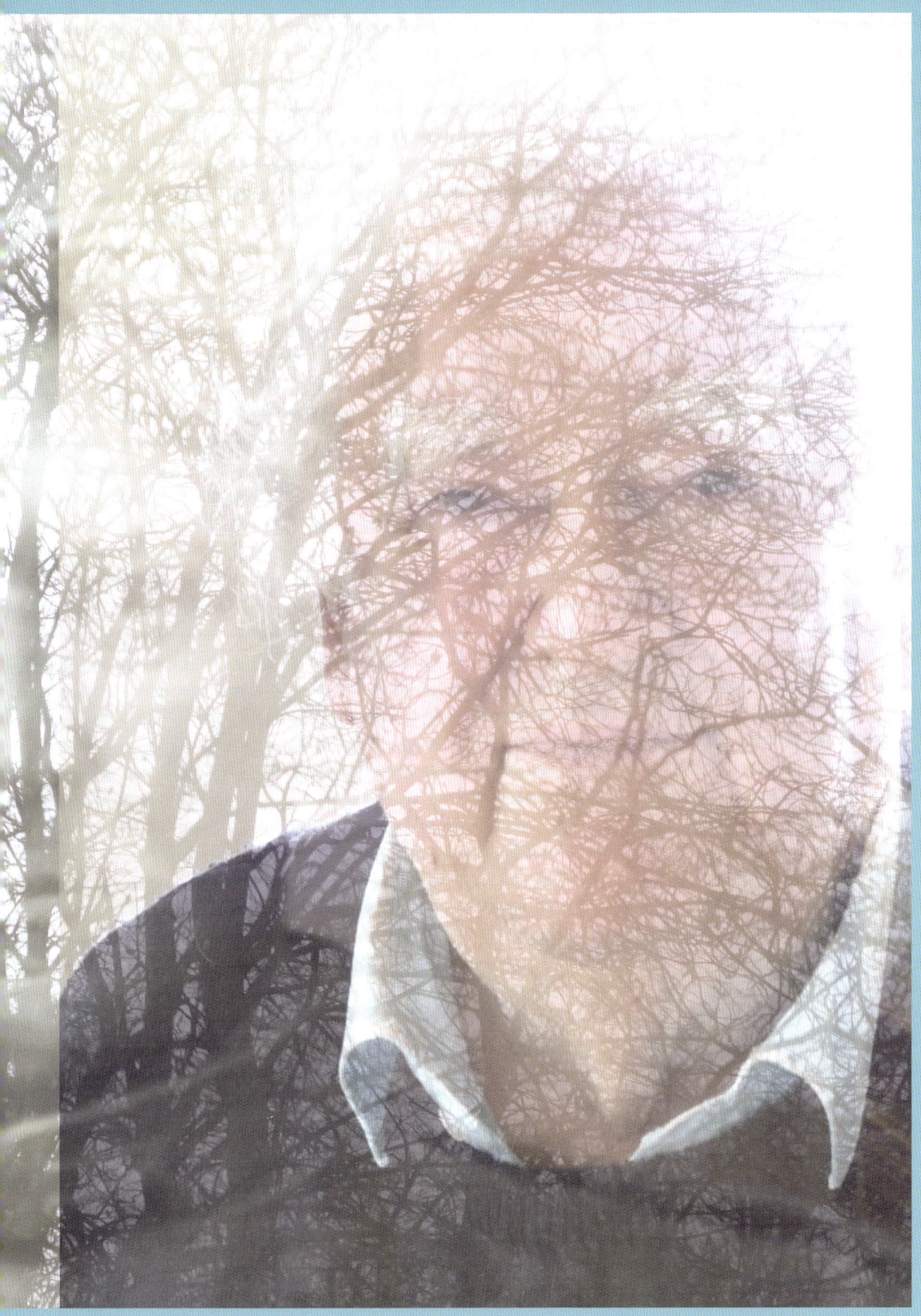

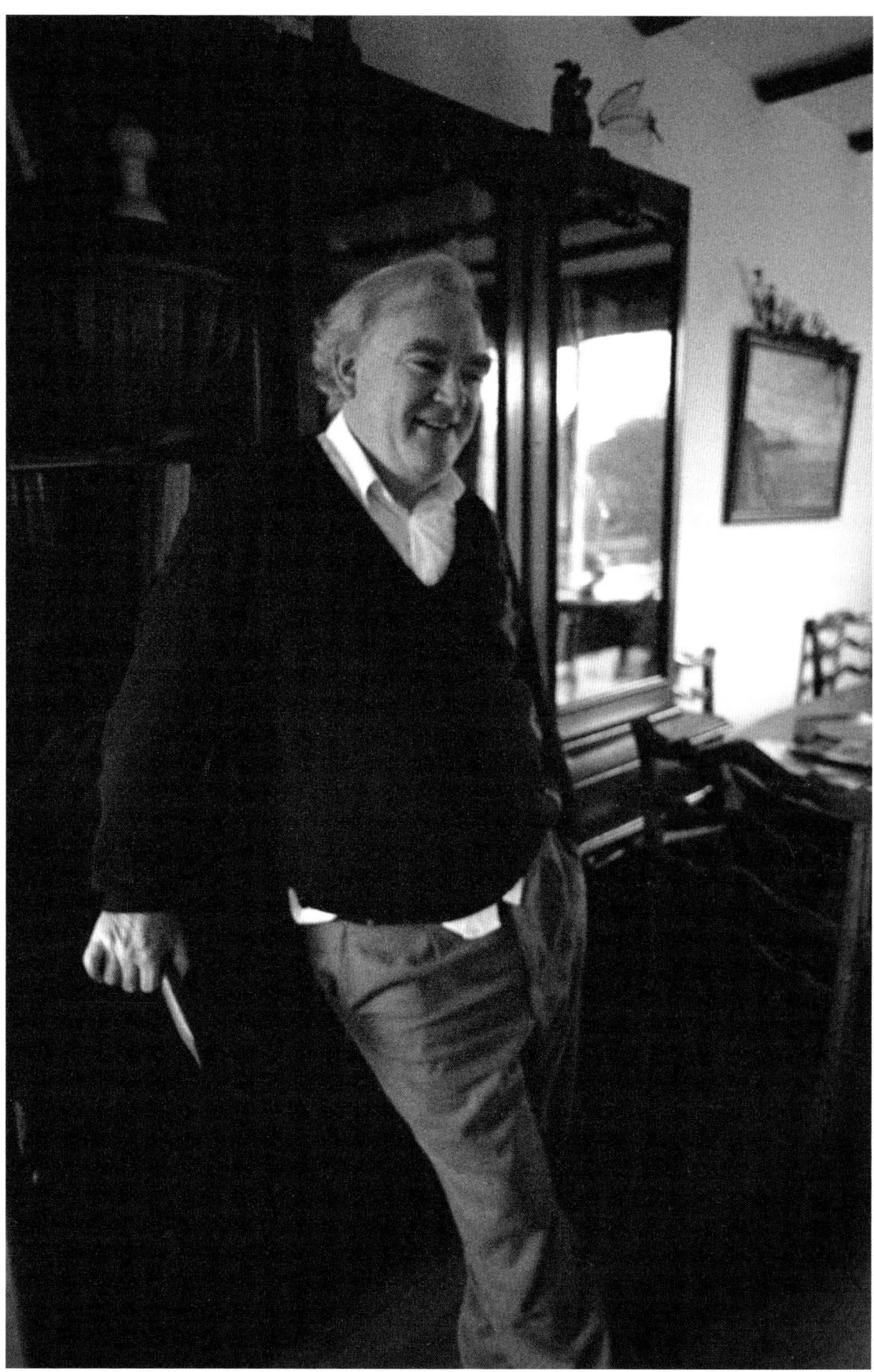

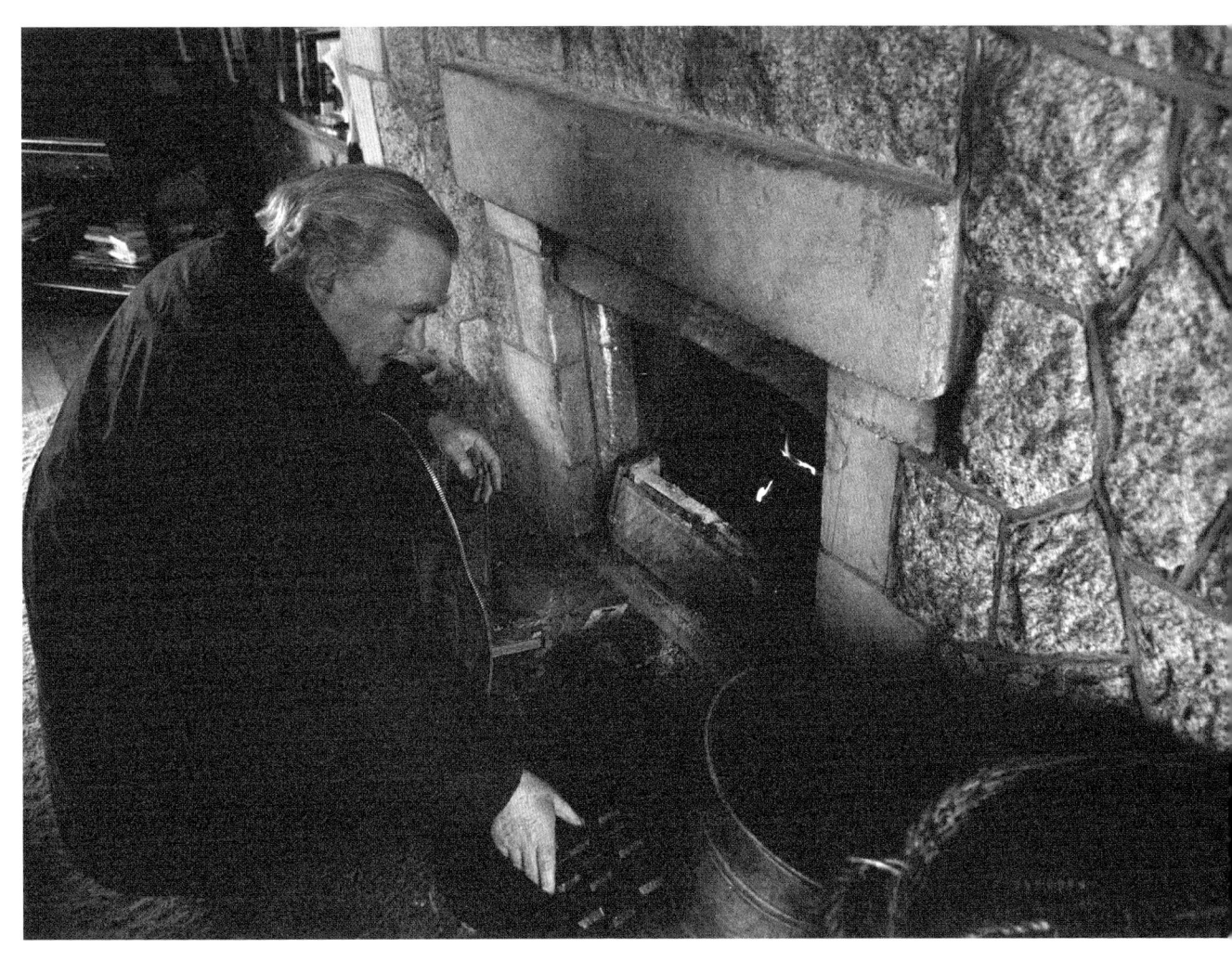

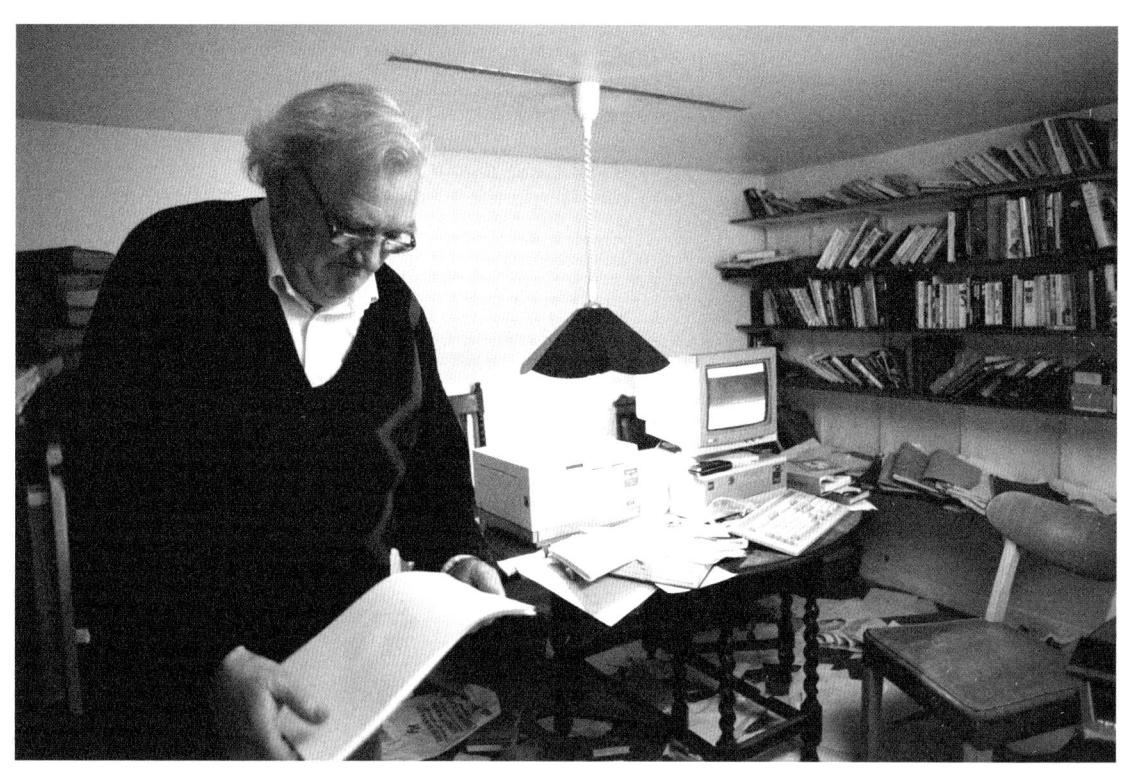

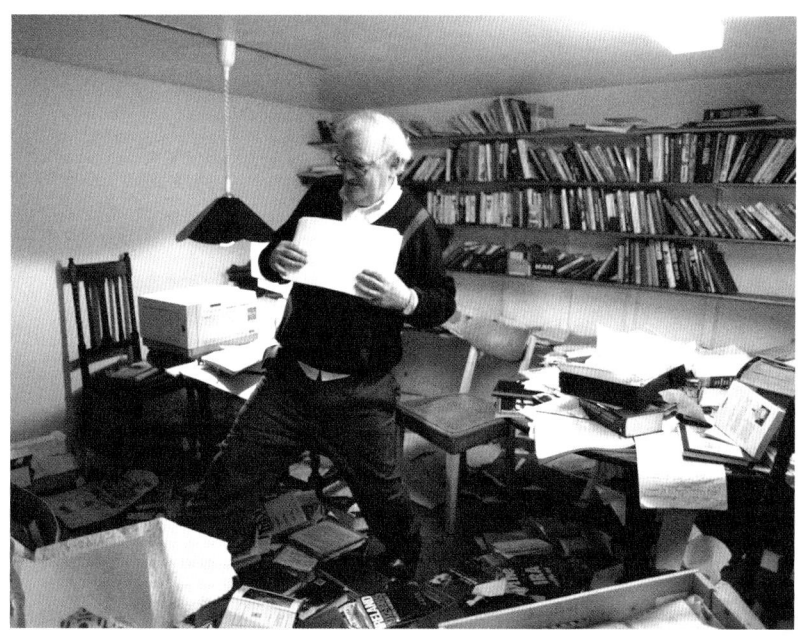

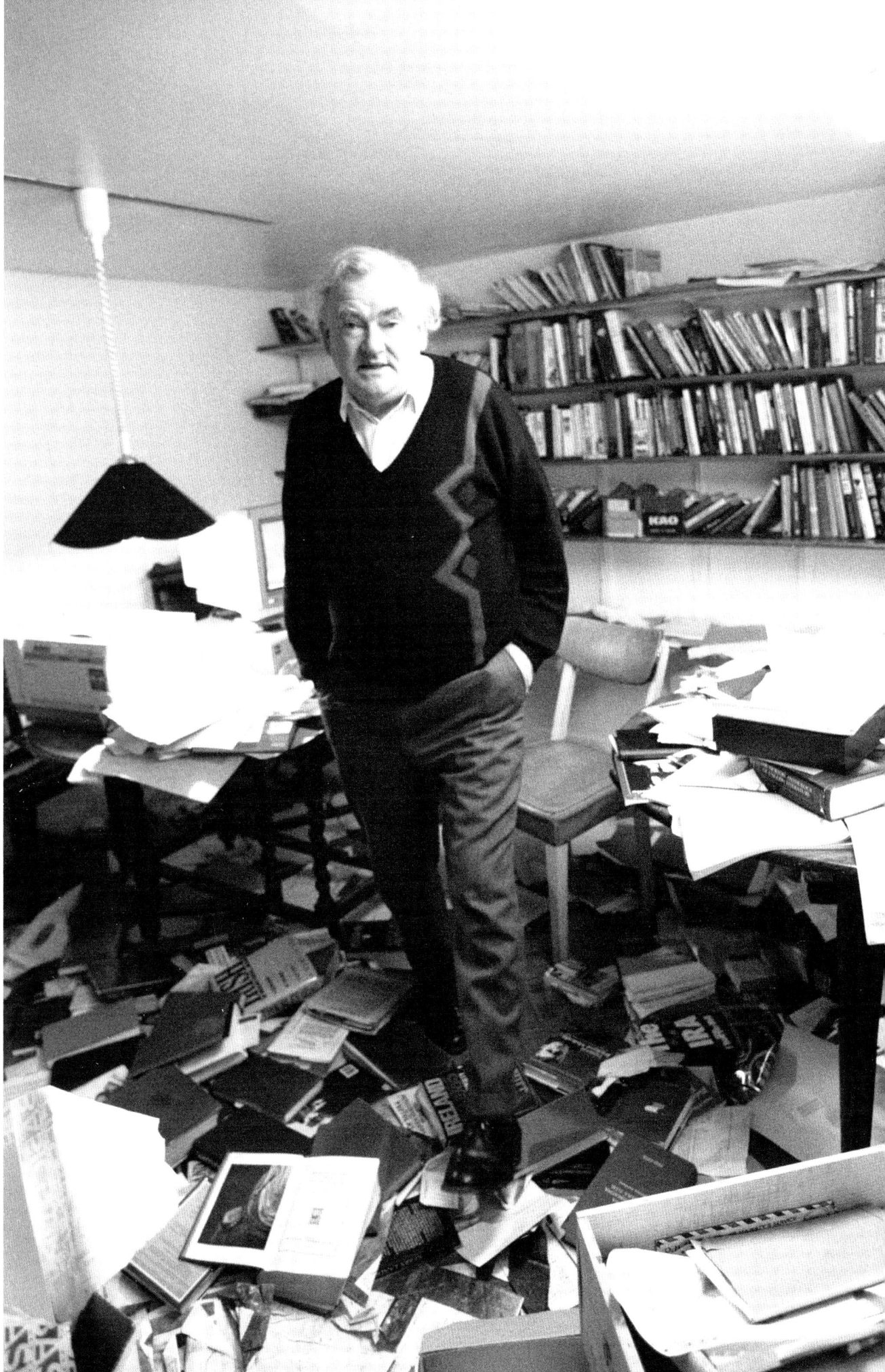

Hector McDonnell

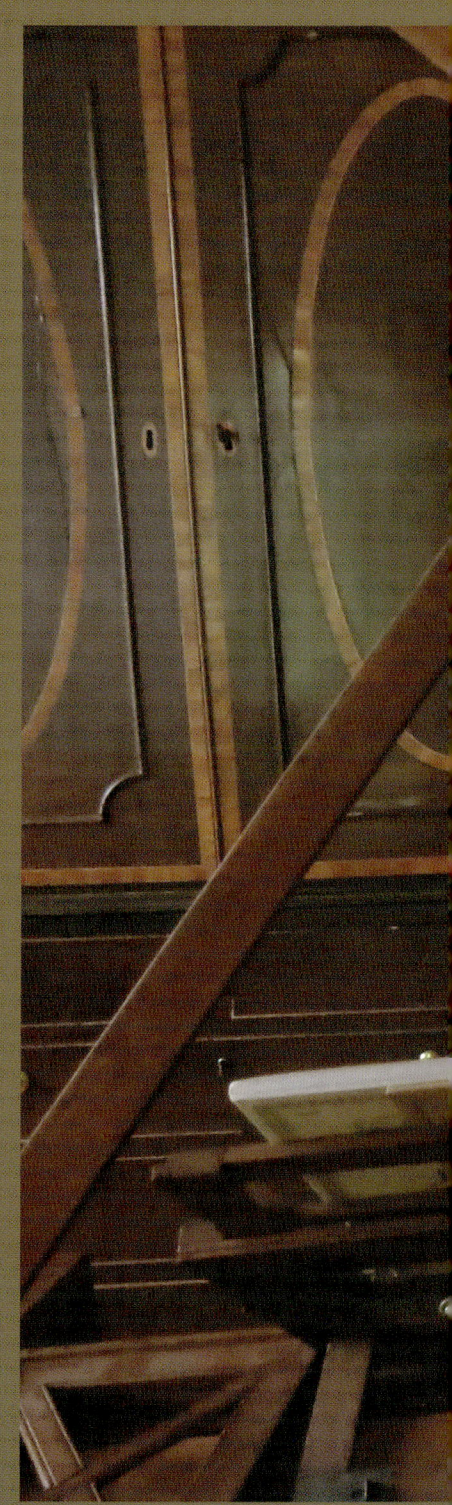

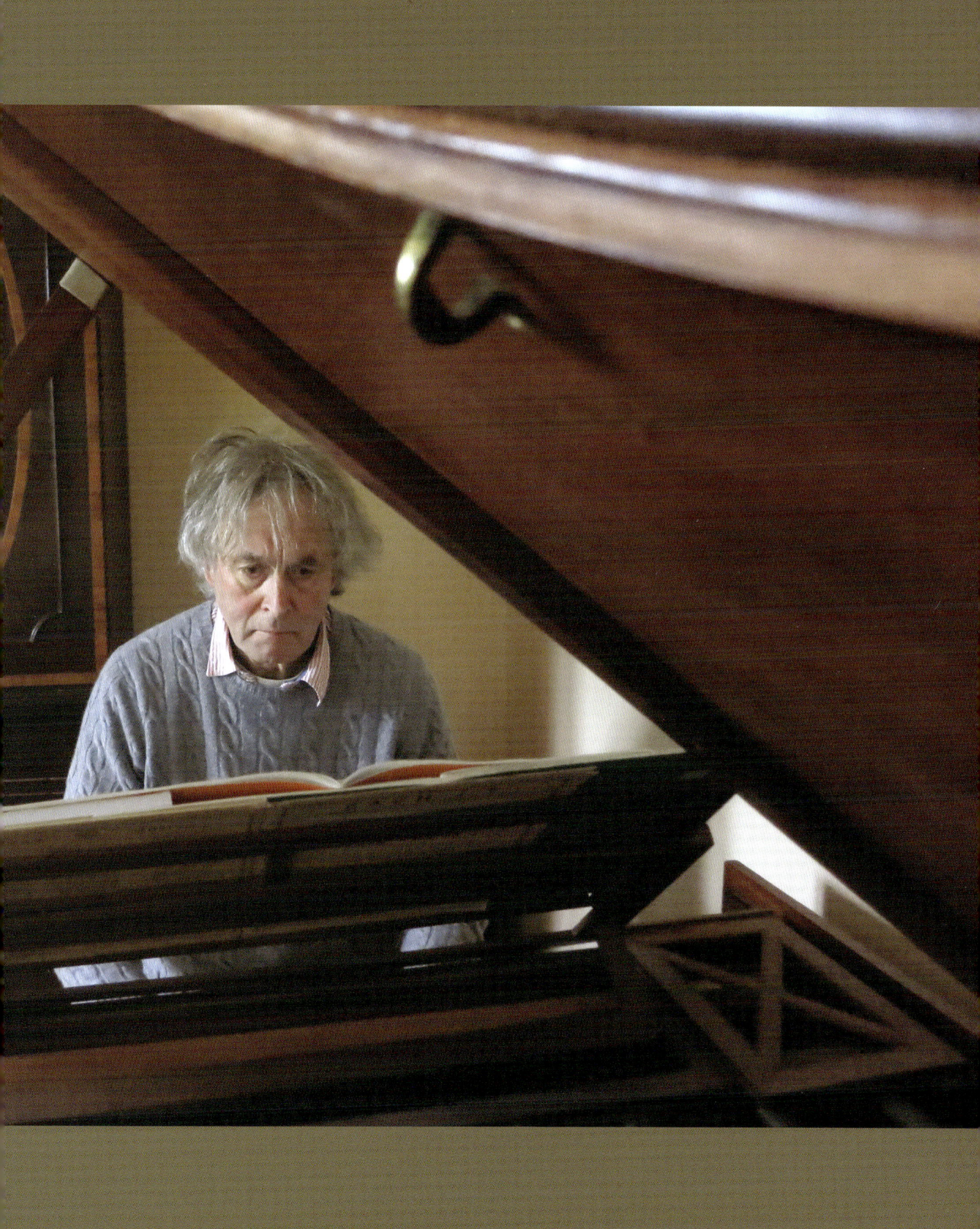

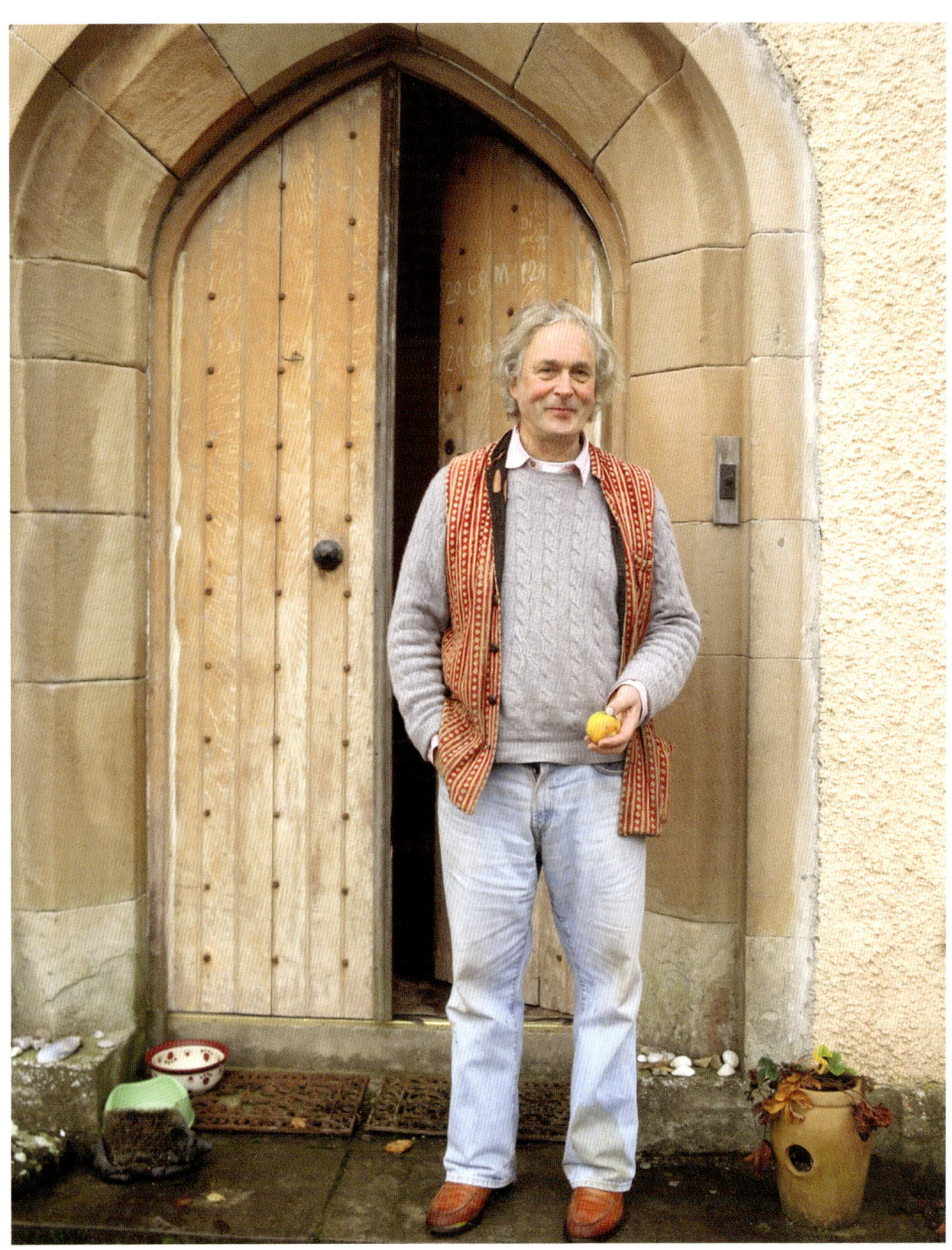

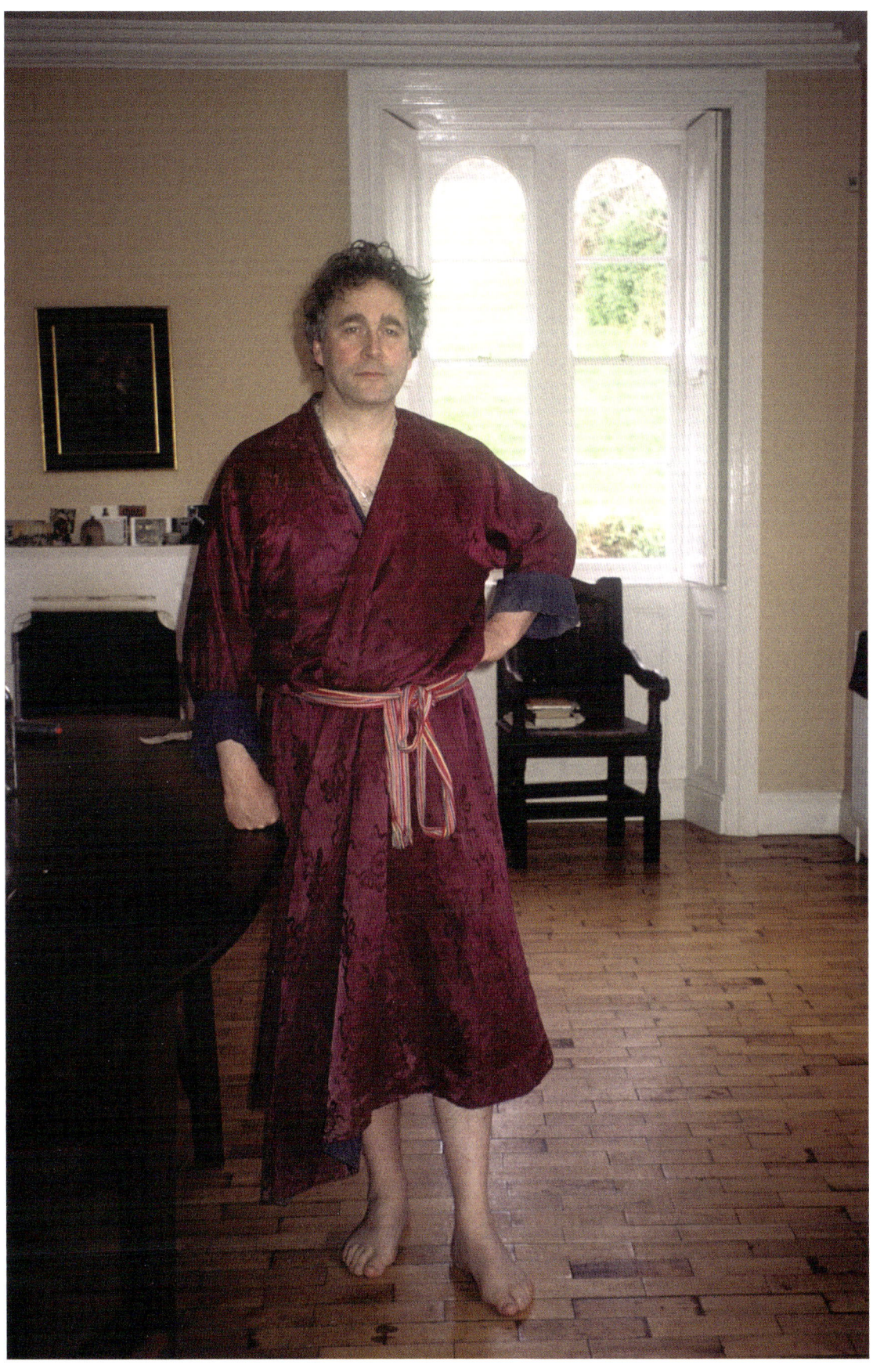

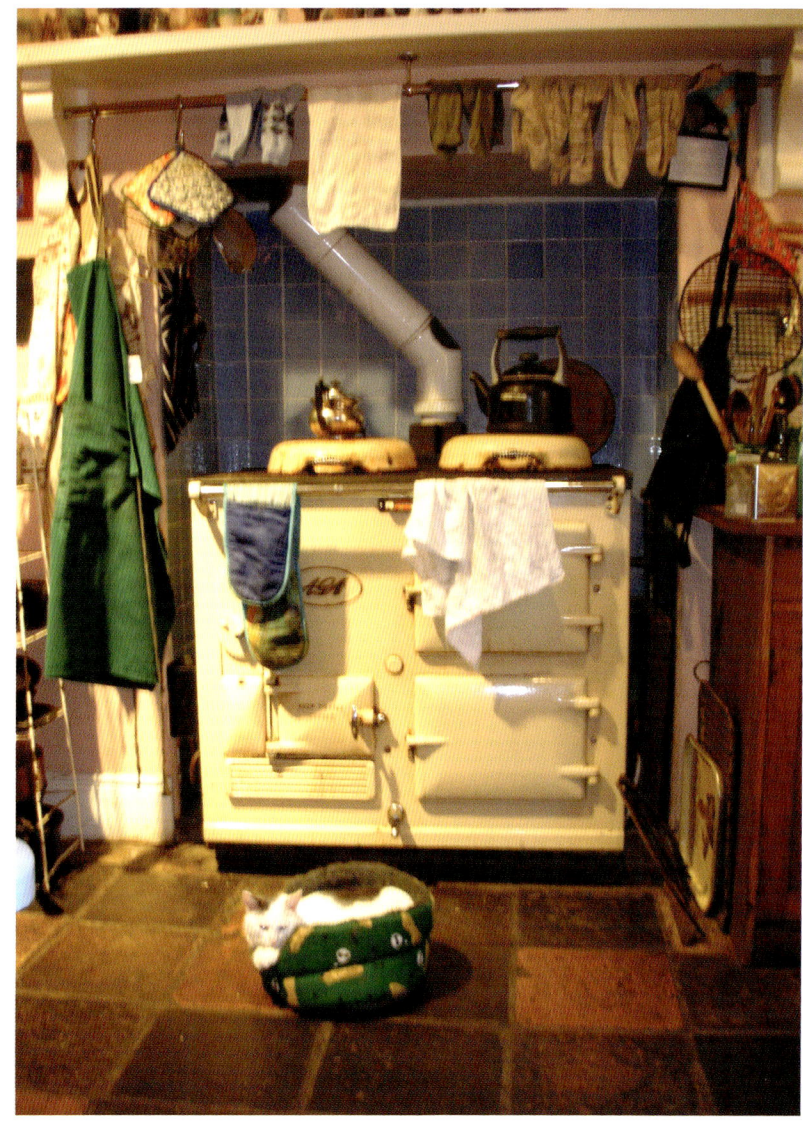
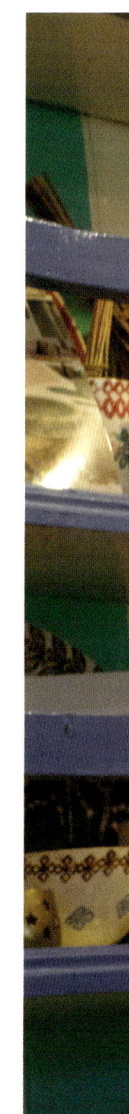

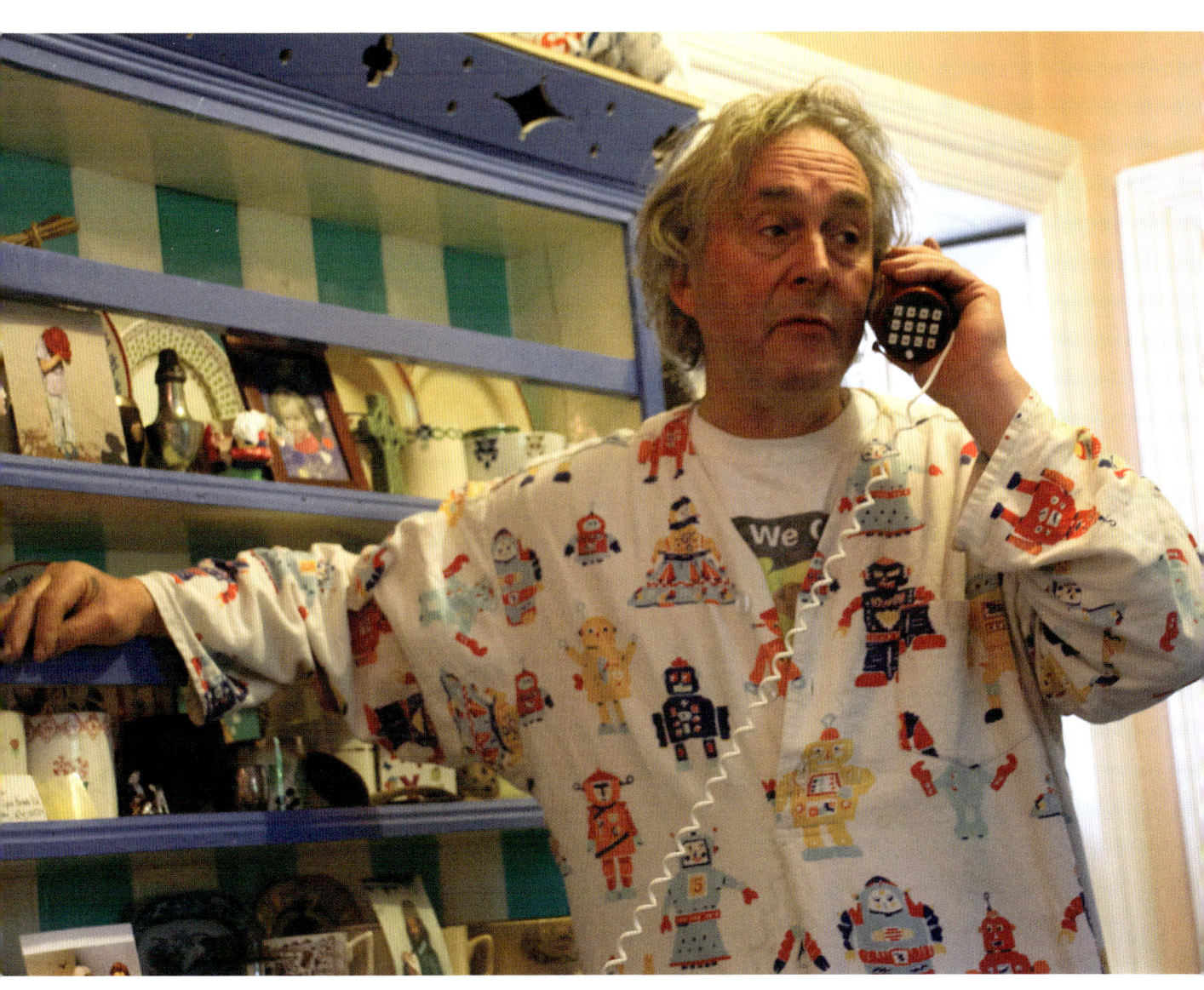

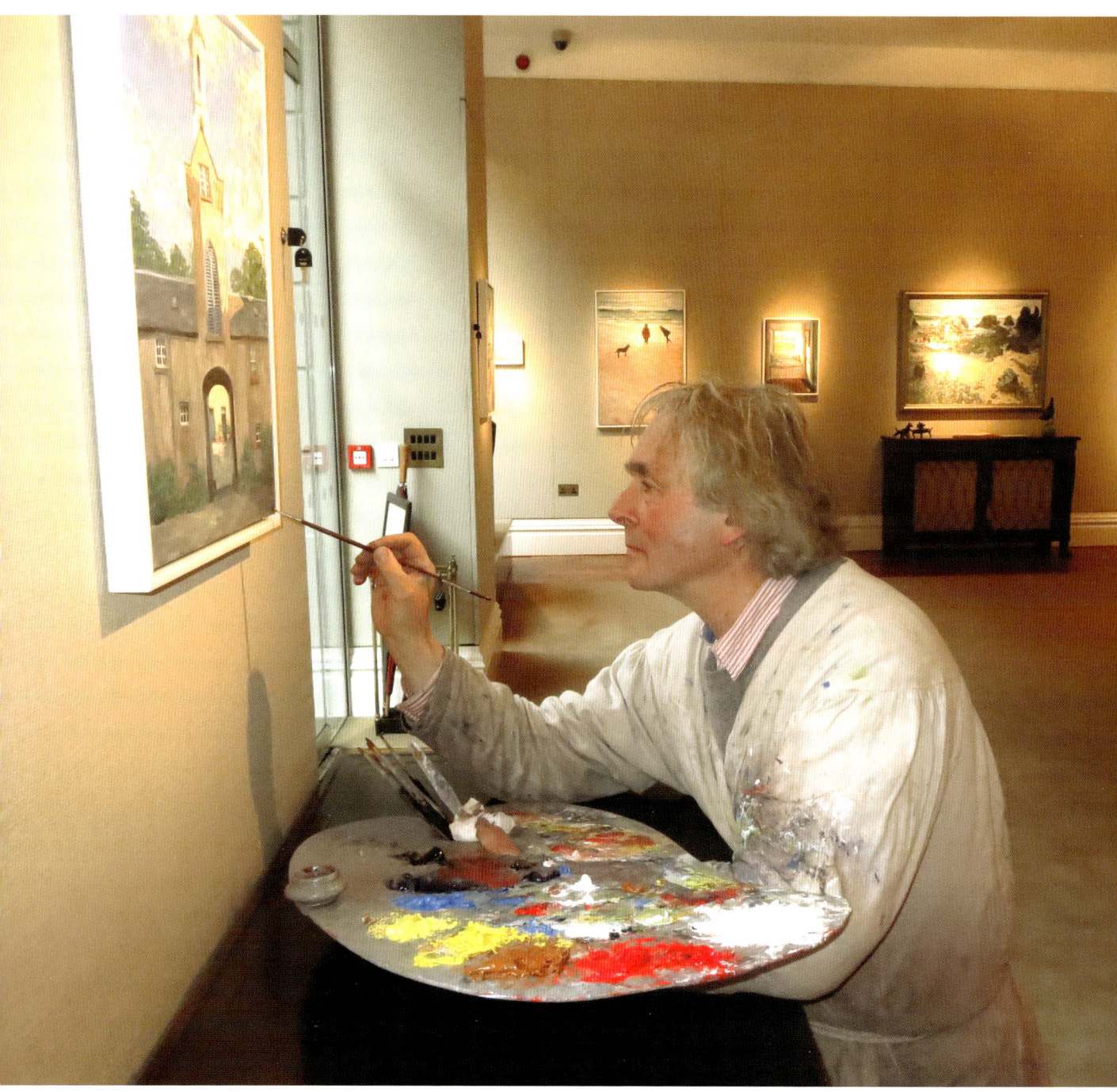

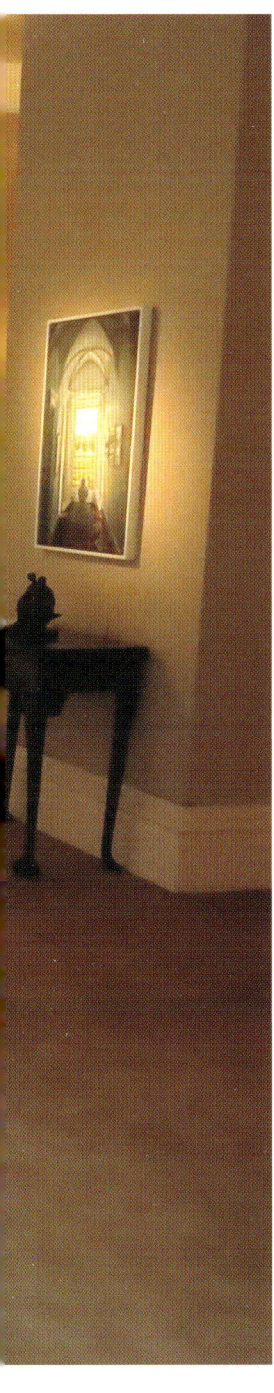
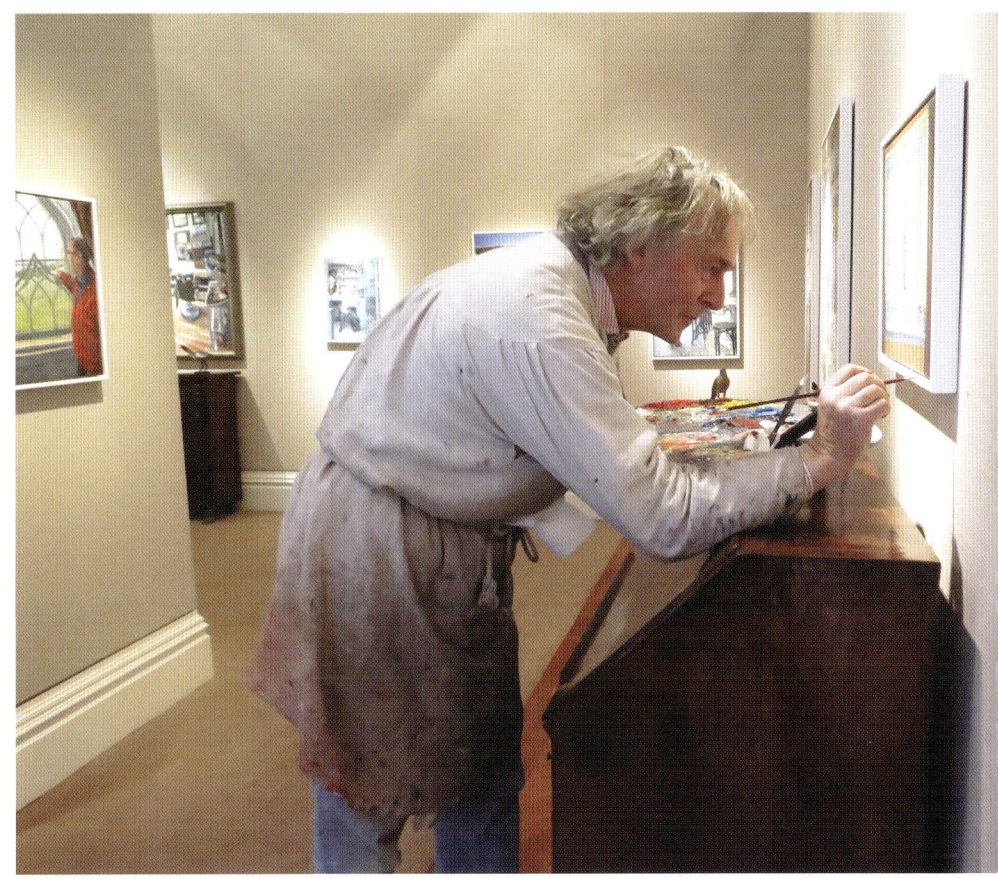

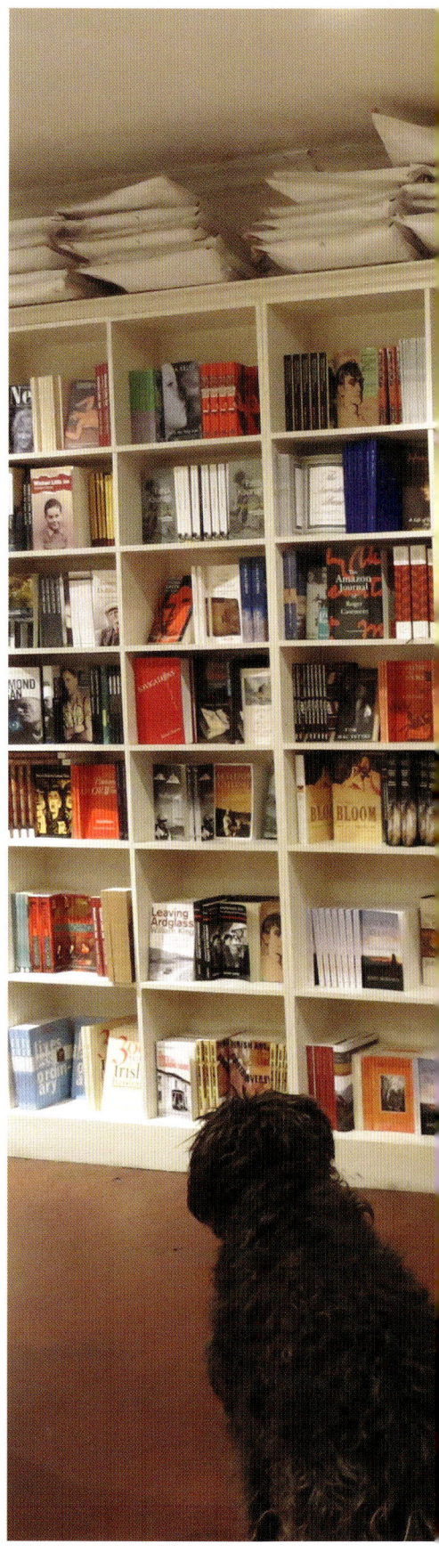

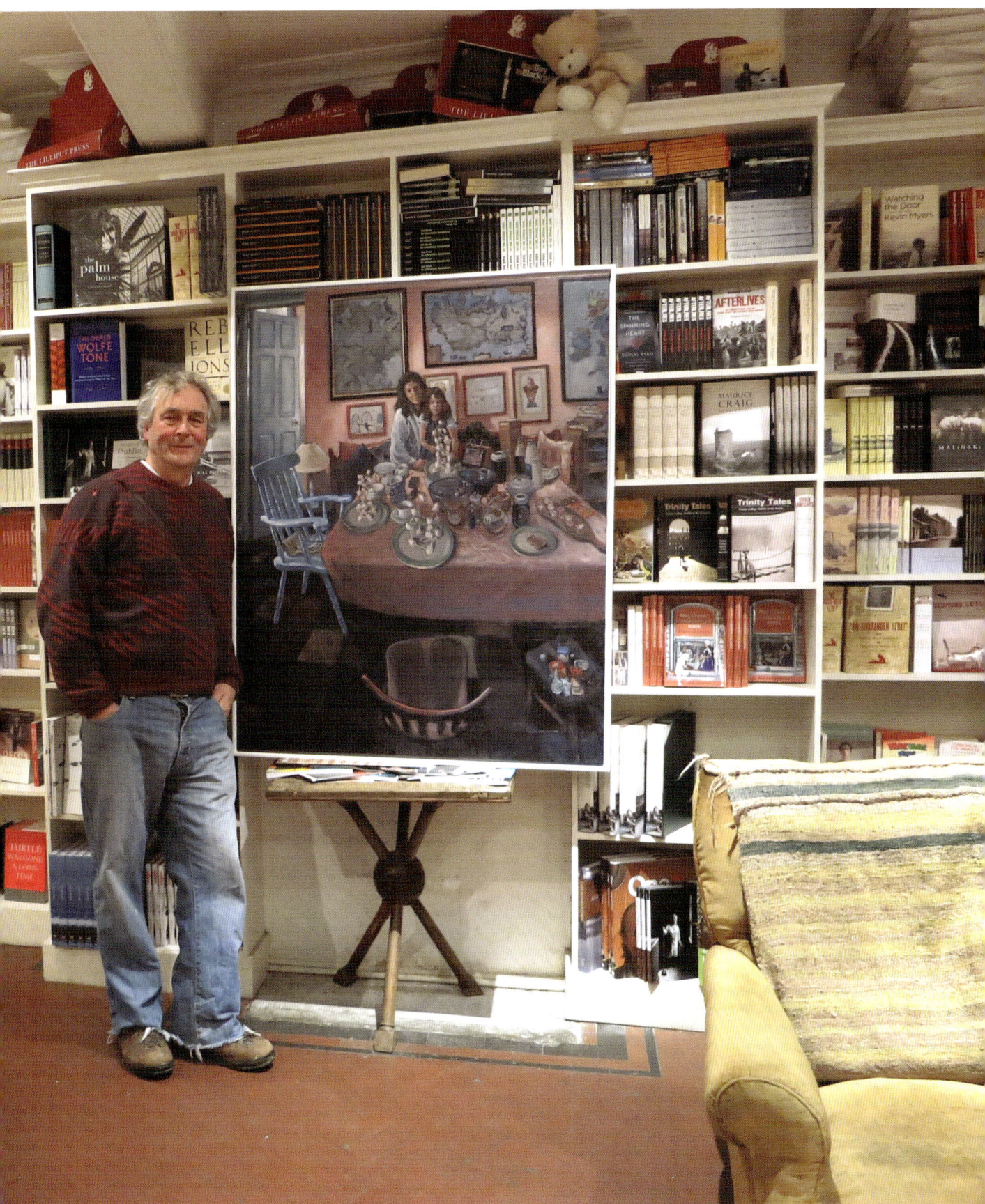

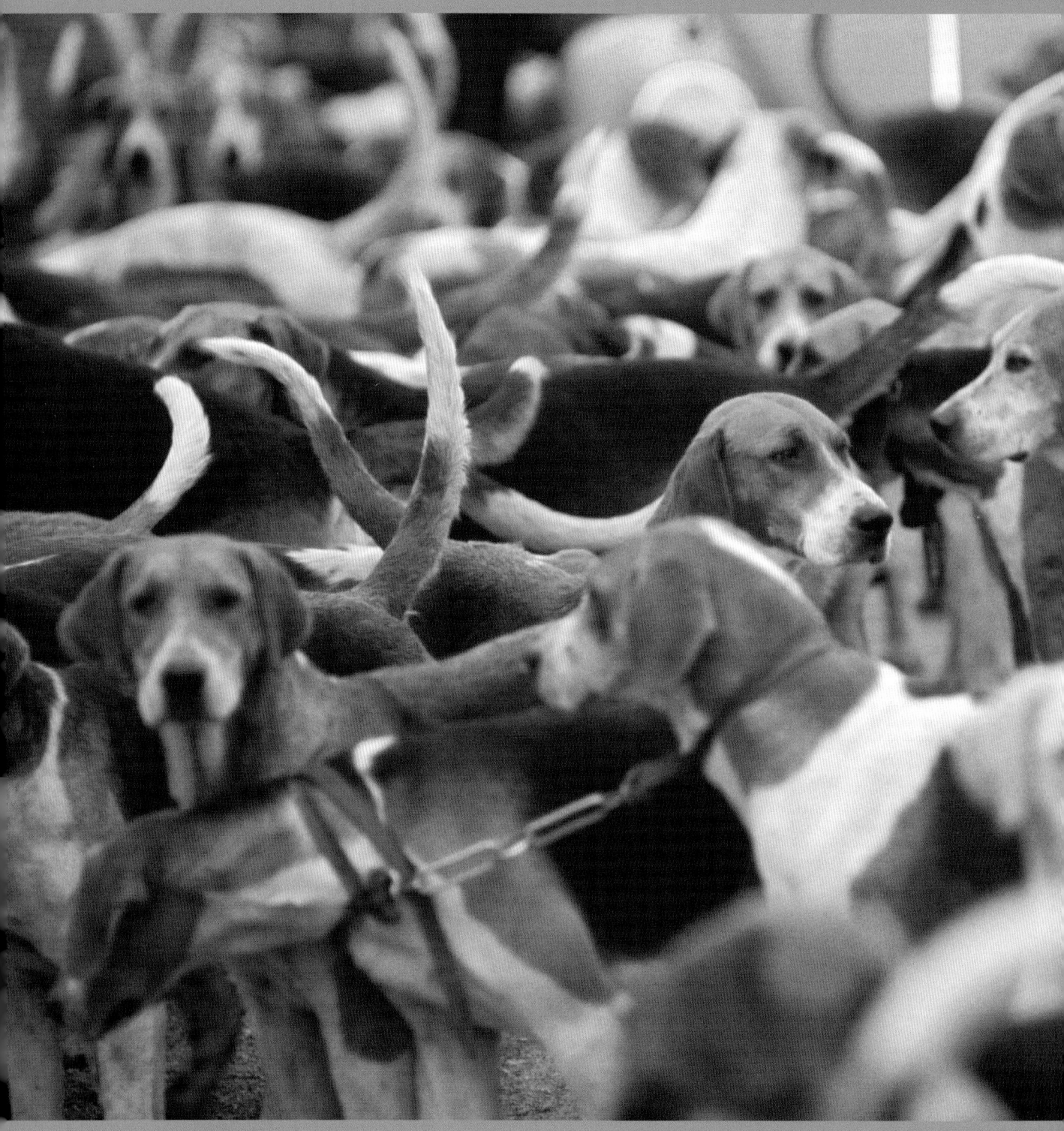

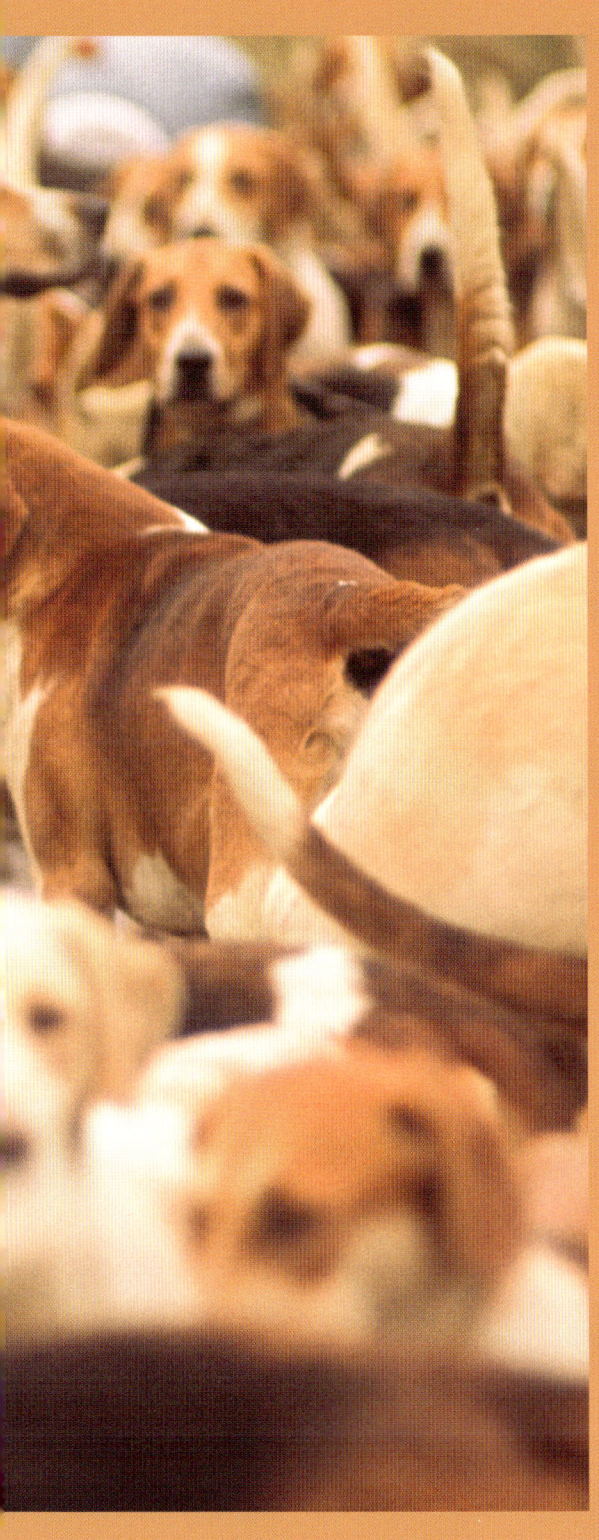

The Hunt

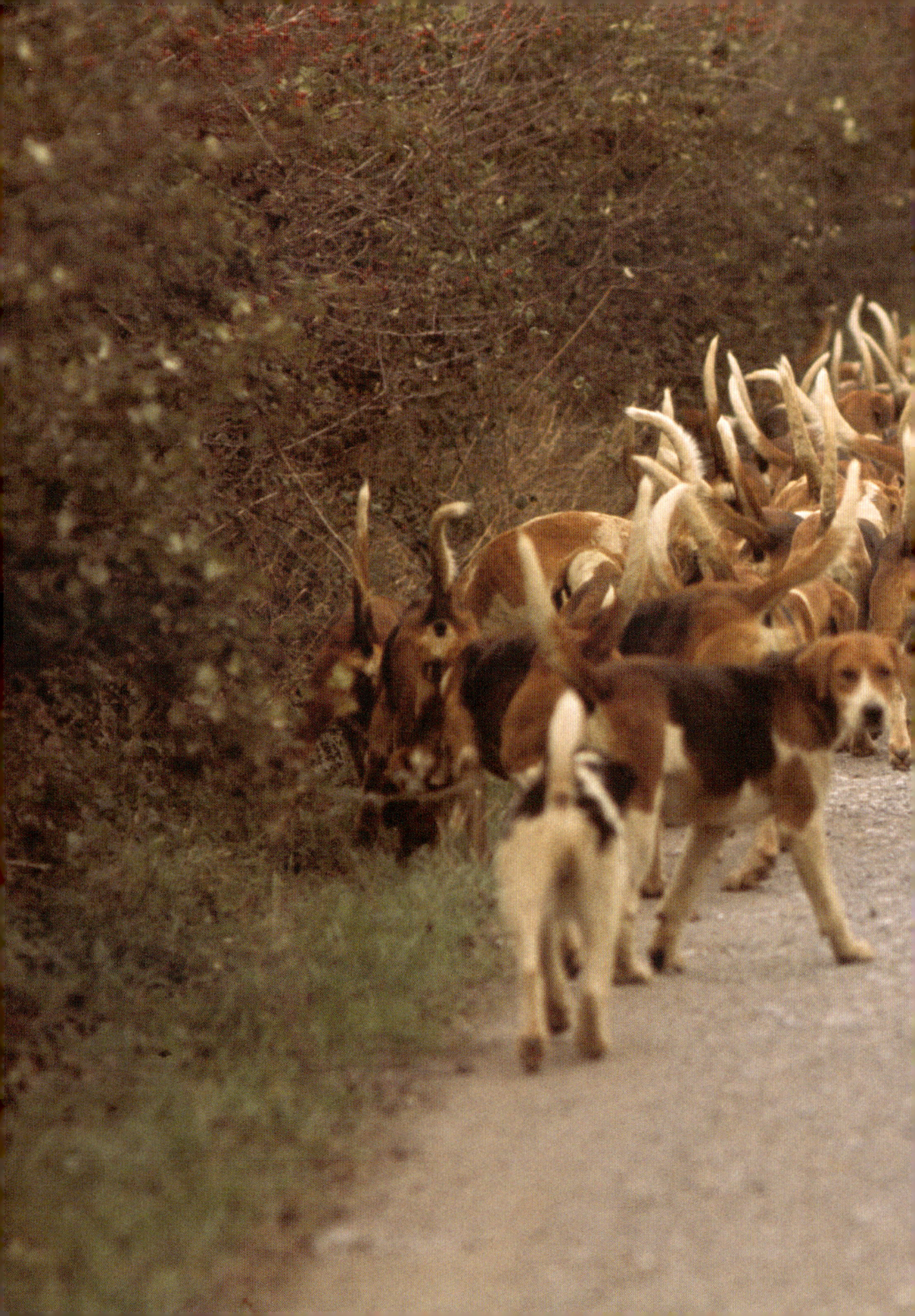

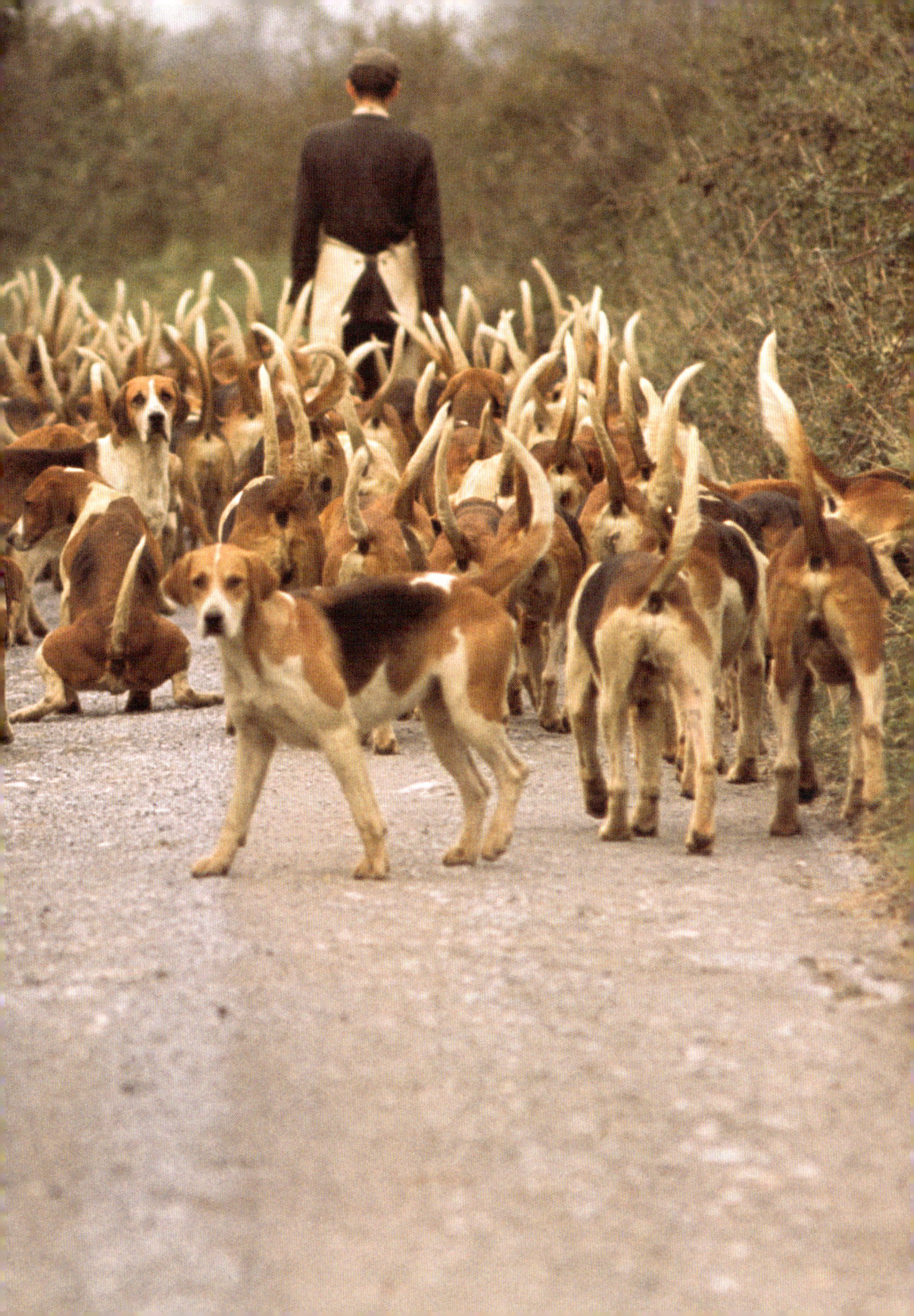

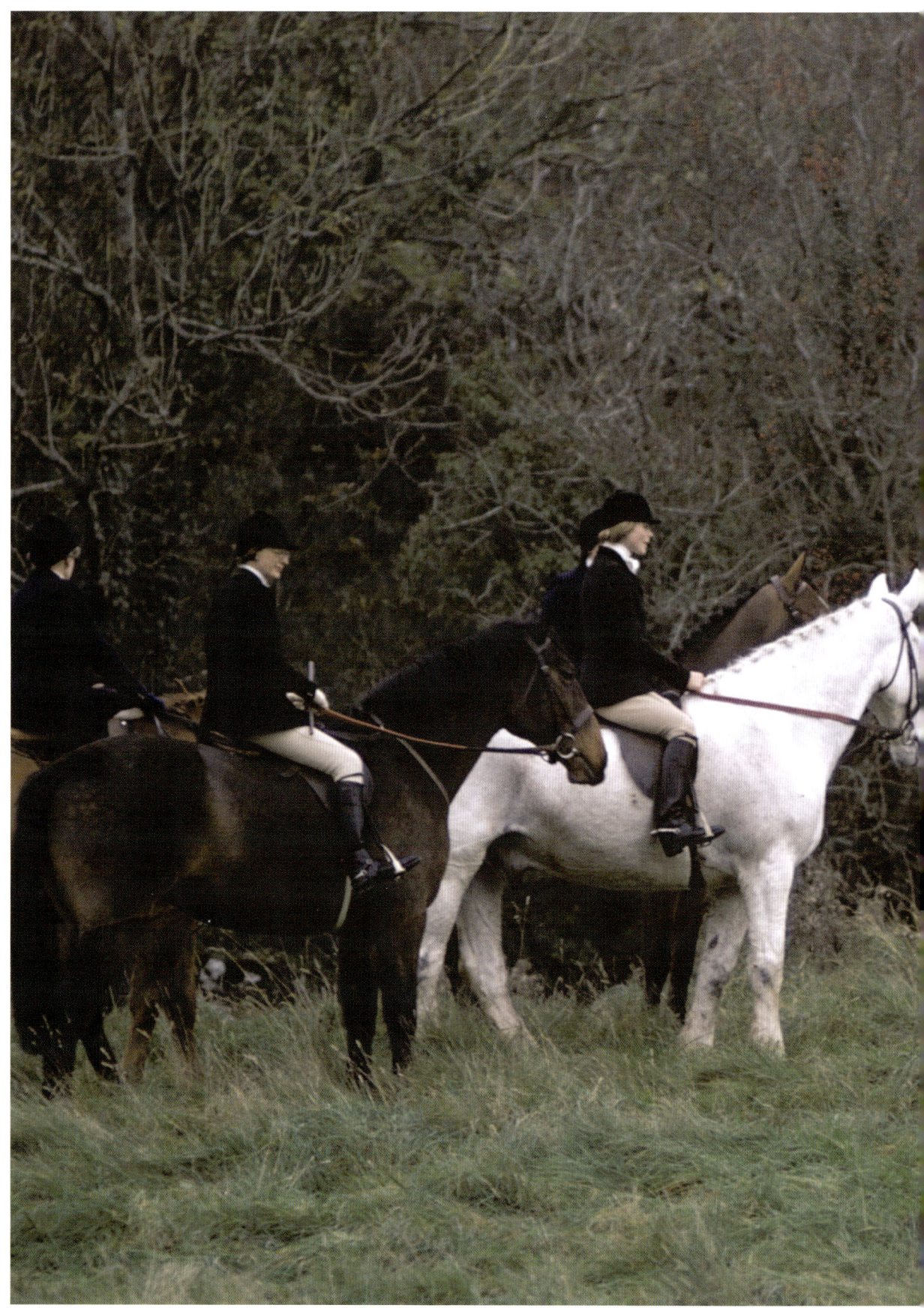

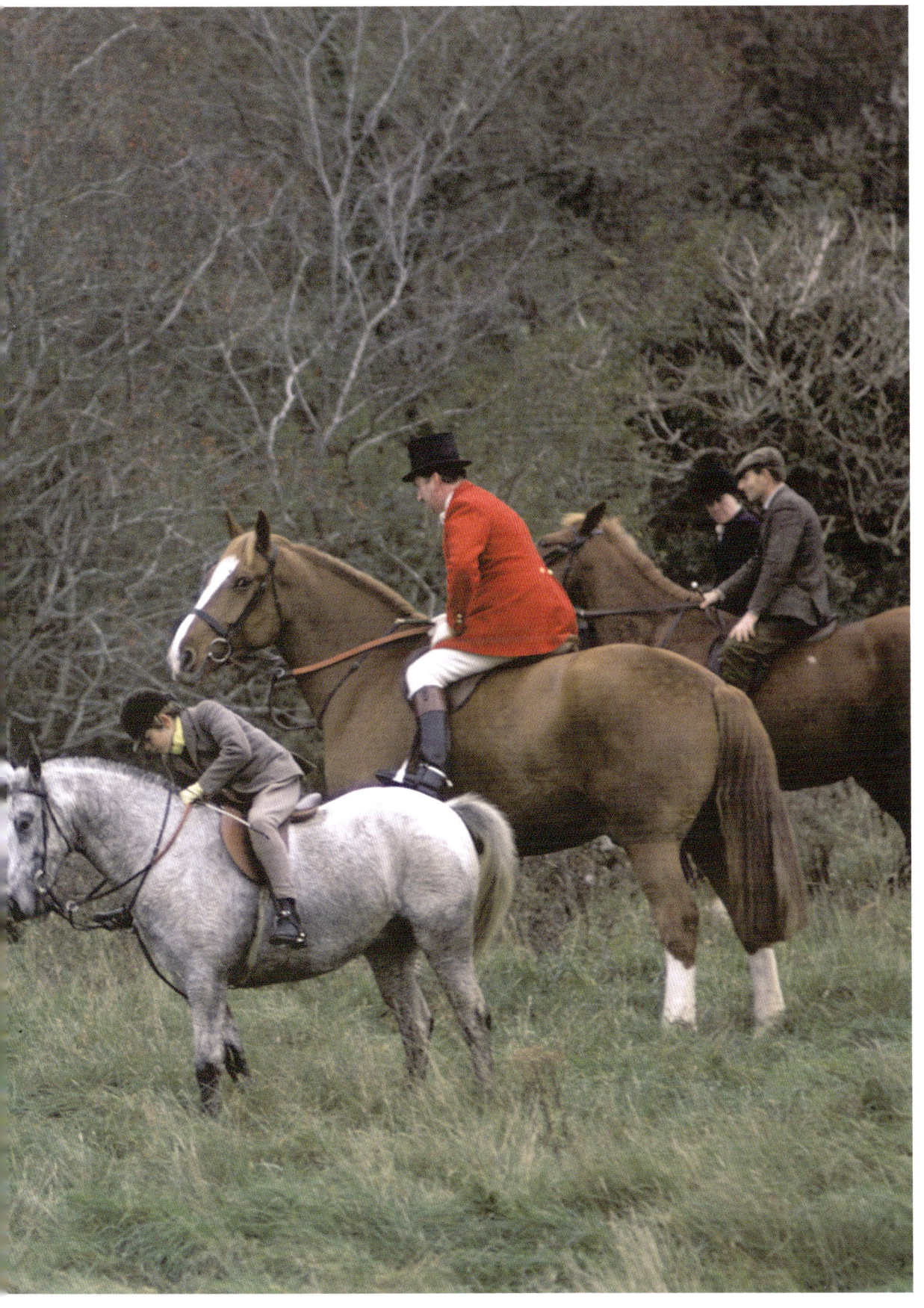

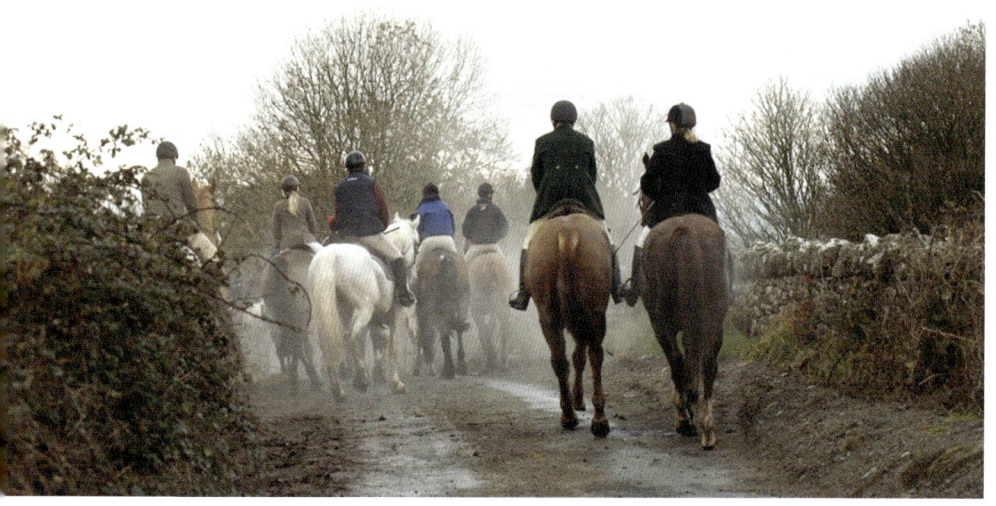
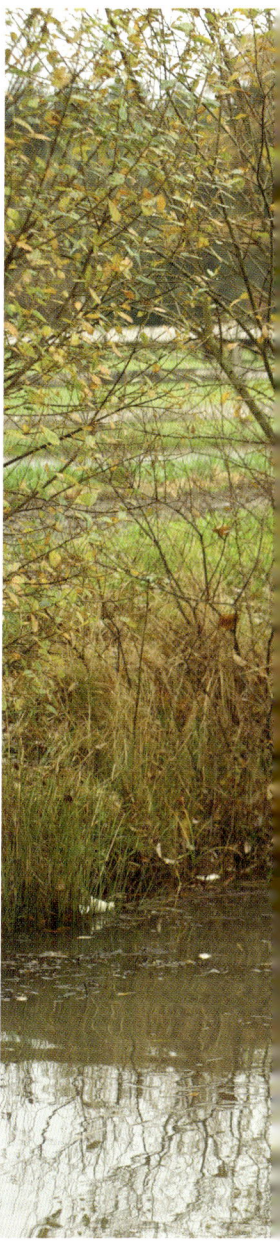

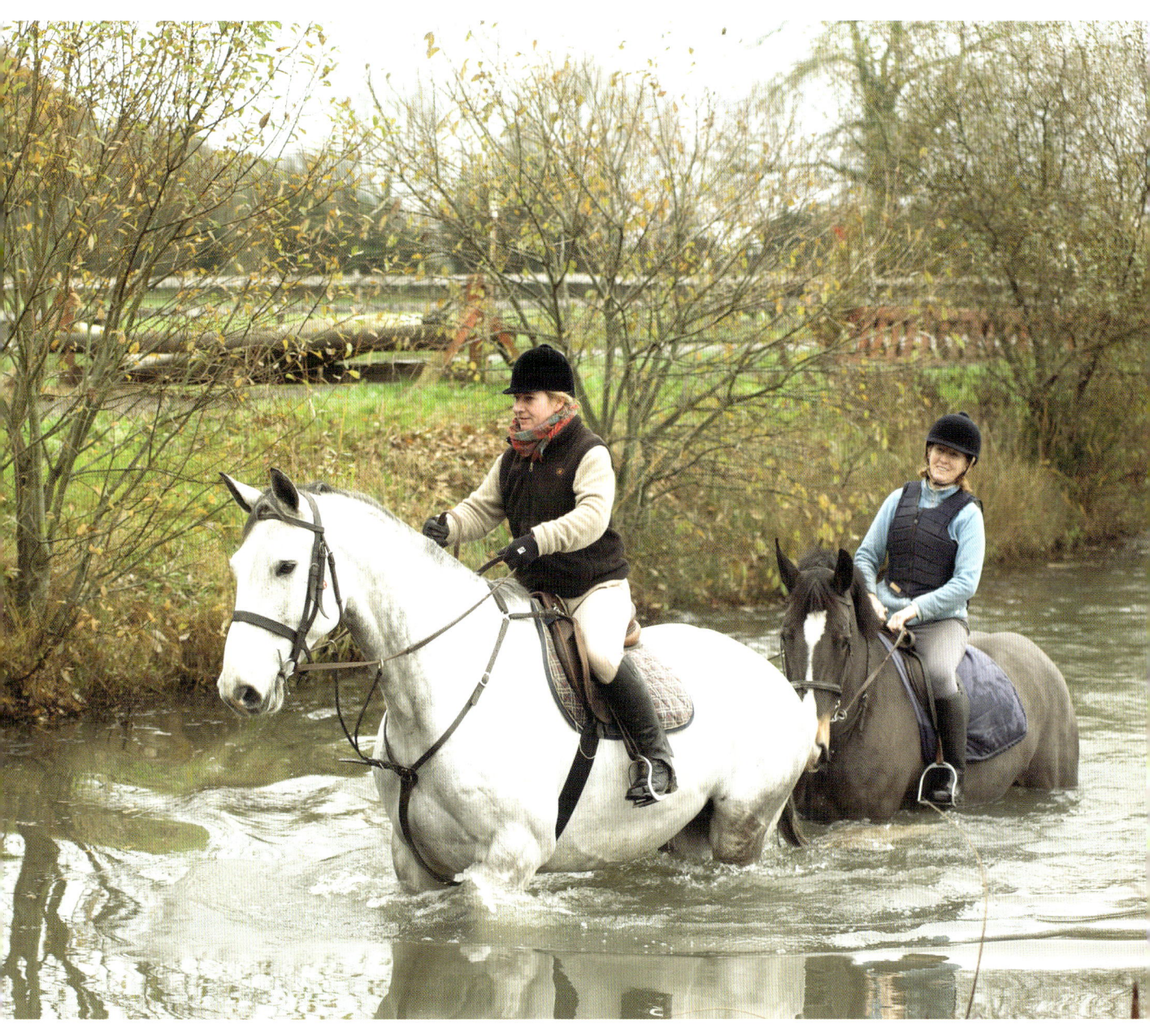

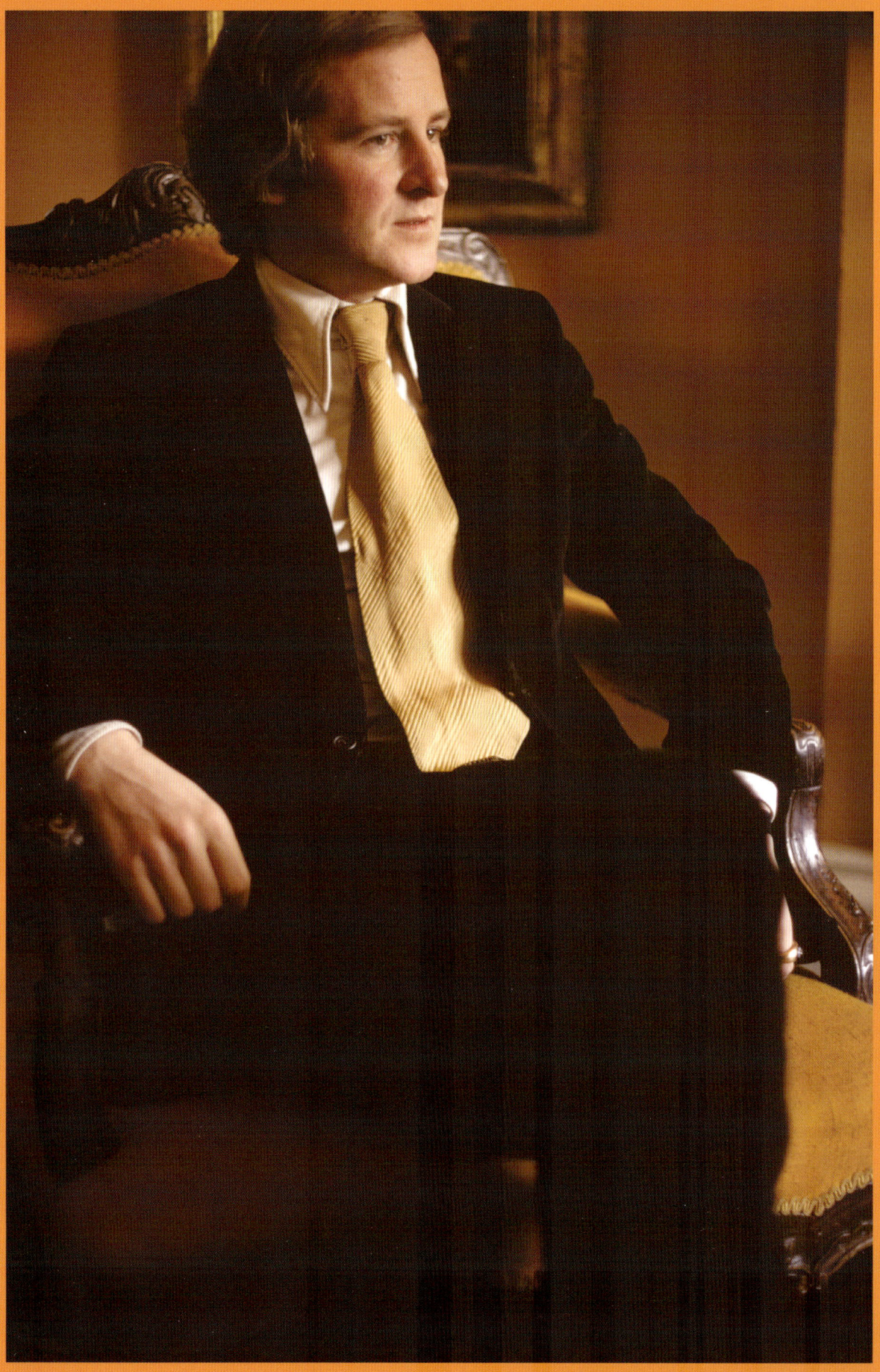

Desmond FitzGerald

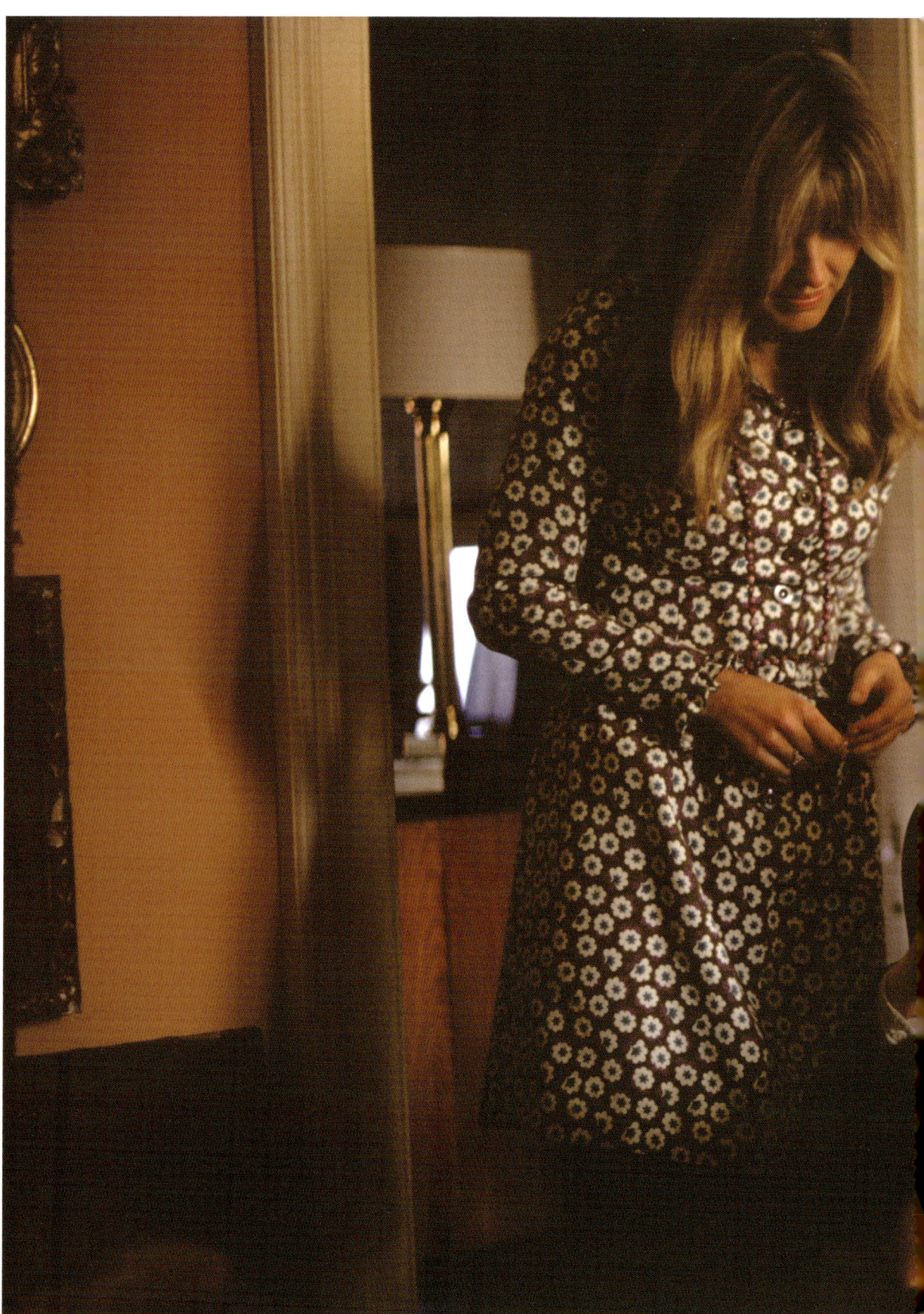

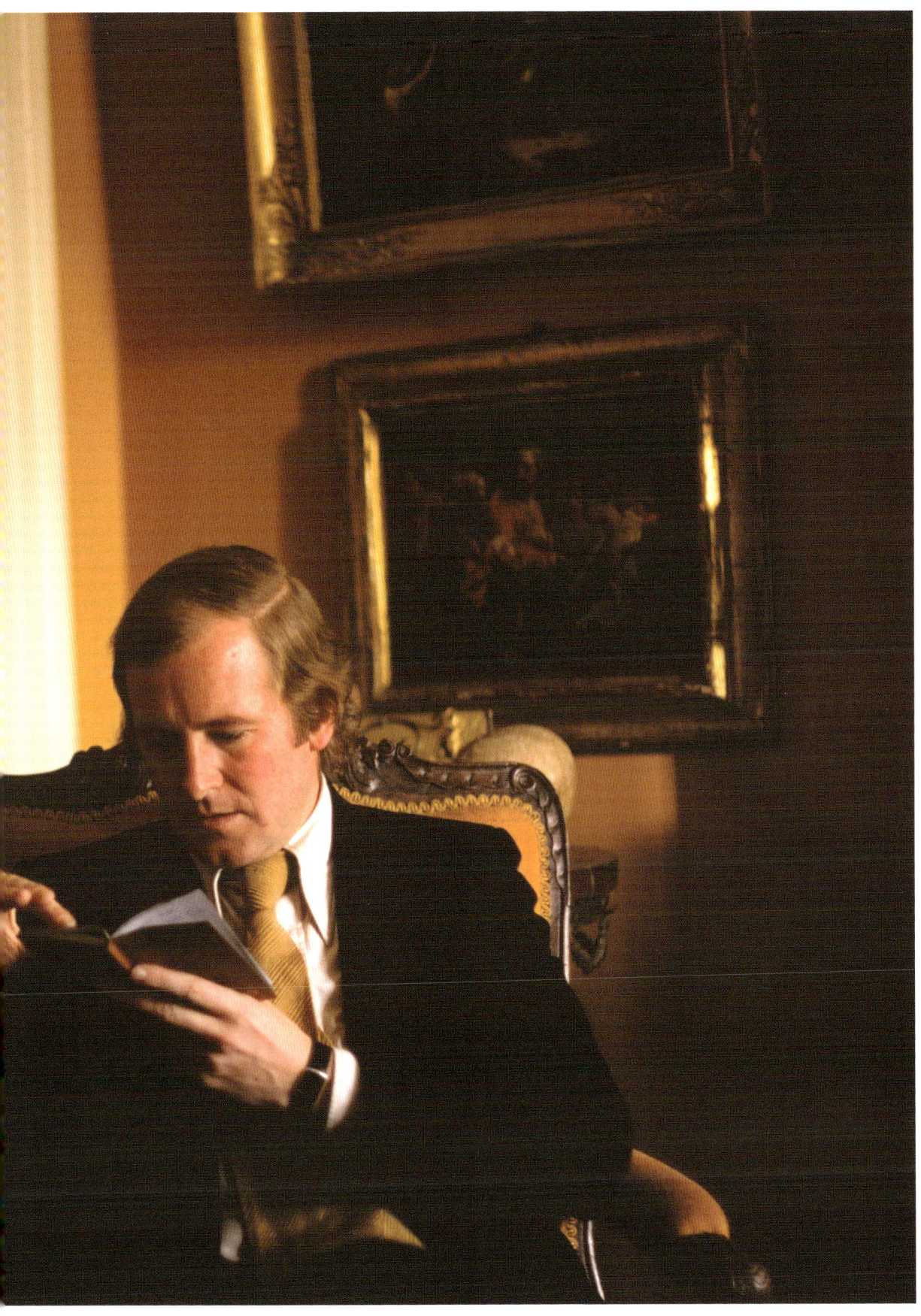

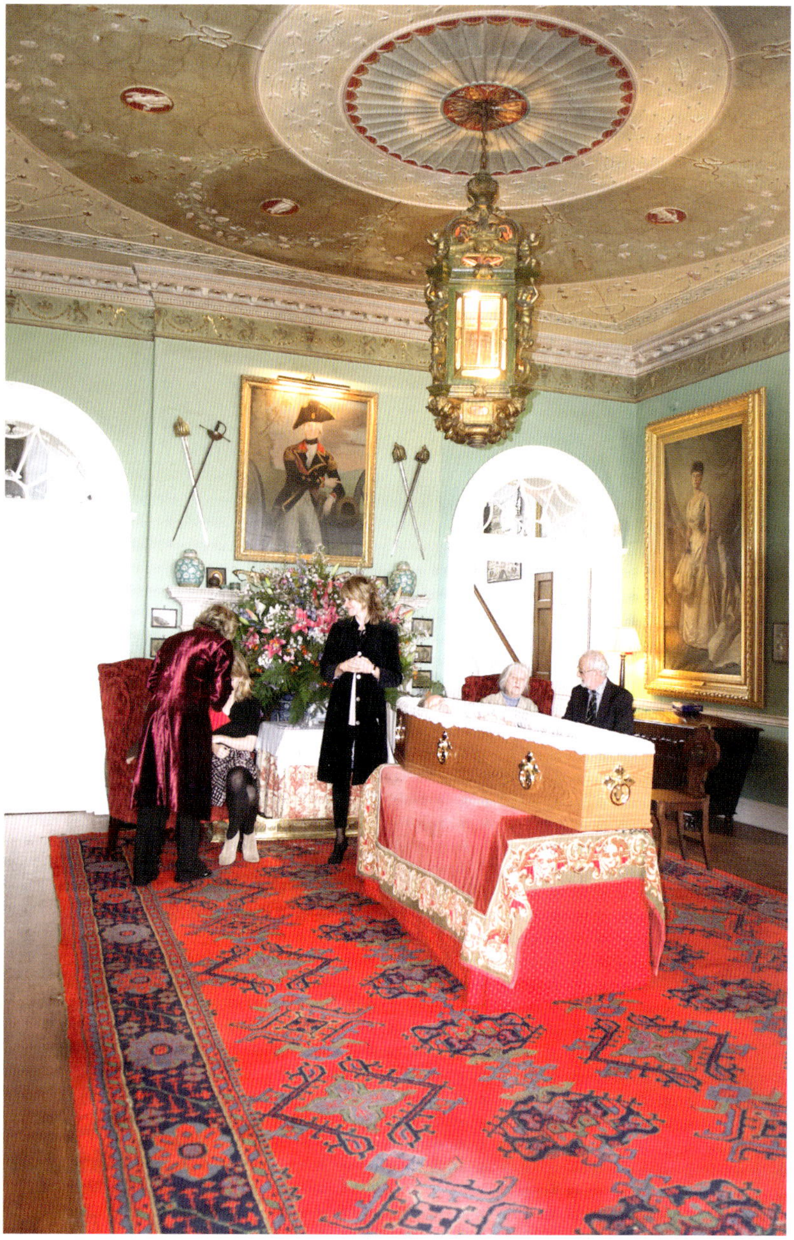

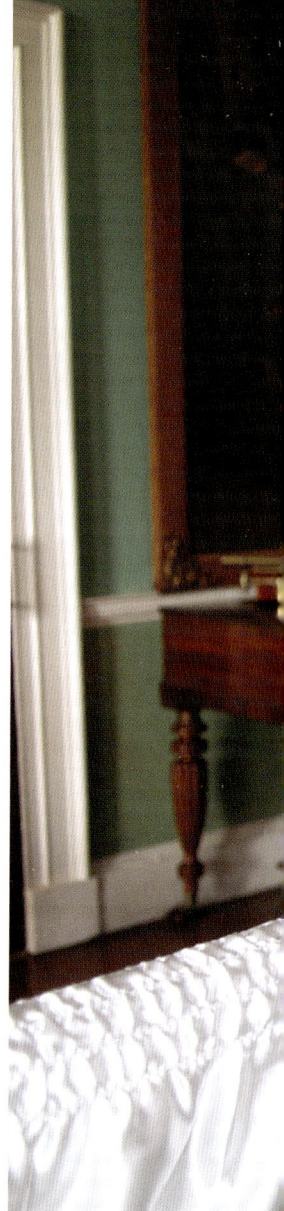

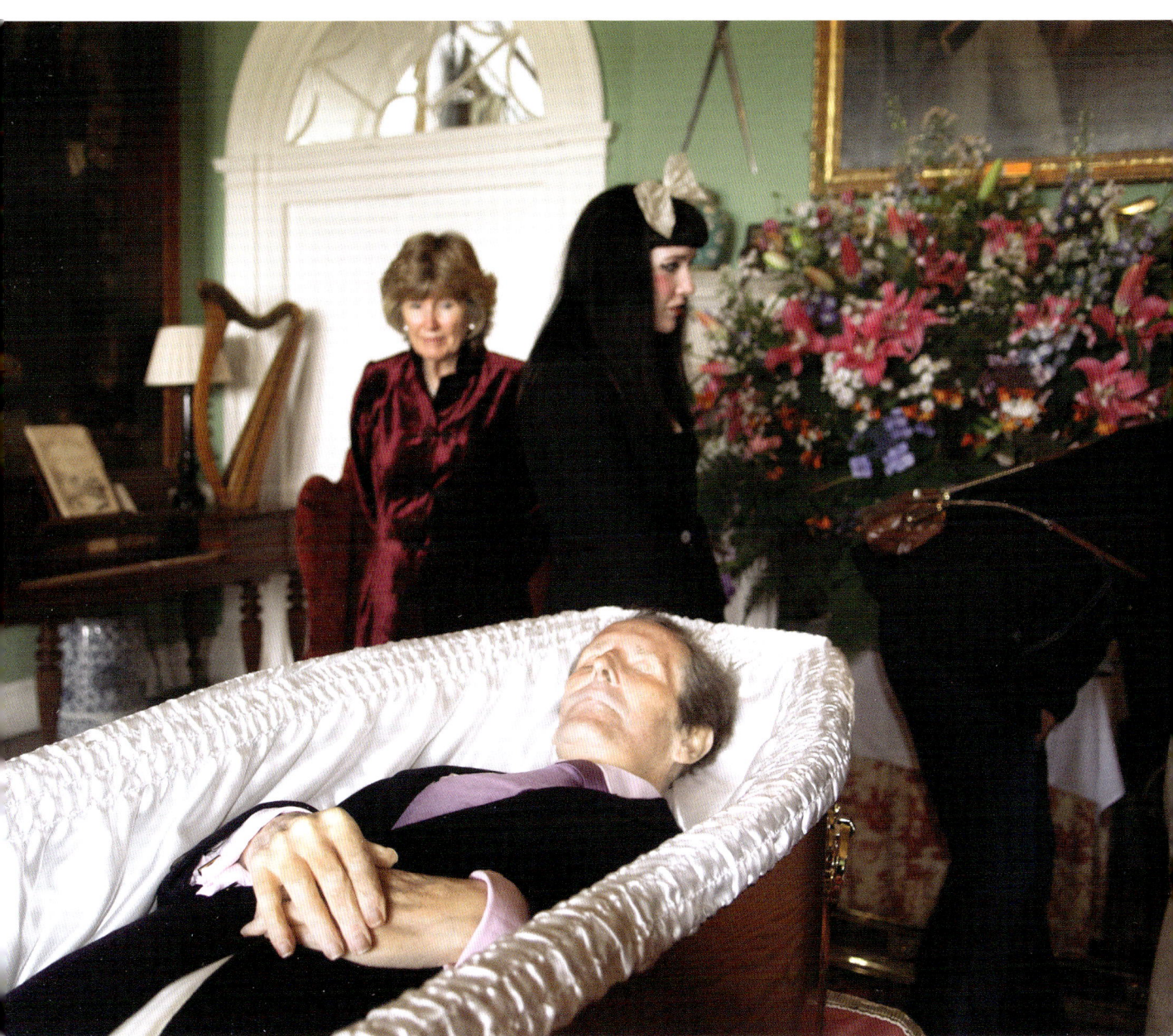

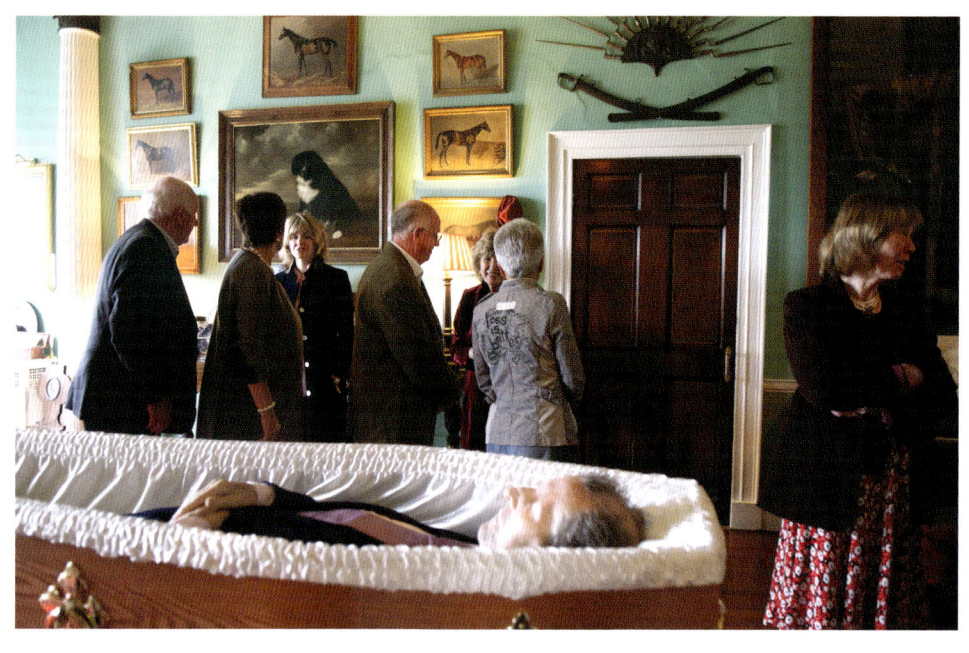

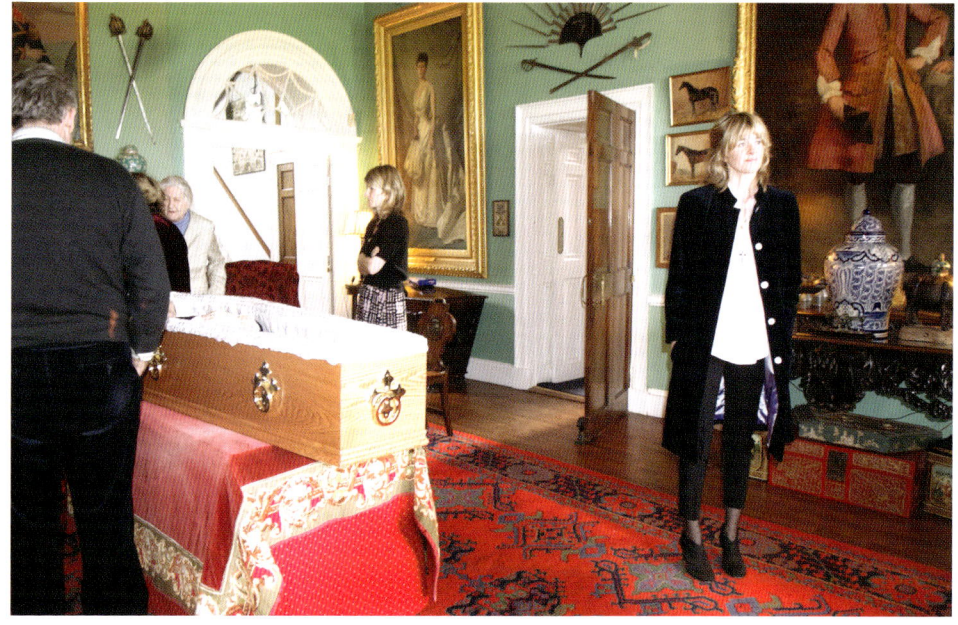

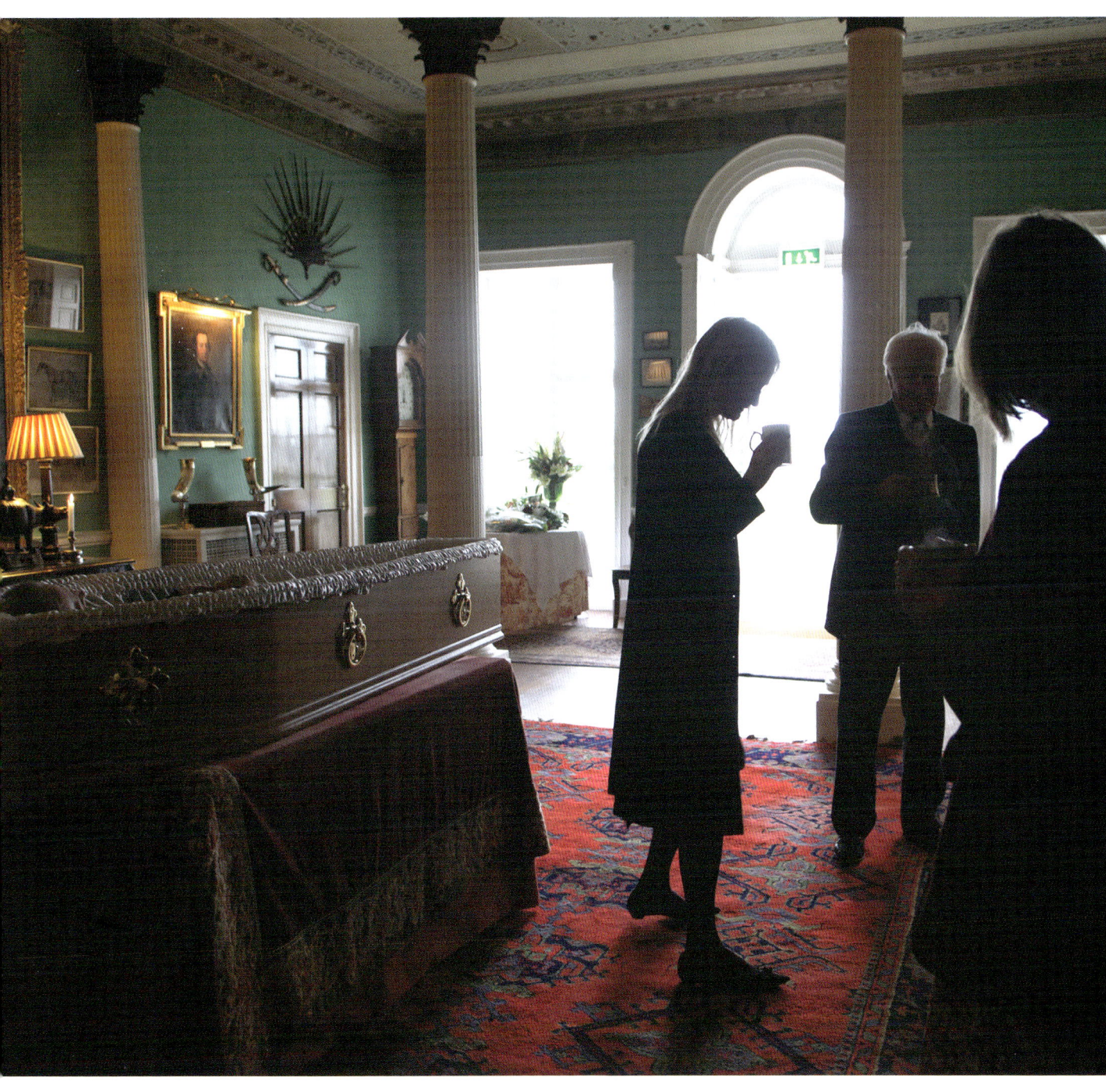

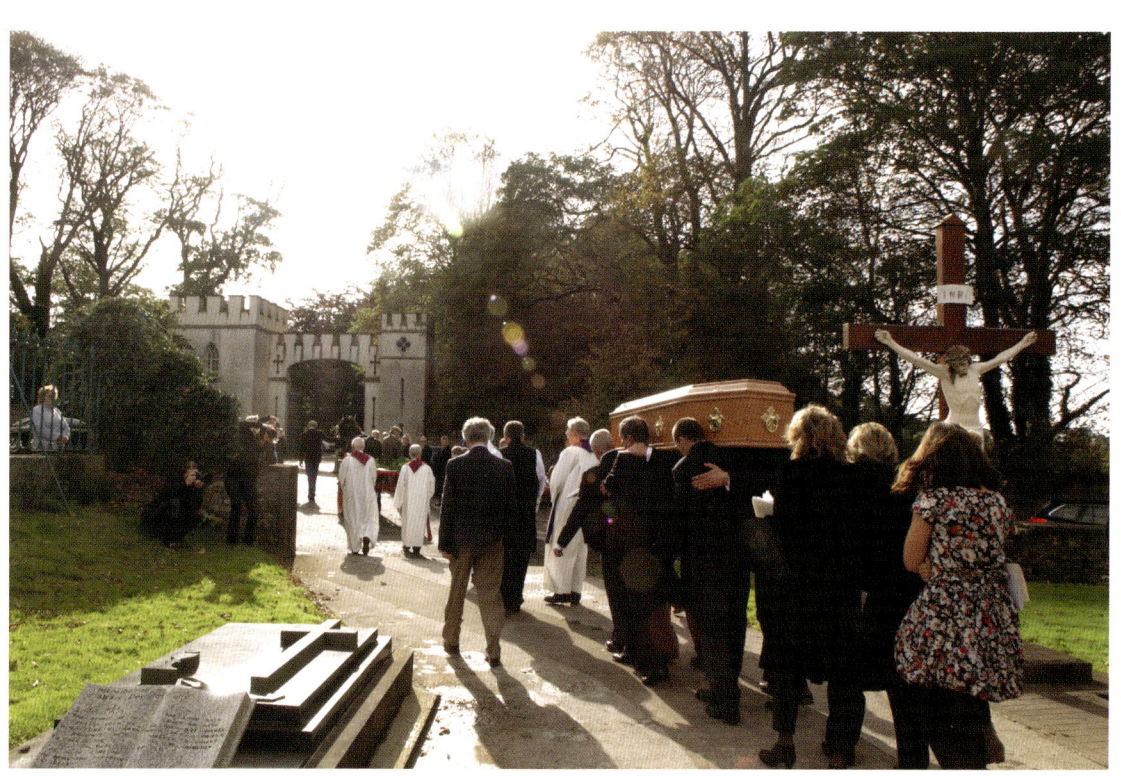

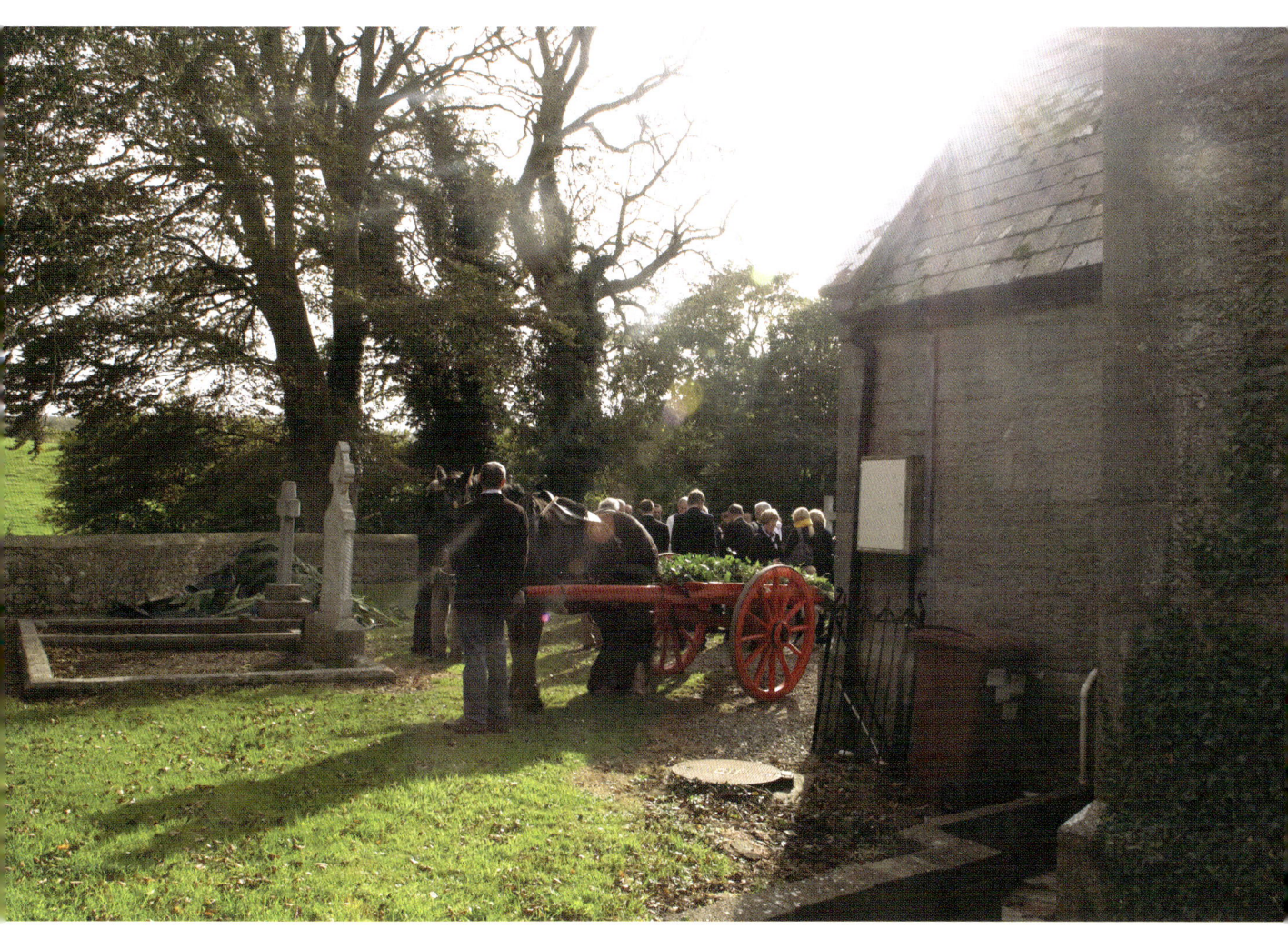

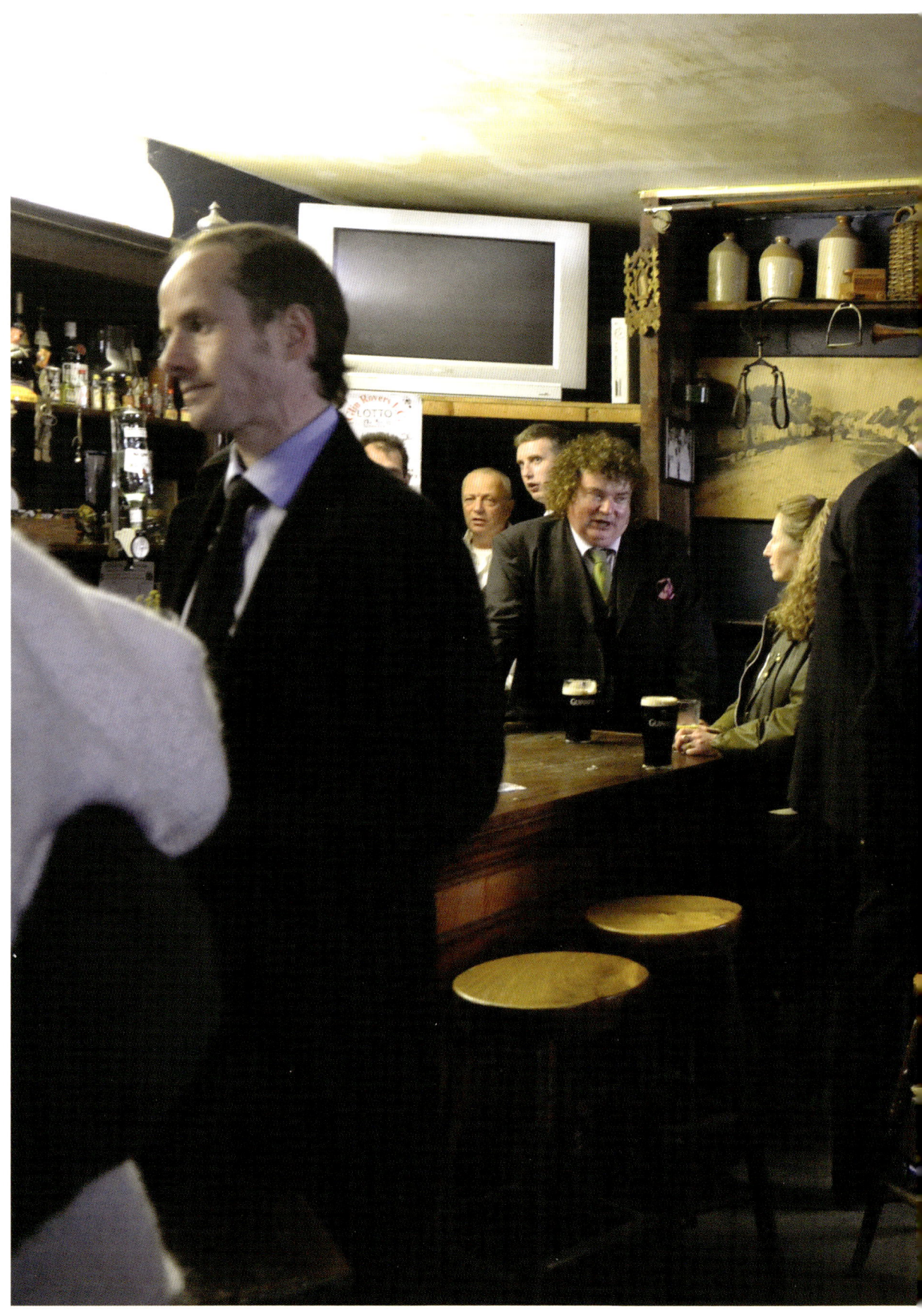

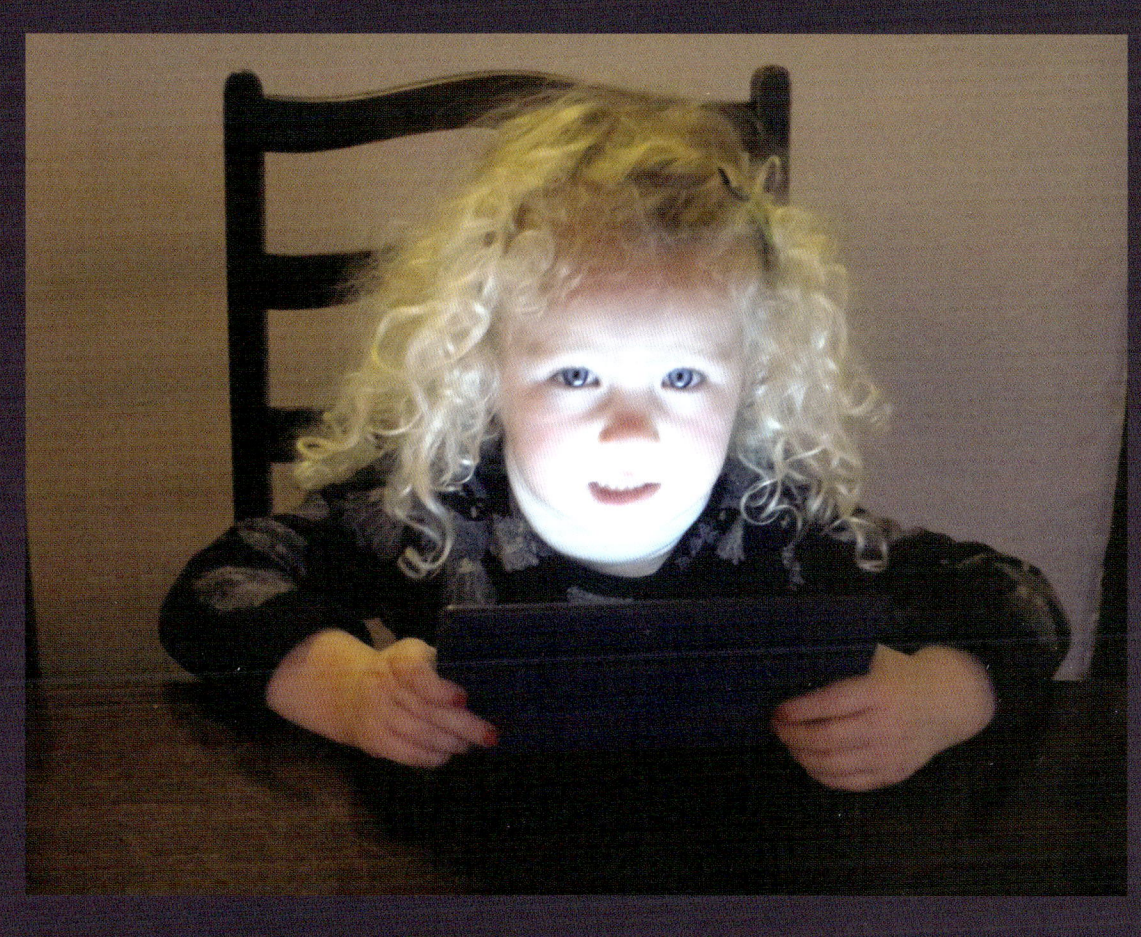

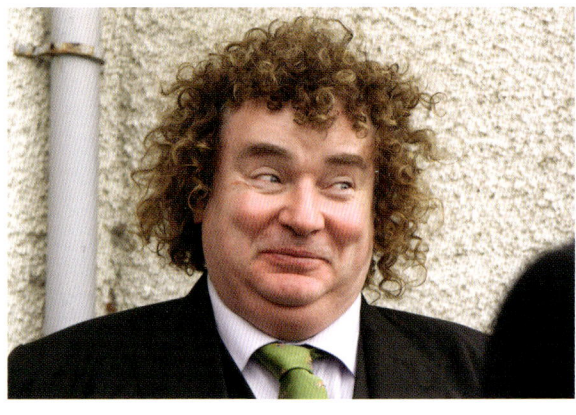
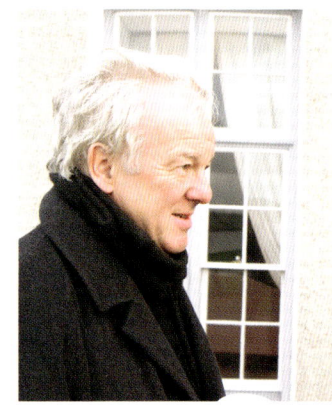
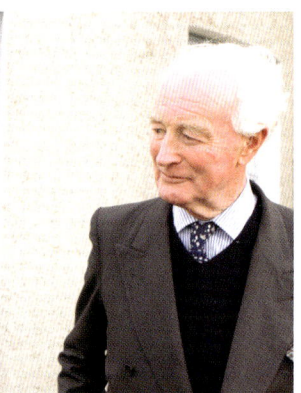
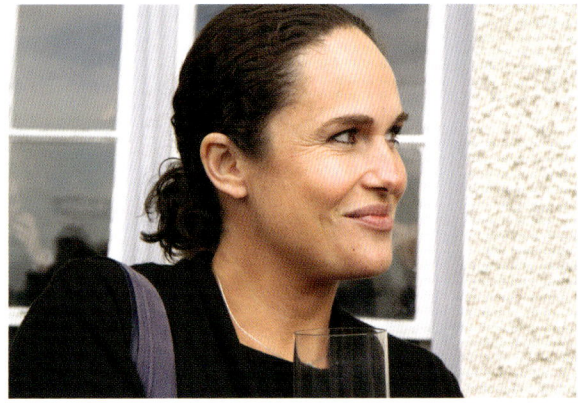
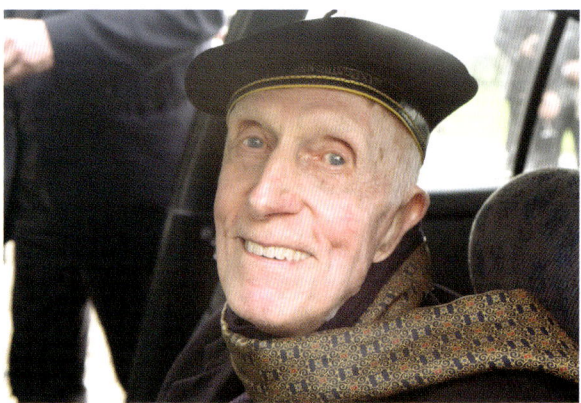

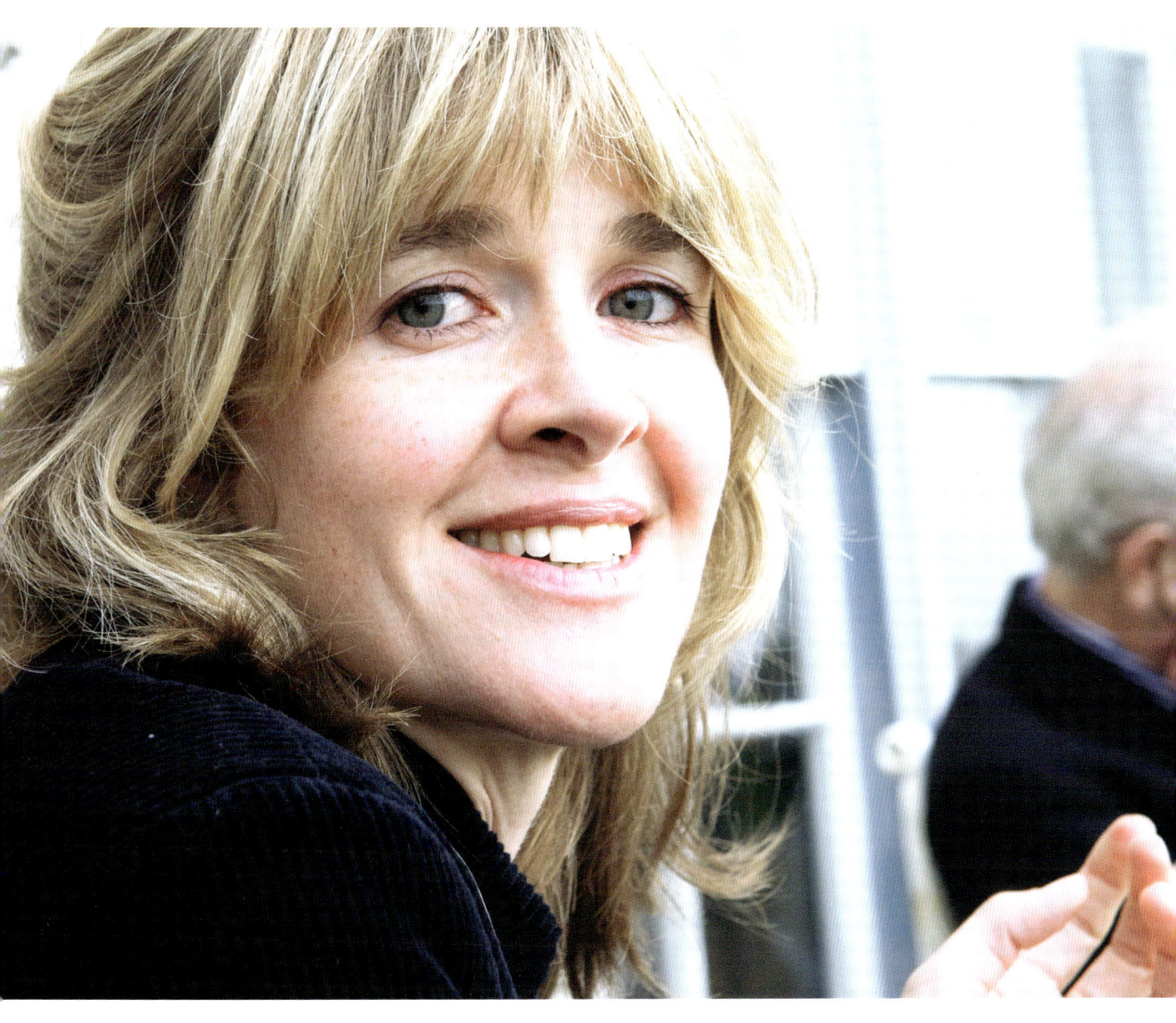

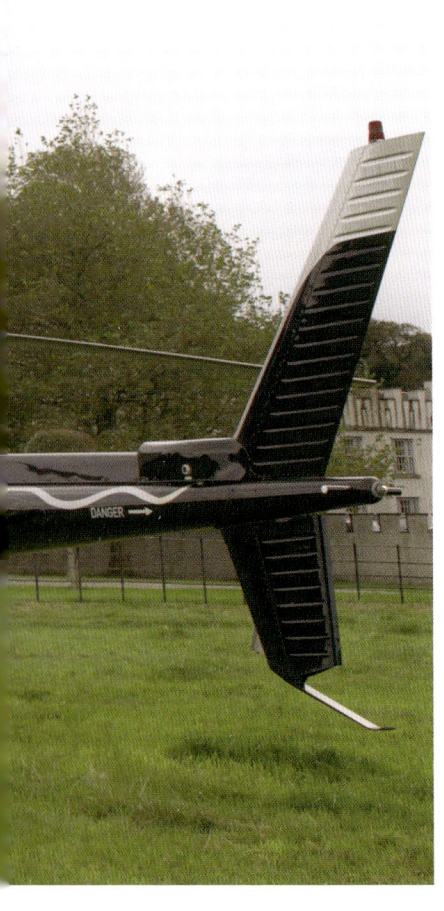
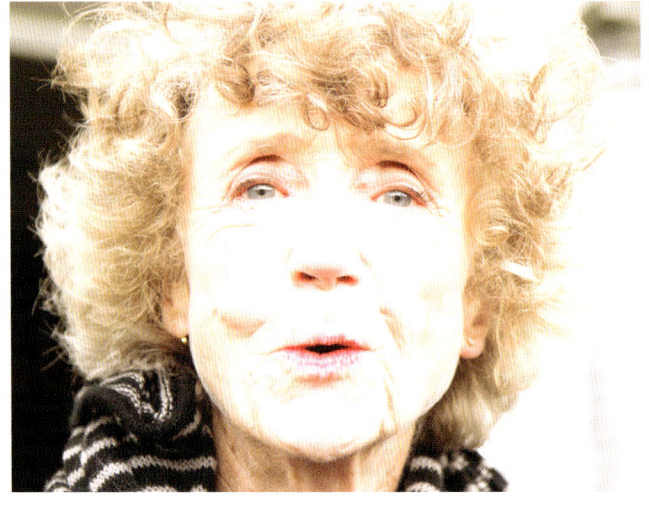

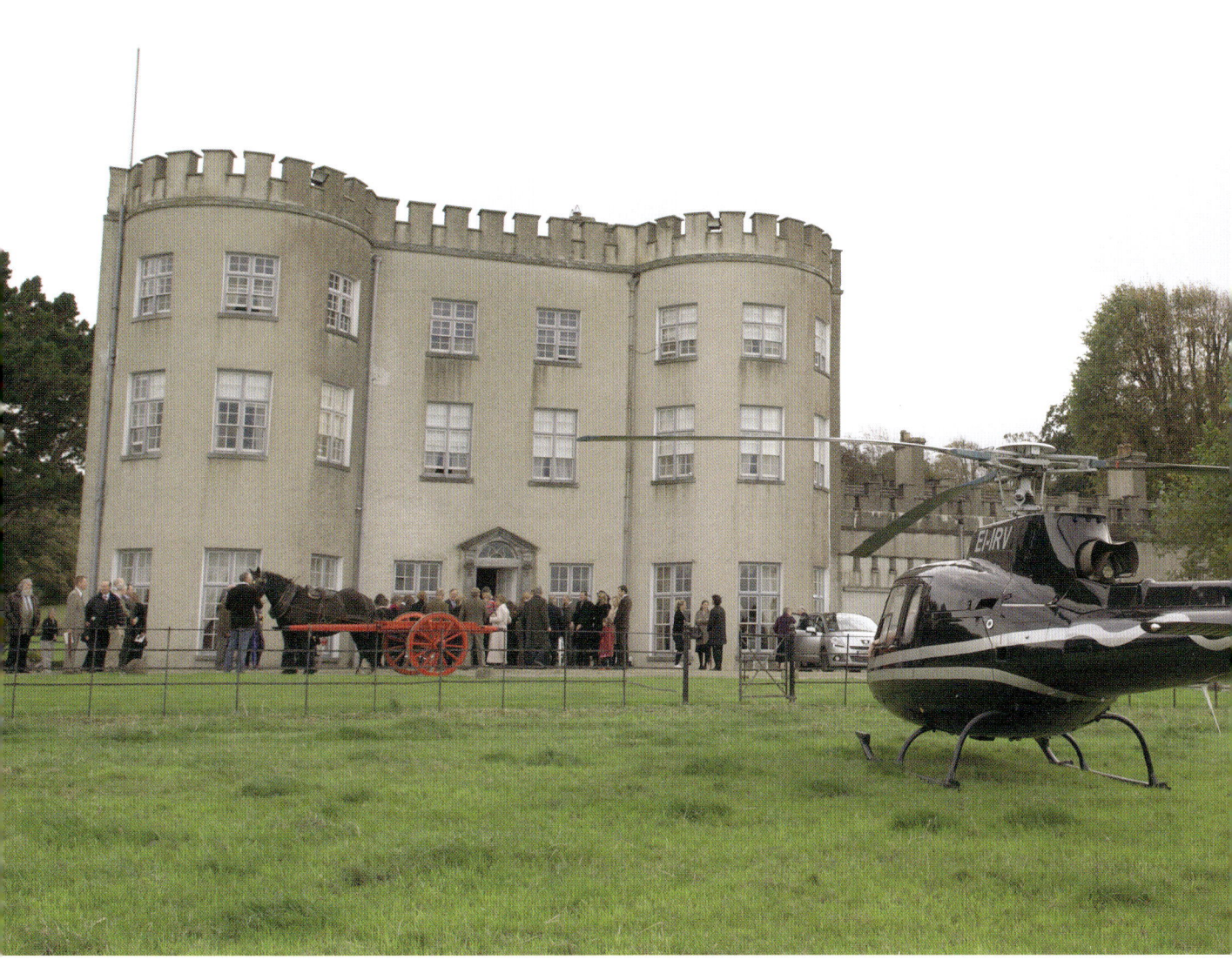

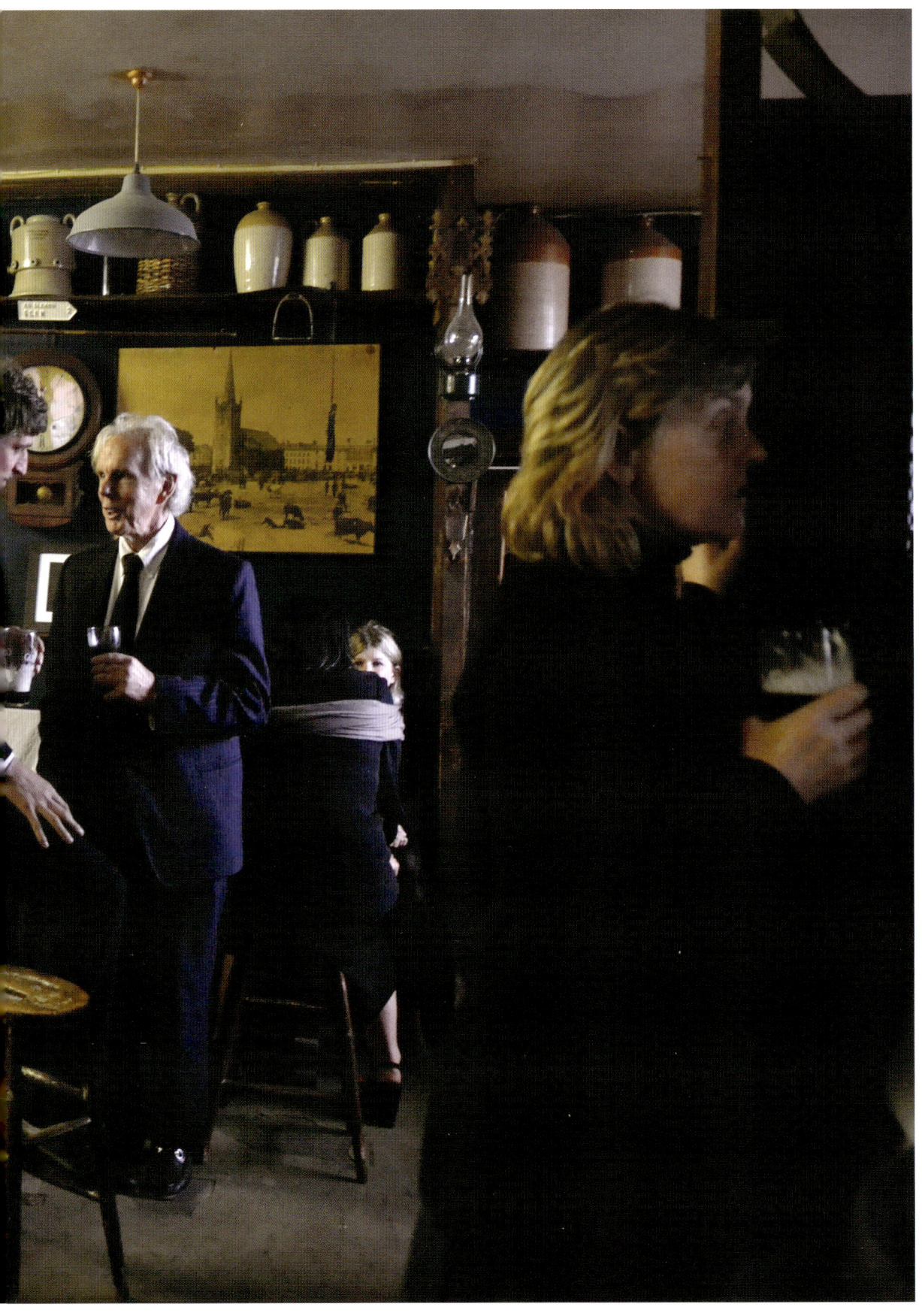

Coda

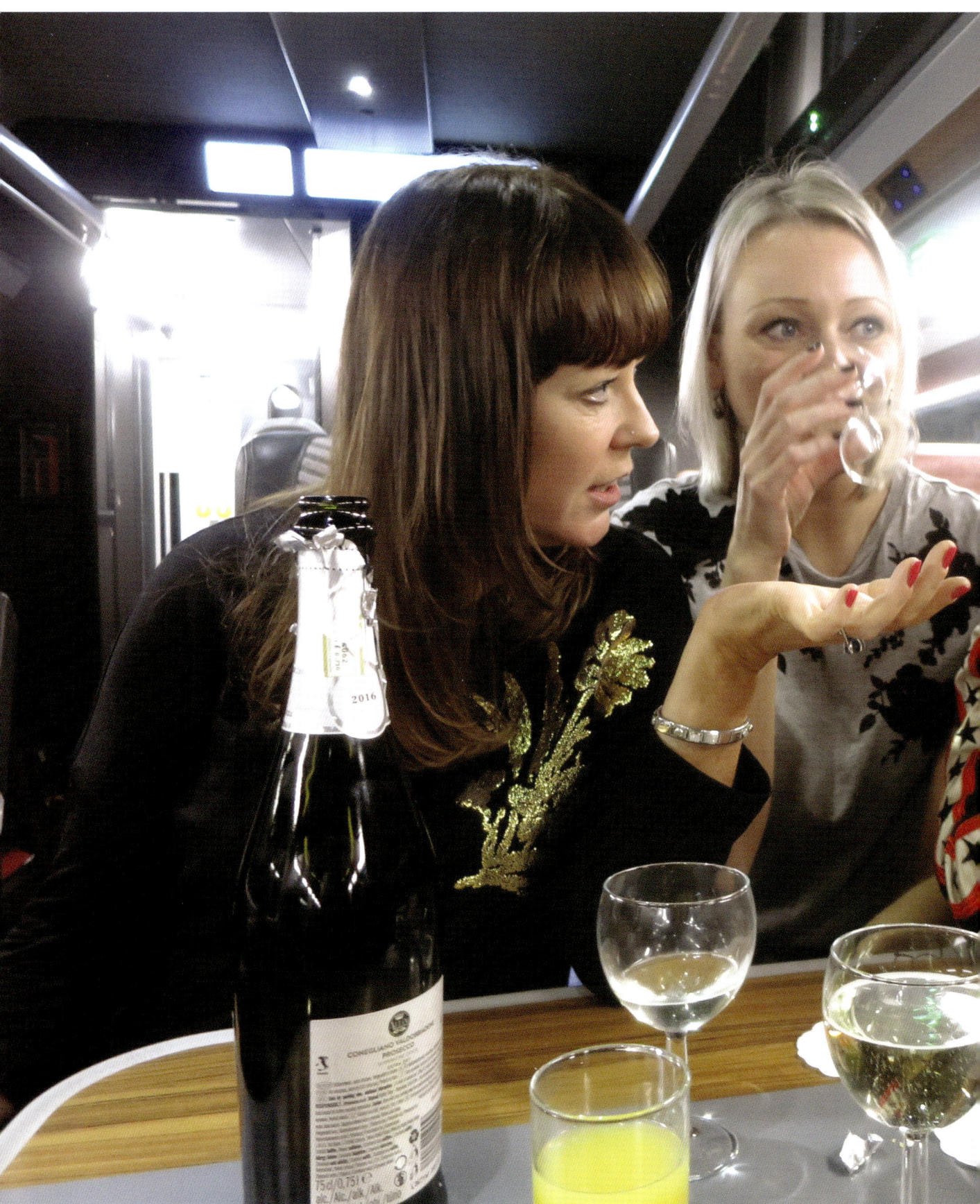

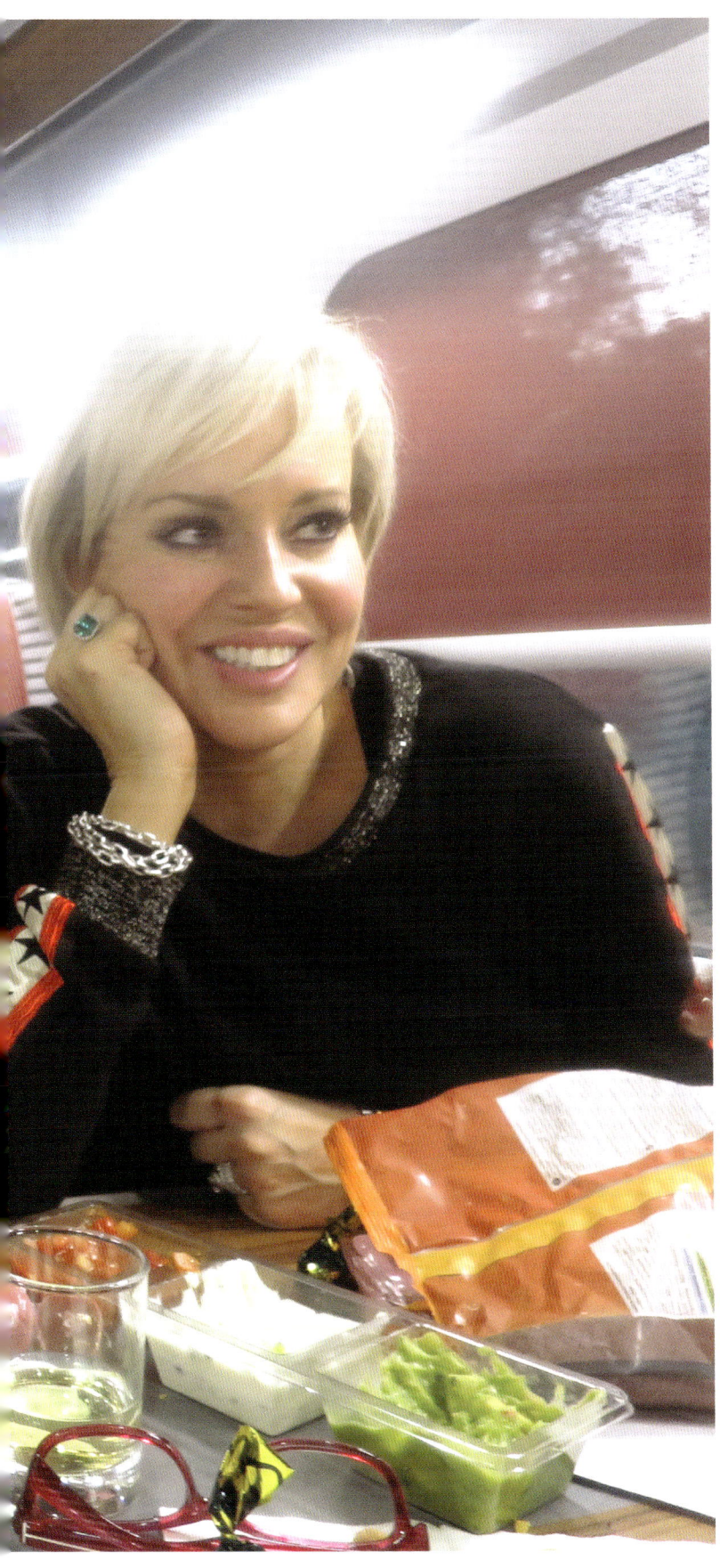

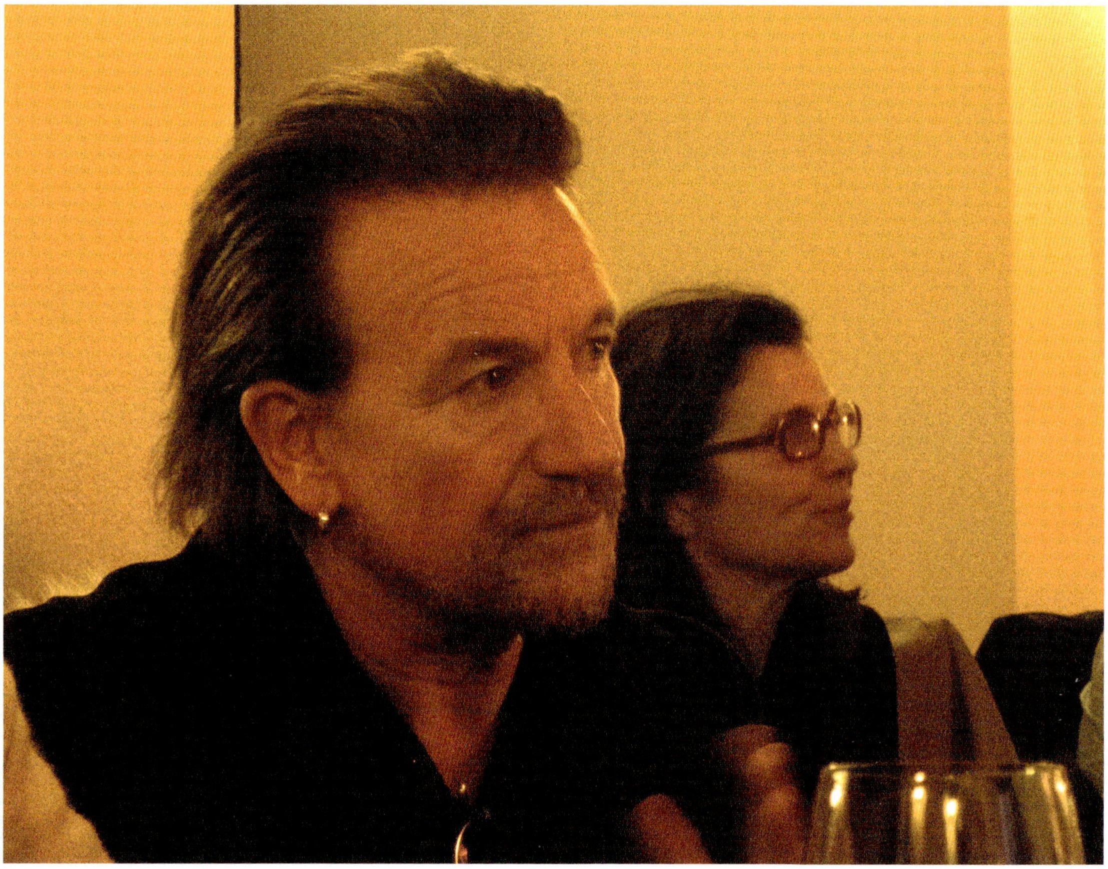

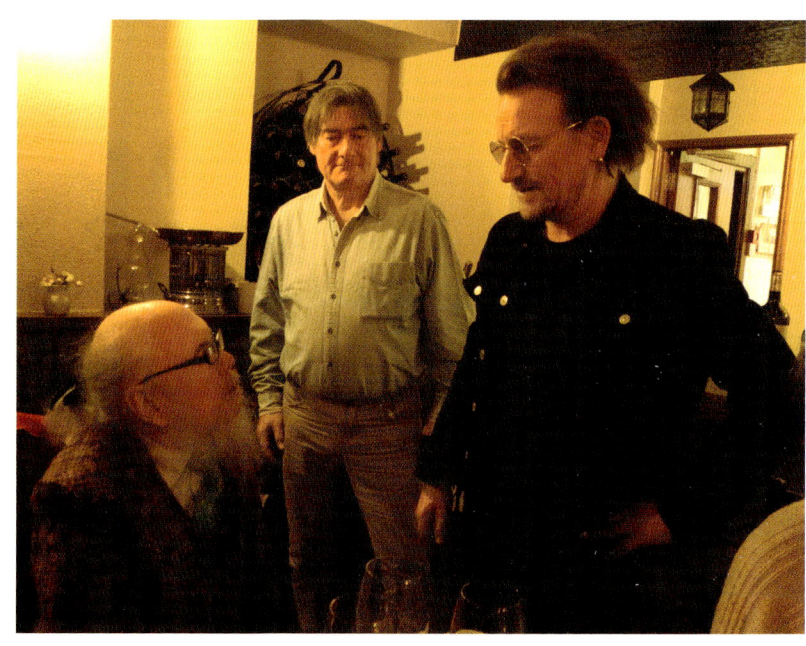

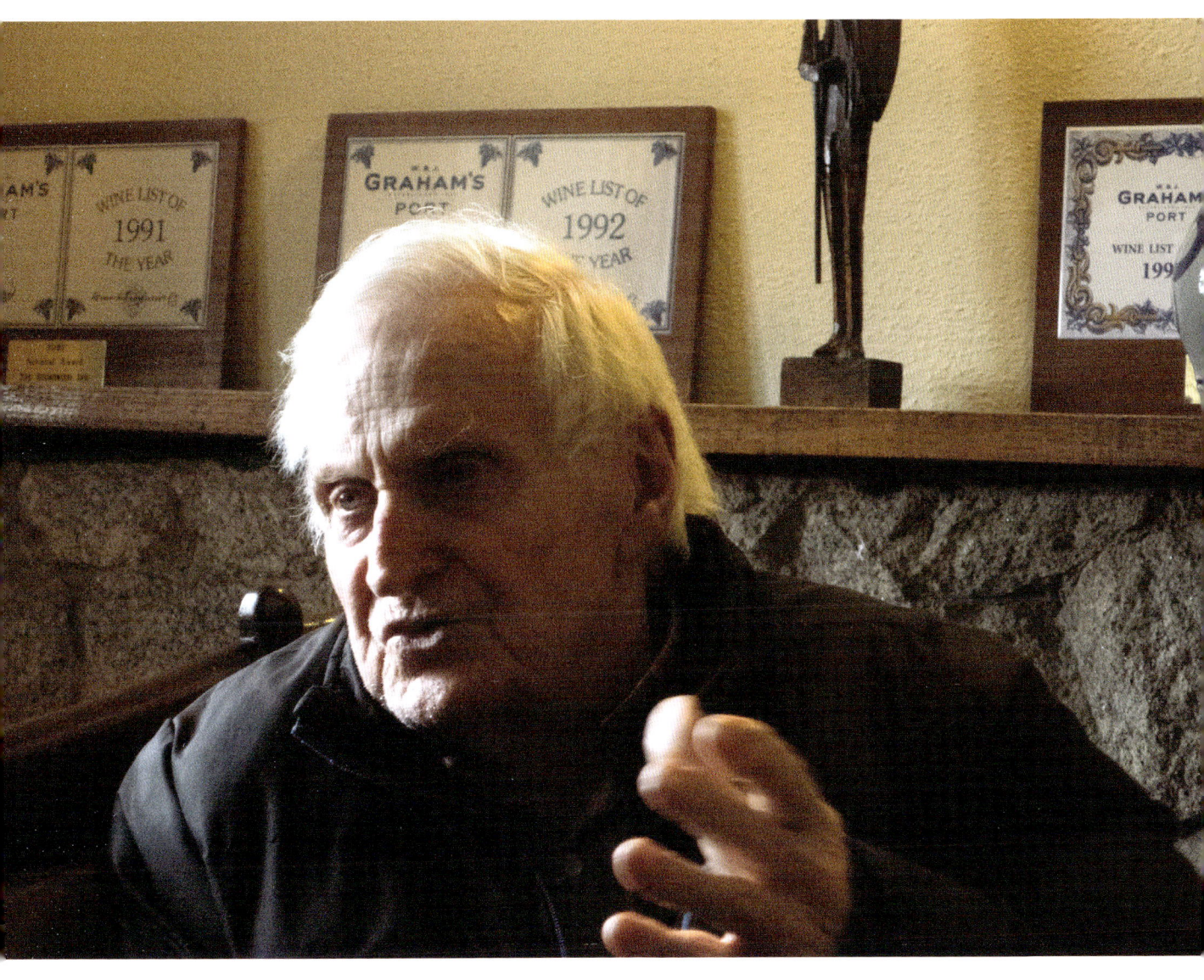

Notes on photographs

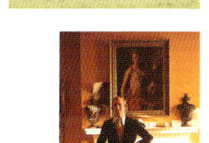

1
Horses by Shannon Estuary with Carrigaholt Castle in the distance
1968

Frontispiece

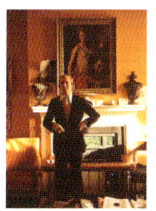

2
Desmond Fitzgerald
London
1968

vvii

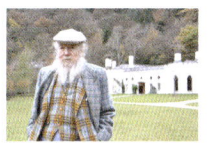

3
Garech Browne
Luggala, Co. Wicklow
2013

page 8–9

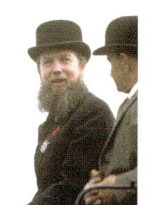

4
Garech Browne
Dublin Horse Show, RDS, Dublin
1973

page 10

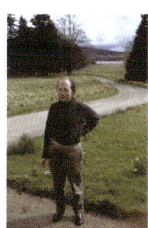

5
Garech Browne
Luggala, Co. Wicklow
1978

page 11

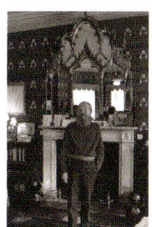

6
Garech Browne
Luggala, Co. Wicklow
1991

page 12

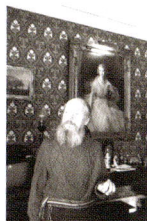

7
Garech Browne
Luggala, Co. Wicklow
1991

page 13

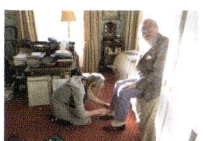

8
Garech Browne & assistant
Luggala, Co. Wicklow
2013

page 14

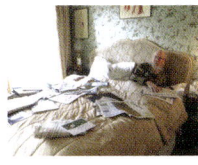

9
Garech Browne on bed with papers
Luggala, Co. Wicklow
2013

page 14–15

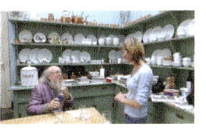

10
Garech Browne & assistant in kitchen
Luggala, Co. Wicklow
2012

page 16–17

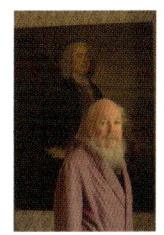

11
Garech Browne
Luggala, Co. Wicklow
2012

page 18

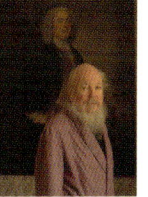

12
Garech Browne reading
Luggala, Co. Wicklow
2013

page 19

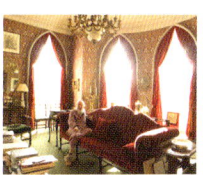

13
Garech Browne on couch
Luggala, Co. Wicklow
2012

page 20

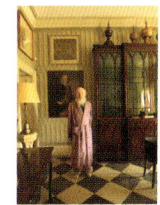

14
Garech Browne in his silk robe
Luggala, Co. Wicklow
2012

page 21

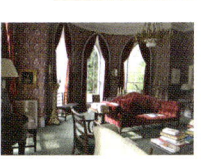

15
The Drawing Room
Luggala, Co. Wicklow
2011

page 22

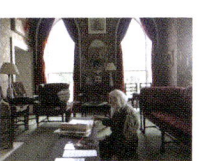

16
Garech Browne in the Drawing Room
Luggala, Co. Wicklow
2013

page 22–23

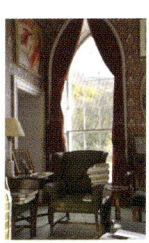

17
Chair with books
Luggala, Co. Wicklow
2013

page 24

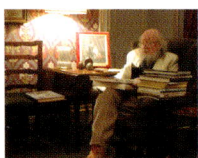

18
Garech Browne reading
Luggala, Co. Wicklow
2013

page 24

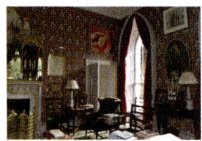

19
The Drawing Room
Luggala, Co. Wicklow
2011

page 24–25

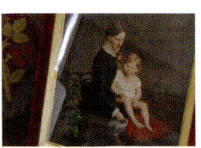

20
Adelaide Viscountess Iveagh with Garech's grandfather Ernest Guinness on her lap
Luggala, Co. Wicklow, 2011

page 26

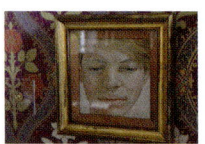

21
Lucien Freud's portrait of Garech Browne
Luggala, Co. Wicklow
2011

page 26

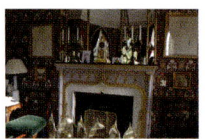

22
Gilded fireplace
Luggala, Co. Wicklow
2011

page 26–27

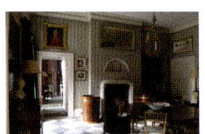

23
Informal Dining Room
Luggala, Co. Wicklow
2011

page 28

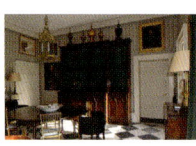

24
Informal Dining Room
Luggala, Co. Wicklow
2011

page 28

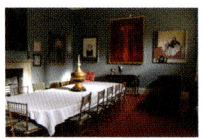

25
Dining Room
Luggala, Co. Wicklow
2011

page 28–29

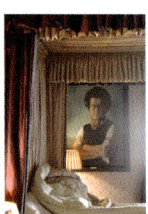

26
Guest room with self-portrait by Anthony Palliser
Luggala, Co. Wicklow
2011

page 30

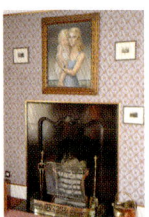

27
Guest room with painting of Garech Browne and his mother Lady Oranmore Browne by Gaetano de Gennaro
Luggala, Co. Wicklow
2011

page 31

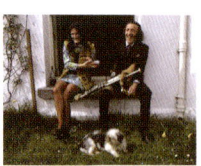

28
Rita and Paddy Moloney
Luggala, Co. Wicklow
1973

page 32

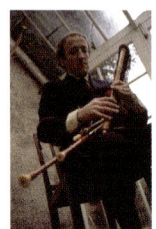

29
Paddy Moloney with pipes
Woodtown Manor, Dublin
1978

page 32

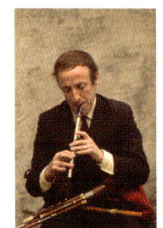

30
Paddy Moloney with whistle
Woodtown Manor, Dublin
1978

page 33

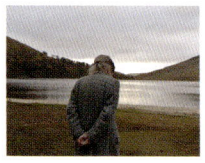

31
Garech Browne by Lough Tay
Luggala, Co. Wicklow
2013

page 34–35

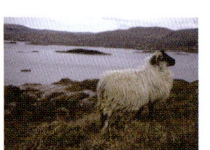

32
Ram
Shannon Estuary, Co. Limerick
1973

page 36–37

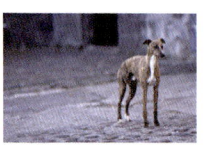

33
Whippet
Mount Coote Stud, Co. Limerick
1968

page 38

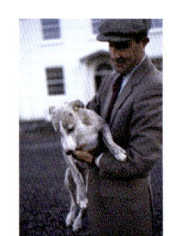

34
Alan Lillingston holding a pet whippet
Mount Coote Stud, Co. Limerick
1968

page 39

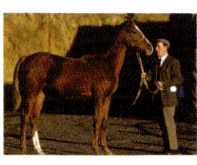

35
Man and horse
Listowel, Co. Kerry
1968

page 40

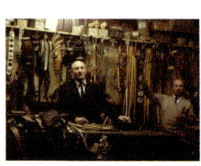

36
Tack shop
Listowel, Co. Kerry
1968

page 41

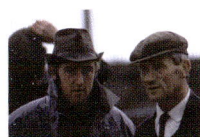
37
Two men at a cattle market
Listowel, Co. Kerry
1968

page 42

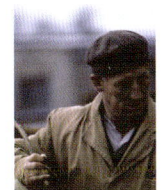
38
Man at cattle market
Listowel, Co. Kerry
1968

page 42

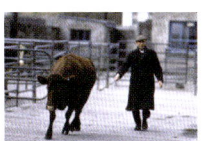
39
Cattle market
Listowel, Co. Kerry
1968

page 42–43

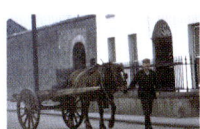
40
Horsedrawn cart
Listowel, Co. Kerry
1968

page 44

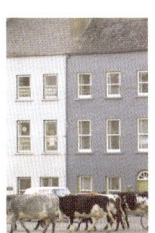
41
Parade of cows
Listowel, Co. Kerry
1968

page 45

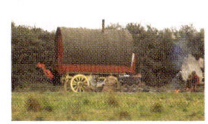
42
Traveller wagon
Monasterevin, Co. Kildare
1968

page 46

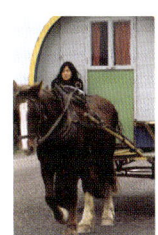
43
Traveller woman with horse
Monasterevin, Co. Kildare
1968

page 46

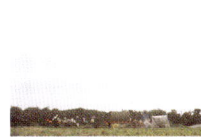
44
Traveller campground
Monasterevin, Co. Kildare
1968

page 46–47

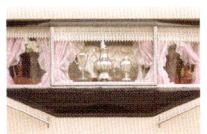
45
Caravan window with silver
Monasterevin, Co. Kildare
1968

page 48

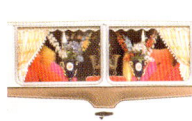
46
Caravan window with flowers
Monasterevin, Co. Kildare
1968

page 49

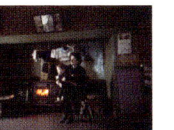
47
Mother and child by fireplace
Co. Clare
1968

page 50

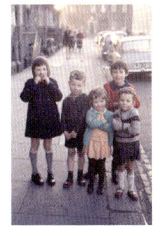
48
City children
Dublin
1973

page 51

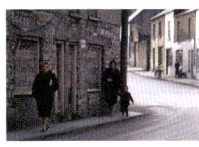
49
Street scene
Co. Kildare
1968

page 52–53

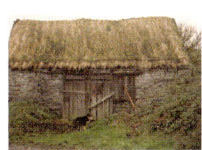
50
Stone house
Co. Roscommon
1973

page 54

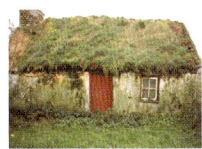
51
Moss roof house
Co. Down
1973

page 54

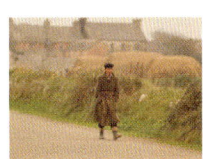
52
Man walking
Ballyguiltenane Lower,
Glin, Co. Limerick
1968

page 54–55

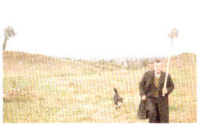
53
Men with dog and shovel
Ballyguiltenane Lower,
Glin, Co. Limerick
1968

page 56–57

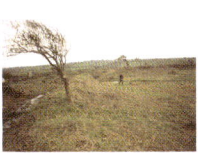
54
Man in field
Ballyguiltenane Lower,
Glin, Co. Limerick
1968

page 58–59

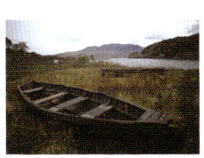
55
Boats by lakeside
River Shannon
1973

page 60–61

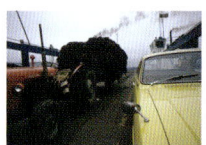

56
Tractor on Killimer Tarbert ferry
1973

page 62–63

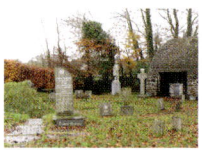

57
St Brigid's Well
Cullion, Co. Westmeath
2012

page 64

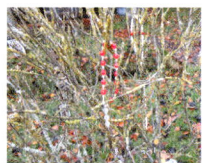

58
St Brigid's Well
Cullion, Co. Westmeath
2012

page 64–65

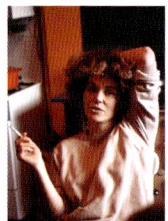

59
Marina Guinness
Pickering Forest, Co. Kildare
1993

page 66

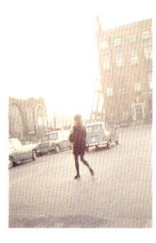

60
Mariga Guinness
Mountjoy Square, Dublin
1969

page 68

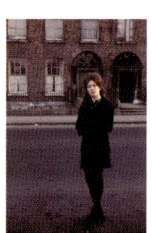

61
Mariga Guinness
Mountjoy Square, Dublin
1969

page 69

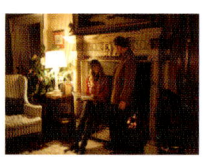

62
Desmond and Marina Guinness by fireplace
Leixlip Castle, Co. Kildare
1968

page 70

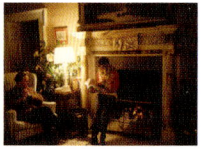

63
Desmond and Marina Guinness
Leixlip Castle, Co. Kildare
1968

page 70

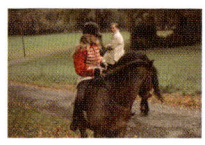

64
Marina Guinness by fireplace
Leixlip Castle, Co. Kildare
1968

page 71

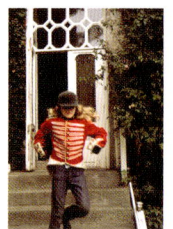

65
Marina riding
Leixlip Castle, Co. Kildare
1968

page 72–73

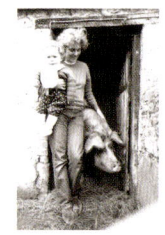

66
Marina running down steps
Leixlip Castle, Co. Kildare
1968

page 73

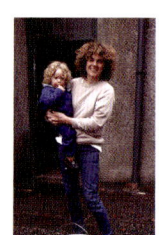

67
Marina holding Finbar
Pickering Forest, Co. Kildare
1990

page 74

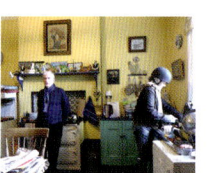

68
Marina holding Finbar
Pickering Forest, Co. Kildare
1994

page 75

69
Tommy and Marina in kitchen
Pickering Forest, Co. Kildare
2013

page 76

70
Marina and daughter
Pickering Forest, Co. Kildare
2013

page 77

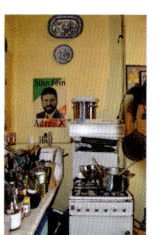

71
Gerry Adams poster
Pickering Forest, Co. Kildare
2013

page 78

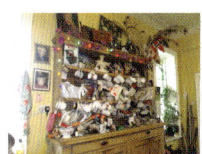

72
Sideboard
Pickering Forest, Co. Kildare
2016

page 78

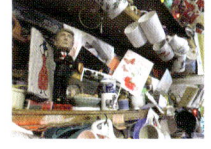

73
Glen Hansard and Marina in the garage
Pickering Forest, Co. Kildare
2009

page 79

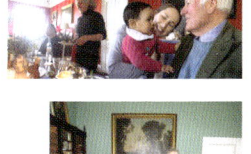

74
Sideboard with Trump bobblehead
Pickering Forest, Co. Kildare
2016

page 79

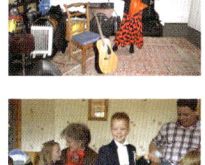

75
Four generations of Guinnesses Marina, Nancy, Violet and Desmond
Pickering Forest, Co. Kildare, 2016

page 80–81

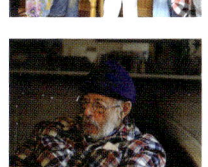

76
Marina holding a balalaika in the studio
Pickering Forest, Co. Kildare
2013

page 82–83

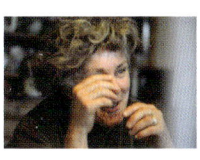

77
Marina at Paddy Doran's confirmation party
Co. Kildare
2013

page 84–85

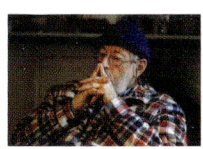

78
J.P. Donleavy
Levington Park, Co Westmeath
2012

page 86–87

79
Marina Guinness
Levington Park, Co Westmeath
2012

page 88

80
J.P. Donleavy
Levington Park, Co Westmeath
2012

page 89

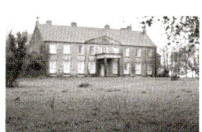

81
Levington Park, Co Westmeath
2012

page 90–91

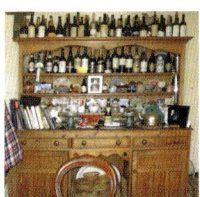

82
J.P. Donleavy
Levington Park, Co Westmeath
2012

page 91

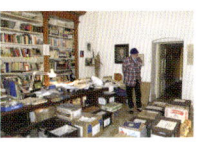

83
Sideboard
Levington Park, Co Westmeath
2012

page 92

84
Philip and Marina in the kitchen
Levington Park, Co Westmeath
2012

page 93

85
J.P. Donleavy in the archive
Levington Park, Co Westmeath
2012

page 94

86
The archive
Levington Park, Co Westmeath
2012

page 95

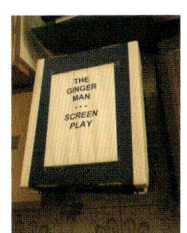

87
***The Ginger Man* screenplay**
Levington Park, Co Westmeath
2012

page 95

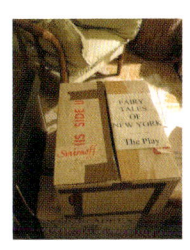

88
***A Fairy Tale of New York* the play**
Levington Park, Co Westmeath
2012

page 95

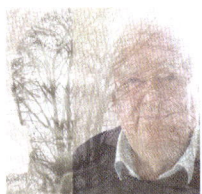

89
**Michael Collins/
Tim Pat Coogan**
2016

page 96–97

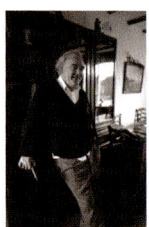

90
Tim Pat Coogan
Dublin
1993

page 98

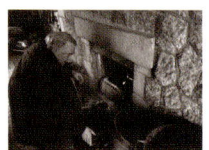

91
Tim Pat Coogan lighting fire
Dublin
1993

page 99

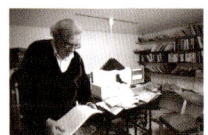

92
Tim Pat Coogan in office
Dublin
1993

page 100

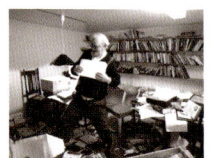

93
Tim Pat Coogan in office
Dublin
1993

page 100

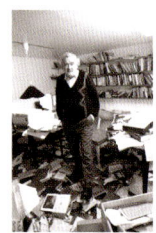

94
Tim Pat Coogan in office
Dublin
1993

page 101

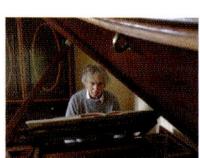

95
**Hector McDonnell
playing piano**
Glenarm, Co. Antrim
2013

page 102–103

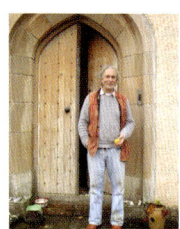

96
Hector McDonnell
Glenarm, Co. Antrim
2013

page 104

97
Hector McDonnell in robe
Glenarm, Co. Antrim
1999

page 105

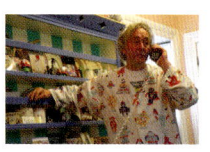

98
Aga stove with cat
Glenarm, Co. Antrim
2007

page 106

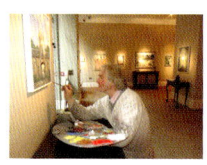

99
Hector McDonnell on phone
Glenarm, Co. Antrim
2013

page 106–107

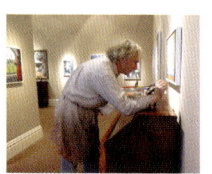

100
**Hector McDonnell touching
up painting**
Belfast
2013

page 108–109

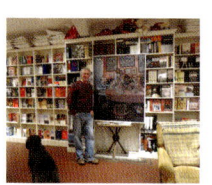

101
**Hector McDonnell touching
up painting**
Belfast
2013

page 109

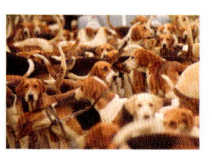

102
**Hector McDonnell in
The Lilliput Press office**
Dublin
2012

page 110–111

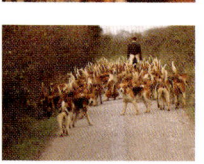

103
Foxhounds being walked
North Tipperary
1968

page 112–113

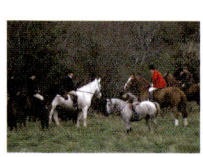

104
Foxhounds being walked
North Tipperary
1968

page 114–115

105
Hunting party
North Tipperary
1968

page 116–117

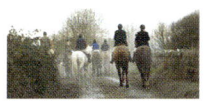

106
Roscommon Hunt
Co. Roscommon
2016

page 118

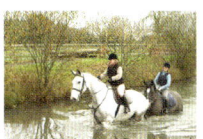

107
Leah Haggerty Clark, Joint Master of the Roscommon Hunt
Dartfield, Co. Galway
2016

page 118–119

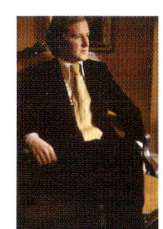

108
Desmond FitzGerald
London
1969

page 120

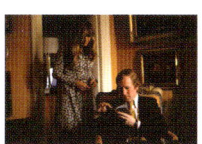

109
Olda and Desmond FitzGerald
London
1969

page 122–123

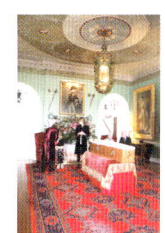

110
Desmond FitzGerald's wake
Glin Castle, Co. Limerick
2011

page 124

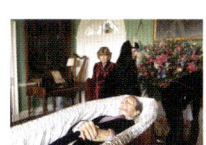

111
Desmond FitzGerald's wake
Glin Castle, Co. Limerick
2011

page 124–125

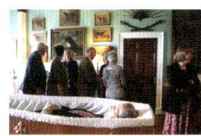

112
Desmond FitzGerald's wake
Glin Castle, Co. Limerick
2011

page 126

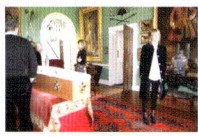

113
Desmond FitzGerald's wake
Glin Castle, Co. Limerick
2011

page 126

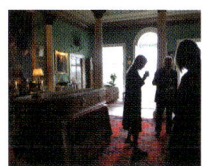

114
Desmond FitzGerald's wake
Glin Castle, Co. Limerick
2011

page 126–127

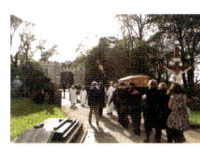

115
Funeral of Desmond FitzGerald
Glin, Co. Limerick
2011

page 128

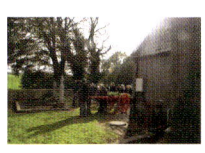

116
Funeral of Desmond FitzGerald
Glin, Co. Limerick
2011

page 129

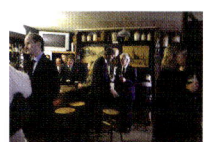

117
O'Shaughnessy's The Ivy House
Glin, Co. Limerick
2011

page 130–131

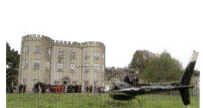

118
Funeral of Desmond FitzGerald
Glin Castle, Co. Limerick
2011

page 132–133

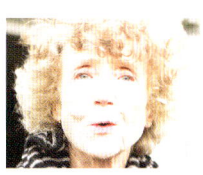

119
Lindy, Marchioness of Dufferin and Ava
Glin Castle, Co. Limerick
2011

page 133

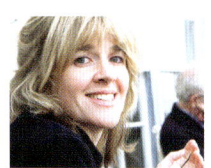

120
Catherine FitzGerald
Glin Castle, Co. Limerick
2011

page 134

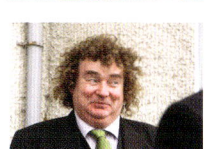

121
Johnny McCoy
Glin Castle, Co. Limerick
2011

page 135

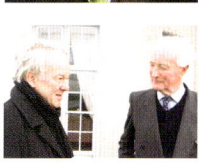

122
Antony Farrell and Ben Jellett
Glin Castle, Co. Limerick
2011

page 135

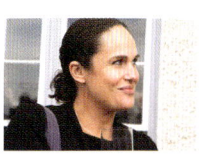

123
Emmeline Henderson
Glin Castle, Co. Limerick
2011

page 135

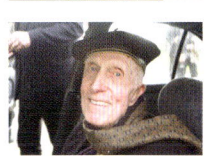

124
Sir John (Jack) Leslie
Glin Castle, Co. Limerick
2011

page 135

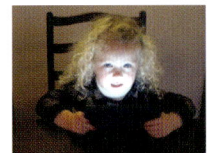

125
Eliza Geoghan
Roundwood, Co. Wicklow
2017

page 136

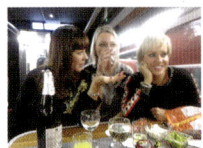

126
Ladies on Belfast to Dublin train
2017

page 138–139

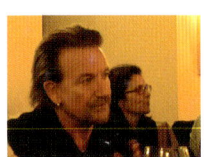

127
Bono and Ali Hewson
Roundwood, Co. Wicklow
2017

page 140

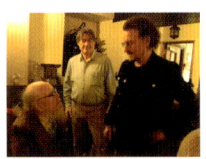

128
Garech Browne, John Rubenstein and Bono
Roundwood, Co. Wicklow
2017

page 140

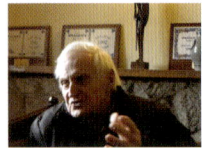

129
John Boorman
Roundwood, Co. Wicklow
2017

page 141

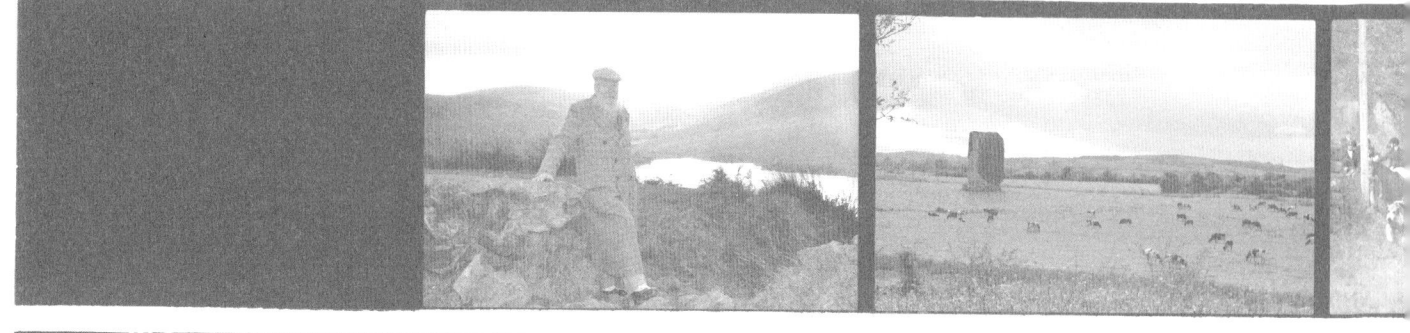

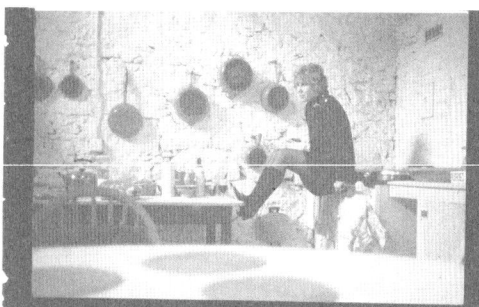
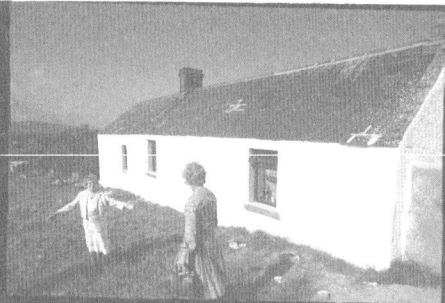
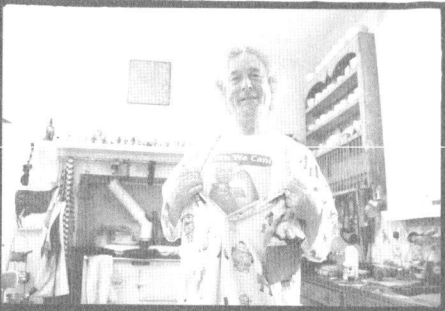
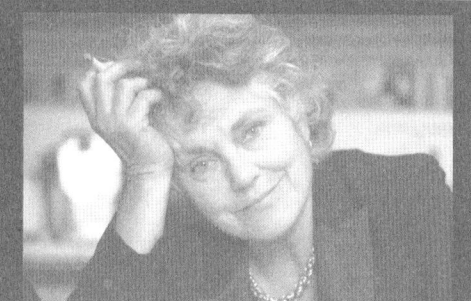
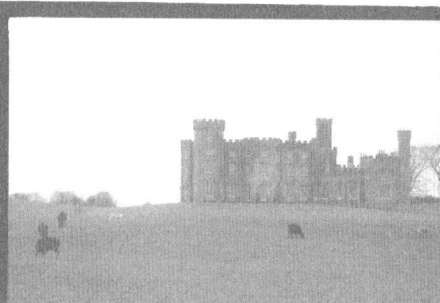
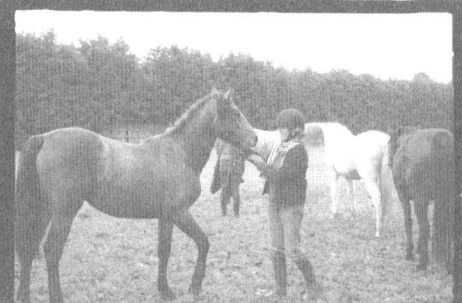
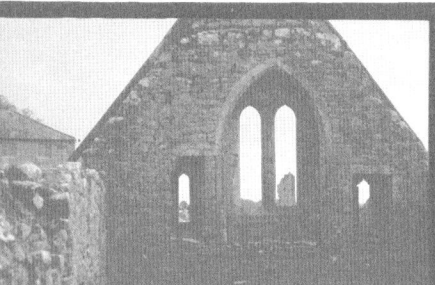
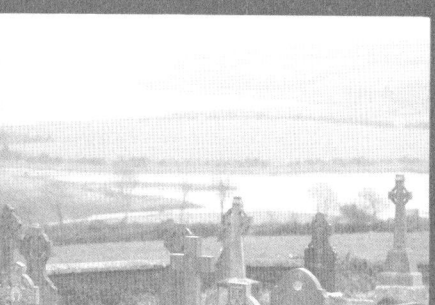
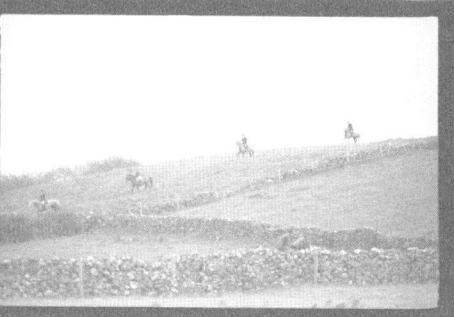

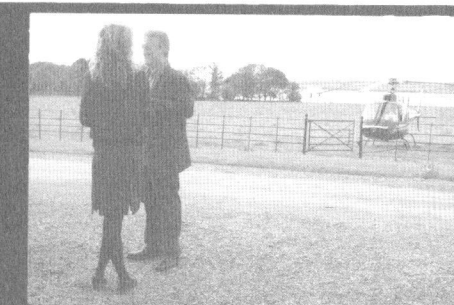
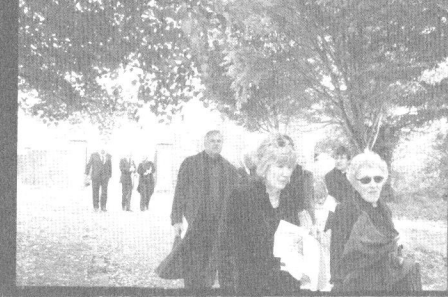
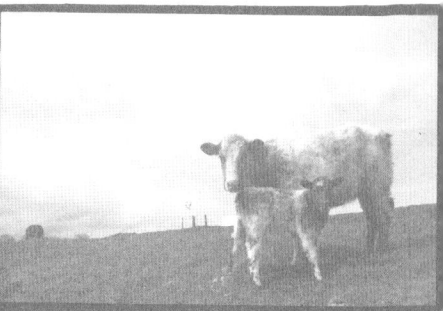